Greenhill Books

THE EAGLE'S LAST TRIUMPH

'I thought I was
striking a great blow but
I was mistaken. From
the sublime [Ligny] to
the ridiculous [Waterloo]
is but one step.'
NAPOLEON, 19 June 1815

THE EAGLE'S LAST TRIUMPH

Napoleon's Victory at Ligny, June 1815

by

ANDREW UFFINDELL

Greenhill Books, London
Stackpole Books, Pennsylvania

The Eagle's Last Triumph
first published 1994 by Greenhill Books,
Lionel Leventhal Limited, Park House, 1 Russell Gardens,
London NW11 9NN
and
Stackpole Books, 5067 Ritter Road, Mechanicsburg, PA 17055, USA.

British Library Cataloguing in Publication Data
Uffindell, Andrew
Eagle's Last Triumph: Napoleon's Victory
at Ligny, June 1815
I. Title
940.27

ISBN 1–85367–182–7

Library of Congress Cataloging-in-Publication Data
Uffindell, Andrew.
The eagle's last triumph : Napoleon's victory at Ligny, June 1815 / Andrew Uffindell.
p.   cm
Includes bibliographical references and index.
ISBN 1–85367–182–7
1. Ligny (Belgium), Battle of, 1815. 2. Napoleon I, Emperor of the French, 1769–1821—
Military leadership. 3. Blücher, Gebhard Leberecht von, 1742–1819.
4. Napoleonic Wars, 1800–1815—
Campaigns.—Belgium—Ligny.   I. Title.
DC240 June 16.U38 1994
940.2'7—dc20   94–12032
                                                        CIP

Typeset by DP Photosetting, Aylesbury, Bucks
Printed and bound in Great Britain by
Butler & Tanner, Frome and London

CONTENTS

Appendices

ILLUSTRATIONS

Pages 129–144

LINE DRAWINGS

SKETCH MAPS

KEY TO MAPS

☐ Prussian (and/or Allied) forces

■ French forces

☐ Infantry

◩ Cavalry

ılı Artillery

♂ Skirmishers

♙ Battalion

♯ Regiment

♙ Brigade

♙ Division

♙ Corps

♙ Army

◪ Headquarters

Examples:

Prussian 2nd brigade

Prussian I Corps' cavalry

Guyot Guyot's French cavalry division

N.B. On some maps two identical Prussian brigade signs appear.
This indicates that the brigade has been split into roughly equal parts.

DIAGRAMS

ORDERS OF BATTLE

This book is dedicated to the memory of:

Lt-Gen Le Capitaine
Brigade commander

Capt von Anders
Commander, 6-pdr battery no. 15

Maj Hervieux
Commander, 30th Regt

2nd Lt von Cordier
19th Regt

Chef de bataillon Richard
30th Regt

2nd Lt von Schmeling
4th Westphalian Landwehr

Chef de bataillon Lafolie
30th Regt

2nd Lt von Lintner
4th Westphalian Landwehr

of the French IV Corps

of the Prussian 4th brigade

Killed in action at the Battle of Ligny 16 June 1815

12

PREFACE

The battlefields of 1815 are living history. Time stands still amidst the crumbling masonry of the ruined farms. At Waterloo town Wellington's headquarters reek with history and a certain timelessness affects the visitor to the domed church. The memorial plaques inside commemorate heroes who might have died last year and not nearly two centuries ago.

The priceless relics of 1815 evoke a past of tumult but also of fascination, of terror but also of grandeur, of slaughter but also of the birth of modern Europe.

The student of war will learn more from the 1815 campaign than from any other clash of arms. 1815 is a fascinating subject which evokes images of a trio of unique commanders and a trio of courageous armies. The arguments on strategy and tactics and the might-have-beens are endless.

The 1815 campaign is well provided with enthusiastic historians, both amateur and professional, and this raises the question of what justification there is for writing yet another book on the subject.

Firstly, Ligny is not a well-known battle. However, it is both an important and an instructive action, and it forms a refreshing case study with many lessons for both the military enthusiast and the army officer.

Secondly, it is valuable for any reader to be able to look anew at the 1815 campaign as a whole, for the story of the campaign has become traditional, stuffy and out of date. Erroneous conceptions about Waterloo are legion. A fresh viewpoint is presented here. The aim is to examine in detail the neglected early stages of the campaign and thus to place the Battle of Waterloo in its proper perspective.

The major revisionist view of this text concerns Allied co-operation against the French. The Prussian contribution to victory gains its due recognition, without being overstated. Wellington's conduct, although faultless on the battlefield of Waterloo itself, was flawed in the early stages of the campaign.

Allied co-operation throughout the campaign was far from perfect on either side. In any coalition, generals inevitably put the interests of their own nation first. If they did not, they would forfeit both the trust of their troops and the support of their government at home. The 1815 campaign, like the campaign in Europe, 1944–5, saw arguments about strategy and national prestige. But in spite of all the disagreements, the two coalitions survived and triumphed. The vital point is that victory was won in the end. Beneath the surface of doubt and suspicion, a great deal of trust and co-operation existed in both 1815 and 1944–5, and that basic co-operation was sufficient to win an Allied victory.

Two main propositions run through this work. The first is that Napoleon's last military victory at Ligny led logically and surely to his final defeat at Waterloo. The second is that Blücher laid the foundations of victory in the 1815 campaign, for his rugged determination and fierce loyalty saved the allies in the crucial early stages and thus made possible Wellington's magnificent defensive battle at Waterloo in the spotlight of history.

ACKNOWLEDGEMENTS

I owe a deep debt of gratitude to my tutors over the years and I would particularly like to thank Dr Geoffrey Ellis of Hertford College, Oxford.

I thank Philip Offord, Fred Rye, James Wilkes and the other members of the Bexhill Hanoverian Study Group, as well as my friends and comrades of the 21st Regiment and of the Napoleonic Association. I am grateful also to Michael Corum, editor of the *Waterloo Journal* and source of much helpful advice. Richard Moore and Lucien Gerke have kindly given their valuable advice on several matters relating to the Waterloo campaign.

David Chandler and Philip Haythornthwaite read through the manuscript of this book; I thank them for their positive criticism and expert advice which has saved me from several errors. In Belgium I received invaluable help from Guy and Janine Delvaux and greatly appreciate the hospitality and valuable information they gave me. I am very grateful to the Renard family for their warm welcome, encouragement and advice on the location of the Bussy mill. I wish to record my deep gratitude to Patrick Maes who lives in Ligny village and is the President of the Association Belge Napoléonienne. Patrick most generously shared with me his detailed knowledge of the battle and battlefield of Ligny and provided me with much invaluable documentation. He himself has written a first-rate booklet, *Ligny: Le Crépuscule de l'Aigle*, which I thoroughly recommend.

I am grateful to both the parish priest of Sombreffe who kindly invited me into Blücher's headquarters and to the ladies of the secretarial staff at Fleurus Town Hall for showing me Napoleon's room.

I thank the first-rate staff of the Bodleian Library. Their cheerful and undaunted spirit was undimmed even after my three years' sojourn in Oxford. I thank also the authorities of All Souls' College, Oxford, for allowing me to conduct research in the magnificent Codrington Library. The Codrington specialises in military history and contains many of the French eyewitness accounts for the 1815 campaign. I thank the staff there for their co-operation.

I am indebted to Lionel Leventhal, Kate Ryle and the other staff of Greenhill Books for their unfailing encouragement and sound advice throughout the publication of this book.

For help in obtaining suitable illustrations, I am most grateful to Peter

Harrington, curator of the Anne S.K. Brown Military Collection at Brown University, Rhode Island, U.S.A., and to Peter Hofschröer.

Finally but by no means least, I am grateful to my family, particularly to Big Brother who forbore to complain when in 1987 I diverted our cycling tour of Dutch polders to the battlefield of Waterloo.

Andrew Uffindell
Battlefield of Ligny
16 June 1994

PART ONE

1

STORMCLOUDS OF WAR

The French Revolution plunged Europe into more than two decades of strife. Anxious to contain the spirit of Revolution, and if possible to reverse the Revolutionary course of events in France, the European powers went to war. The French responded with the execution of their king, Louis XVI, and with conscription. This gave French Republican generals the weight of numbers with which to defend their fatherland's frontiers and to extend both French power and Revolutionary ideas.

The chaotic conditions in France, the breakdown of the old social hierarchy and the chances of gaining military renown made the Revolutionary era one of opportunism. Napoleon Buonaparte, the most skilful and determined opportunist of all, was a rising star, fresh from a victory at Toulon and about to gain laurels in Italy. Victory followed victory, political advancement led to political advancement and through a combination of ambition, ruthlessness and good fortune, Napoleon became Emperor of the French in 1804.

However, Europe's strife continued, partly because Napoleon's enemies refused to recognise him as the ruler of France (the would-be King Louis XVIII was in exile in Britain). Moreover, the Revolution had begun a cycle of French expansion and Napoleon needed to conquer new lands in order to pay for his gifts to loyal servants, and for his large standing army. For several years Napoleon was the master of Europe. He crushed the Austrians and Russians at Austerlitz in 1805, the Prussians at Jena-Auerstädt in 1806 and the Russians again at Friedland in 1807.

Then the cracks in the mighty edifice of the French Empire appeared. Britain held out, protected by the English Channel and by her powerful fleet. In Spain, guerrilla fighters helped a British army under the Duke of Wellington to defy and eventually defeat the French. In Russia, Napoleon's Grand Army of 1812 was swallowed up, frozen by the winter, harassed by Cossacks and all but destroyed.

The years 1813 and 1814 saw French forces in fighting retreat all over Europe. In spite of a brilliant defensive campaign in 1814 on French soil itself, Napoleon was finally finished, defeated militarily by a coalition of the rest of Europe and internally by a revolt of French politicians and marshals. Napoleon abdicated from the throne of France on 6 April 1814. With a small, faithful escort of crack Imperial Guardsmen, the fallen French Emperor departed for exile on the Italian island of Elba.

He was not in exile for long. The European powers squabbled and danced the time away at the Congress of Vienna. In France itself, the restored Bourbon monarchy was unpopular. The French people were bored and dissatisfied. 'All France regrets me and wants me', was Napoleon's accurate verdict of the mood of the nation.[1] In February 1815 he saw his chance and seized it.

Lightning is the only word to describe it: a swift voyage by sea to the south coast of France followed by a fantastic twenty-day march across country to Paris while collecting troops, marshals, and support like pennies falling into his cap.

'The Eagle will fly from steeple to steeple up to the towers of Notre-Dame', promised Napoleon, and so it did.[2] His carriage clattered into the Tuileries on 20 March 1815 with that of Louis XVIII having scampered out the day before. Then came Napoleon's frantic race against time to revitalise the French army and to place the French nation on a war footing.

For the sovereigns of Europe rejected Napoleon's overtures of peace. To Europe, Napoleon was an unbridled warmonger, the dangerous product of the feared Revolution. Now he was back on the throne of France. Already, the allied powers had condemned the French Emperor as having 'placed himself outside the pale of civil and social relations' and that 'as the disturber of world repose he had exposed himself to public vengeance.' Now they mobilised their armies for war. They created the Seventh Coalition of the Revolutionary and Napoleonic Wars – the signatories being Russia, Great Britain, Spain, Portugal, Prussia, Austria, Sweden and some of the German states – and determined on restoring Louis XVIII by force of arms. Europe was ranged against Napoleon.

Four huge armies, with smaller supporting formations, marched on the frontiers of France, gathered strength and prepared to invade. In the north, in Belgium (part of the Kingdom of the United Netherlands), two armies built up their strength. The first was a composite force of soldiers from Britain, the United Netherlands and various small German states, the whole being commanded by England's foremost general, Field Marshal Arthur Wellesley the Duke of Wellington. The second army was Prussian, under Field Marshal Prince Blücher. Further south, a Russian army and a force of Austrians and German contingents marched across the plains towards the River Rhine. The invasion plan involved these four huge armies making for Paris, with supporting units in the south capturing Lyons, the other important French city. The emphasis was on a co-ordinated steam roller approach with armies pushing on at all costs and crushing the French opposition by brute force and numerical superiority.

Mobilisation and concentration of the allied armies required time. In

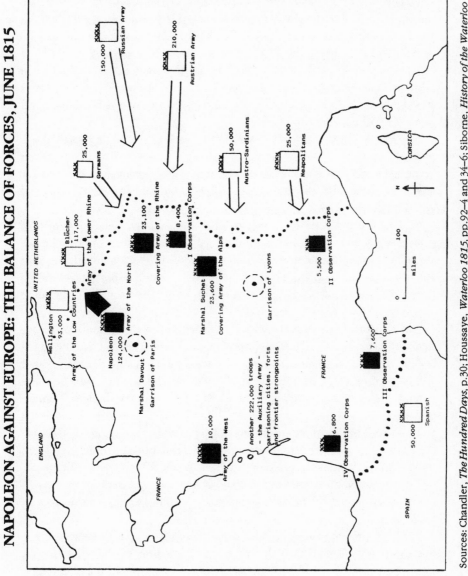

NAPOLEON AGAINST EUROPE: THE BALANCE OF FORCES, JUNE 1815

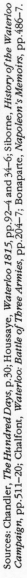

Sources: Chandler, *The Hundred Days*, p.30; Houssaye, *Waterloo 1815*, pp.92–4 and 34–6; Siborne, *History of the Waterloo Campaign*, pp.511–20; Chalfont, *Waterloo: Battle of Three Armies*, pp.204–7; Bonaparte, *Napoleon's Memoirs*, pp.486–7.

particular, the Russians had to march all the way from the River Vistula. Only Wellington and Blücher's armies were ready, stationed as they were in Belgium facing the French border. In short, the allied invasion could not begin until July 1815. That gave Napoleon time.

Napoleon had a choice. He could remain on the defensive, building up further forces before the allies invaded in mid-July, and repeating his brilliant 1814 campaign with more chances of success. The invaders would have to detach troops to invest the French frontier forts. Consequently, they would arrive before the gates of Paris and Lyons lacking food and a sufficient numerical superiority, only to face powerful counter-attacks. Wellington later stated this had been Napoleon's best chance of success but 'the fact is, he never in his life had patience for a defensive war.'[3]

Yet the political drawbacks of fighting on French soil outweighed the military advantages. After his fall in 1814, Napoleon was no longer an omnipotent dictator. His only sure power base was the army, and he could not afford to antagonise the shifting sands of public opinion or the political opposition in Paris.

Napoleon decided it was better to seize the initiative. The best form of defence was attack. Until July the only allied armies on the frontiers of France would be those of Wellington and Blücher. Napoleon hoped to invade Belgium and to knock these two armies out of the allied coalition. In short, it would be a daring pre-emptive strike designed to start the war with a glorious lightning campaign.

Having dealt with Wellington and Blücher, Napoleon would face a considerably weakened allied onslaught on France in July. The plan had the added benefit of seizing Belgium, whose people were mostly sympathetic to France and hated their enforced union with Holland. Besides gaining valuable troop reinforcements from the Belgians, the seizure of the country would be popular in France.

The defeat, or if possible the destruction, of Wellington's army could topple the British Tory Government, bringing the Whigs to power. Unlike the Tories, the Whigs did not insist on the need to restore Louis XVIII as a condition of making peace. With Britain out of the war and the vital British subsidies no longer forthcoming, the other coalition powers might likewise withdraw from the fight.

But if the pre-emptive attack on Belgium was a gamble with great prizes, it was also one with great risks. It was a gamble because if it failed, Napoleon would fall back on Paris with an army ravaged by casualties and a nation ravaged by demoralisation. France in this state would be ill fitted to meet the coalition invasion in July.

But Napoleon was a born gambler.

In the two months since his return to power on 20 March, Napoleon had achieved wonders. Cloth factories were restarted to churn out uniforms. Horses were purchased. Muskets were produced in remarkable numbers. France became infected with a patriotic fervour, and at parades spectators handed Napoleon banknotes to help pay for the war preparations. Unemployment dropped; Napoleon's popularity soared.

In the course of April and May, nearly 7000 soldiers were raised every day. By September, the French army would hopefully consist of 800,000 armed and trained men. By June, the total was already 506,000. Of this figure, 222,000 formed the Auxiliary Army of National Guardsmen and other second line troops, who garrisoned coasts and fortresses. This left an active army of 284,000. This fighting army was to guard the frontiers and also to form a strike force, known as the Army of the North, 124,000 men strong, to invade Belgium.

Napoleon's next task was complex and formidable. He had to surprise Wellington and Blücher. He had to launch a sudden onslaught on their unsuspecting armies before they could concentrate and unite for battle. The accomplishment of this task was remarkable. Wellington himself later admitted to admiration: 'Bonaparte's march upon Belgium was the finest thing ever done – so rapid and so well-combined.'

In twelve days, starting on 2 June, Napoleon concentrated the 124,000 men of the Army of the North south of the Belgian frontier without any allied defensive measures being taken. He himself left Paris in the early hours of 12 June to join the army. A total security blackout had been imposed on the entire operation. French agents spread false intelligence. The secret concentration was so successful that as late as 13 June, Wellington wrote that Napoleon's joining his army from Paris was 'not likely to be immediate. I think we are now too strong for him here.'[4] Just two days later Napoleon attacked.

Notes

1. Brett-James, *The Hundred Days*, p.1
2. Chalfont, *Waterloo: Battle of Three Armies*, p.27
3. Stanhope, *Conversations with the Duke of Wellington*, p.60
4. Longford, *Wellington: The Years of the Sword*, p.405

2

THE FOES

The Rival High Commands

Napoleon stood at the head of the French army. 'I used to say of him that his presence on the field made the difference of forty thousand men', remarked the Duke of Wellington.[1] The French Emperor's genius lay not merely in his military skill as a general but in his ability to inspire his troops. 'It is with baubles that men are led', he declared, bestowing lands and gifts on his marshals and generals and lavishing his troops with praise and the coveted medals of the Legion of Honour. Napoleon encouraged, cajoled and lauded his troops. He led them by offering to all a glittering vision of glory, fame and riches.

But Napoleon the leader of men had another side to his character. The violent rages of temper, the crushing rebukes, the ruthless application of the adage 'divide and rule' were as much part of Napoleon's method as were the rewards for loyalty and bravery. 'Men must be led by an iron hand in a velvet glove', declared Napoleon. His penetrating eagle-eyes and harsh words could break hardened soldiers.

Napoleon believed in personal reconnaissance of enemy positions, as well as in being seen and heard by his troops in order to boost their morale. His ability to inspire loyalty and devotion in his troops depended not a little on his photographic memory, which enabled him to recall statistics and faces and records of old soldiers.

Napoleon admired the famous generals of history Alexander the Great, Julius Caesar and Frederick the Great, and from them he borrowed stratagems and schemes of war. He had learnt from notable theorists of his day and perfected his own set of campaign systems. He outwitted, outflanked, outmarched and outgeneralled his opponents. He seized the initiative and imposed his will on the enemy.

Surprise, rapid movement and a swift and decisive victory were the ingredients of a successful Napoleonic campaign. Napoleon disliked attrition as it wasted both men and time. Yet in the later years of the Empire, his battles became more attritional. The decline in quality of troops with conscripts replacing dead or wounded veterans was one cause of this unfortunate development. A decline in Napoleon's freshness and hitherto unflagging mental energy was another.

Ulm and Austerlitz in 1805 had been won by manoeuvre but Wagram in 1809 and Borodino in 1812 were head-on attacks on formidable and staunchly held enemy positions. Ligny and Waterloo in 1815 would both be costly attritional battles. Increasingly, Napoleon came to mass both his artillery and his attacking formations; his battles came to lack their old finesse and skill.

'Activity! Speed! Speed!' an energetic Napoleon had urged in earlier campaigns. But on several key occasions in 1815 the Emperor would delay and do nothing. 'The Napoleon we knew is no more' whispered one of his generals.[2] Indeed, Napoleon was no longer the rising star who had won Marengo and Austerlitz and Friedland. 'Men of genius are meteors destined to be consumed in illuminating their own century', he had written in 1790. By 1815 the meteor was becoming burnt out. His overall level of energy was on the decline. He was ill with cystitis and piles. 'Napoleon's stoutness had increased rapidly', wrote one French officer of 1815. 'It was noticeable in this campaign that he remained on horseback much less than in the past.'[3]

Moreover, Napoleon had become deluded by his own propaganda. He came to believe in his own infallibility and fatally underestimated at least the tenacity if not the skill of Wellington and Blücher, his opponents of 1815. Napoleon tended, over-optimistically, to believe all was going according to his plan, not crediting evidence to the contrary unless he were on the spot to see it for himself.

Yet in many respects, the Napoleon of 1815 was the same master of war as before. His supreme qualities of leadership were intact; so too was his unrivalled capacity for organisation. His secret concentration of the French army at the Belgian border and the sudden, well planned invasion of 15 June, were nothing short of masterly. Napoleon in 1815 was still 'a giant surrounded by pygmies.'

Napoleon's generals in 1815 were not the best with whom he had campaigned. Too many of his fine marshals were either dead, exiled or retired. Other marshals, namely Louis-Nicolas Davout the Prince of Eckmühl and Louis-Gabriel Suchet the Duke of Albufera, were superb commanders in their own right, but Napoleon assigned them to important posts outside his 'Army of the North.' Davout, for example, was War Minister and Governor of Paris. Suchet had been entrusted with one of the French armies guarding the eastern frontier of France.

It is possible that Napoleon left Davout and Suchet behind because he underestimated his adversaries in Belgium. The Emperor believed the shock of his sudden invasion would send Wellington and Blücher reeling back and that Brussels would fall without a difficult campaign. The important fighting would come later, against the Austrian and Russian invaders. By then, the most brilliant marshals would be already in place – Davout to defend Paris and Suchet to defend Lyons – and would be familiar with the ground and their troops.

But Marshal Joachim Murat, the finest cavalry leader in the world, the dashing General Patton of the Napoleonic wars, received no command, either in the Army of the North or on the eastern frontier of France; Napoleon still bitterly resented Murat's treachery of 1814 in temporarily joining the Austrians.

Perhaps Napoleon deliberately did not appoint Murat and his other best marshals to commands in the Army of the North so that their skill would not detract from his own glory and success. The campaign in Belgium had to be a brilliantly decisive Napoleonic victory. It had to be Napoleon's personal triumph in order to overawe the enemy coalition, and to unite France behind him. 'He thought', commented the German historian Major Karl von Damitz, 'that he would master events and would be, alone, the saviour of France.'[4]

So in 1815 Napoleon had only four, second-rate, marshals with him for his last military campaign. One of these, Mortier, would fall ill on the eve of hostilities and would play no part. The other three were Nicolas Soult, Emmanuel de Grouchy and Michel Ney.

Napoleon's appointment of Marshal Nicolas Jean de Dieu Soult the Duke of Dalmatia as Chief of Staff was a mistake. Soult was no adequate replacement for the reliable, if not infallible, Marshal Louis-Alexandre Berthier the Prince of Neuchâtel and of Wagram, who had recently died. Although Soult had a good understanding of the Emperor's strategy, he would fail dismally in interpreting Napoleon's wishes to his subordinates. Soult's orders would lack precision, clarity and detail.

Soult conspicuously failed to work as a member of a team. He disagreed and argued with colleagues. This boded ill for 1815 when, as Chief of Staff, he had not merely to work as part of a team but also had to use the tact and diplomacy he had never possessed to manage a team composed of generals who distrusted him. Soult was particularly disliked by Marshal Ney, yet on 16 June, Soult's communications to Ney, and Ney's obedience of them, would be of the utmost importance.

Marshal Michel Ney, Prince of the Moskowa, Duke of Elchingen, was forty-six years of age and destined to command the French left wing in the 1815 campaign. He would therefore have a key role to play.

Ney was a legend in his own lifetime. Ney's greatest asset was his remarkable popularity with the ordinary French soldier, who admired Ney's bravery and his uncomplicated personality. Limitless personal courage, immense energy and tactical skill had carried Ney by 1804 to the heights of Napoleon's military hierarchy – the marshalate.

Ney's finest hour came in 1812 when he led the French rearguard during the horrific retreat from Moscow. This was Ney at his best; the defeats of 1814 would bring out the worst in him. Ney became caught up in the political turmoil of France, forced Napoleon's abdication and served the restored Bourbon monarchy to the extent of promising Louis XVIII, when Napoleon returned from Elba, to capture the Corsican and bring him to Paris in an iron cage.

Although in the event Napoleon won the tempestuous Ney over to his side by an emotive letter recalling the marshal's bravery at Borodino, he did not consider taking Ney with his army until four days before the campaign began. Ney's treason rankled deeply, but the Emperor was short of commanders. 'Send for Marshal Ney,' Napoleon instructed Davout on 11 June, 'and tell him that if he wishes to be present at the first battles, he ought to be at Avesnes on the fourteenth.'[5]

Napoleon was not to give Ney the command of the French left wing until the afternoon of 15 June, with the campaign already under way. Ney had insufficient time to familiarise himself with his troops and generals and to discuss plans in detail with Napoleon. Nor did he have time to set up a proper staff team. In 1815, he no longer had the brilliant General Baron Antoine-Henri de Jomini as his Chief of Staff to assist him in matters of strategy.

Napoleon's delay in giving Ney a command in the army was potentially disastrous. Furthermore, the command offered to Ney, that of 50,000 troops, was not the right one. After Waterloo, Napoleon's verdict was that Ney 'was good for a command of 10,000 men, but beyond that he was out of his depth.'[6] Ney's boldness in battle bordered on rashness. He risked losing sight of the battle or campaign as a whole by immersing himself in the front line rough and tumble. Ney lacked the intellect for an independent command; he needed to be under direct and constant supervision by Napoleon.

The faults in Ney's tempestuous personality were destined to be demonstrated to the full.

The other French marshal to participate in the 1815 campaign was Emmanuel, marquis de Grouchy. The last of Napoleon's twenty-six marshals, Grouchy was promoted only on 15 April 1815. He would fail to live up to expectations. Although steady and determined and a cavalry commander of genius, Grouchy lacked dash and imagination in the realm of strategy. In 1815, Grouchy would command the Reserve Cavalry of Napoleon's army. He would also command the French right wing, except when the Emperor was present in person as he would be at Ligny. Grouchy was to be a more important figure in the campaign on 17 and 18 June than at Ligny; nevertheless, he would be a noteworthy participant there.

Usually, Napoleon would place a marshal at the head of each corps. But with marshals in lamentably short supply for this campaign, Napoleon had to rely on ordinary generals. Some of these were talented and reasonably young men who inspired their troops to great deeds of military valour, but others were over-cautious. This was particularly true of those who had taken hard knocks at the hands of their redoubtable British foes in the Peninsular War of 1808–14.

For instance, both Jean-Baptiste Drouet, Count d'Erlon, the commander of I Corps, and Count Honoré Reille of II Corps were cautious generals who had been repeatedly drubbed by Wellington in the Peninsula. D'Erlon in particular was indecisive and lacking in confidence and dash. He had neither initiative nor flair.

Dominique Vandamme the Count of Unsebourg and commander of III Corps, on the other hand, was a hard-bitten and loyal veteran who had joined the army in 1788 and had risen from the ranks. A foul-mouthed looter, whose greed was matched only by his ambition, Vandamme was touchy and rebellious but eager to fight for France, for glory and for his Emperor.

Count Maurice Gérard had volunteered in 1791 for service in the French Revolutionary armies. In 1815 he was at the head of the IV Corps. Napoleon rated him as one of the three best French generals and after Ligny intended, he said, to create Gérard a marshal.

Georges Mouton, the Count of Lobau, commanding VI Corps, was a distinguished veteran with years of service in the Revolutionary and Imperial armies. He had particularly distinguished himself against the Austrians in 1809.

The commanders of the four cavalry corps were Count Claude Pajol, Count Rémy Exelmans, François Kellermann the Duke of Valmy and Count Edouard Milhaud. All were veterans. Pajol was a brilliant and reliable tactician with a flair for seizing enemy-held bridges by a magnificent cavalry *coup de main*. Kellermann, the son of a marshal, had emerged as a celebrated cavalryman who helped save the day at Marengo (14 June 1800) with a decisive charge on the Austrians.

Count Antoine Drouot, an experienced artilleryman, was at the head of the Imperial Guard. The son of a baker, Drouot had joined the army in 1793. Present at numerous battles, including Trafalgar and Borodino, Drouot had decided the victory of Hanau in 1813 by his brilliant employment of the Guard artillery.[7] A brave and simple soldier, Drouot had shared Napoleon's exile on the island of Elba.

Such were the marshals and generals Napoleon had with him in 1815. No longer did he have a galaxy of glittering, ambitious stars in the ascendant, but a collection of survivors, some good, others faulty. Several were worn out. Many of the French generals, wrote Count Fleury de Chaboulon, Napoleon's secretary, 'were no longer those youthful and ambitious men who generously gave their lives to gain promotion and fame; they were men tired of war and who, having reached the highest rank and enriched by loot from enemies or by the generous gifts of Napoleon, desired only to enjoy their fortune in peace and in the shade of their laurels.'[8]

Yet much talent remained in the majority of Napoleon's generals. Many of the corps commanders of 1815 became Marshals of France in later life. Above all, every one of Napoleon's generals was a veteran with years of experience.

The main disadvantage experienced by the generals was the lack of trust placed in them – except a favoured, popular few such as Marshal Ney – by the rank and file. The political turmoil of Napoleon's abdication and the return of the Bourbons in 1814, during which many generals had taken office under Louis XVIII, left many troops suspicious of the trustworthiness of their commanders.

The Prussian high command laboured under an entirely different set of problems and contained men whose characters contrasted sharply with those of the French generals.

'The French are before me, glory behind, and a explosion will come soon!'[9] Thus promised the Commander-in-Chief of the Prussian army, Field Marshal Gebhard Leberecht von Blücher the Prince of Wahlstadt. No ordinary commander was he. Indomitable, resilient, exuberantly optimistic, Blücher was always wanting to attack. He was a veteran of dozens of scraps, a drinker, a gambler and a swearer.

In spite of his seventy-two years, Blücher was energetic and ferociously intent on capturing his hated foe, Napoleon, and executing him by firing squad. Blücher's vendetta against the French and their Emperor brought him to the verge of insanity. In 1811, he had believed he was pregnant with an elephant. This fantasy was to return shortly after Waterloo, following a fall from a horse that resulted, characteristically, from showing off in front of the ladies.

Aged Blücher enjoyed the active life of a youth and the popularity of a saviour of the nation. His unlimited capacity to inspire his troops, as much as any skills of generalship, had led to his appointment as Commander-in-Chief of the Prussian army.

His career was chequered but colourful. Born at Gross-Renzow near Rostock in 1742, he had enlisted fifteen years later in the Swedish hussars. Captured by a regiment of Prussian hussars in 1760, he entered its ranks, under the guardianship of the Prussian colonel. This introduction to soldiering fixed Blücher's attitudes. It gave him for life a 'hussar complex' that showed itself even when he was a general commanding a force of all three arms. The cavalry always remained Blücher's favourite arm and, according to one who knew him, even 'as a field-marshal he put himself at the head of a squadron as readily as at the head of an army.' He would employ infantry as if they were cavalry, hurling battalions into spirited bayonet charges rather than placing them in coolly chosen defensive positions.

Blücher participated in the Seven Years' War (1756–63) against the French, but Frederick the Great took offence at young Blücher's peacetime pastimes of duelling, gambling, wenching and drinking, told Blücher he could 'go to the devil' and in 1773 sent him to become a farmer. Blücher was allowed to return to the army in 1786 and led Prussian cavalry against the powerful armies of the French Revolution after 1793.

In 1806, he commanded the Prussian advance-guard at Auerstädt. Blücher did not perform well at this battle, failing to co-ordinate his attacks and being beaten by numerically inferior French forces. Worse was to follow and, obliged to surrender at Lübeck, he retired to his estates. From these years stem Blücher's intense vendetta against Napoleon, and his desire to avenge the humiliations he and Prussia had undergone in 1806.

Blücher's chance came in 1813, when Napoleon was in fighting retreat through Europe consequent to the disaster in Russia of 1812. Blücher soon proved himself to be the outstanding leader of the sixth European coalition against Napoleon. He was popular not merely with his own Prussian soldiers but also with the Russians, Austrians and Swedes. Blücher habitually exchanged coarse, jovial banter with his devoted troops:

'Good morning, children', he would address them. And they would roar in delighted reply, 'Hurrah, Father Blücher!' His pipe was always in his mouth, the word 'Forwards' always on his lips and the smell of powder always in his nostrils. Often Blücher suffered defeat – at Lützen and Bautzen in 1813, at Brienne and Vauchamps in 1814 to name just a few – but he always returned for another scrap.

A dogged, fierce persistence won Blücher his victories in the end: at Leipzig, at La Rothière, at Laon until, eventually, he had driven, cajoled, led and swept the allied armies into Paris, forcing Napoleon to abdicate on 6 April 1814.

Now, in 1815, Napoleon was back in France, and Blücher was once more at the head of a Prussian army eager to do battle and eager to stand by his friend the Duke of Wellington. For Blücher worked well as part of a team, and his loyalty was fierce and unswerving. 'Wellington is obligingness itself', Blücher commented on his new ally for this campaign. 'He is an extremely resolute man, we shall get along very well together.'[10]

For all his undoubted assets, Blücher did have drawbacks as a commander. He was a hussar general who waged war by instinct rather than reasoned logic. Even so, Blücher could muddle through a battle with some credit to his name; it was in the realm of strategy that the aged field marshal was truly out of his depth. He was incapable of reading a map and was nearly illiterate. A subordinate asserted that Blücher understood so little of the conduct of war that he was unable to judge whether a plan of operations was good or bad.[11]

Fortunately, therefore, Blücher was blessed with a superb Chief of Staff, Lieutenant-General Count Neithardt von Gneisenau. Seventeen years younger than Blücher, Gneisenau nevertheless shared his chief's intense hatred for the French and equally intense dedication to Prussia and victory. Gneisenau and

Blücher made a superb command team – as they had proved in the campaigns of 1813 and 1814. For Gneisenau possessed the intellectual power and knowledge of strategy his chief badly needed. Blücher once joked that he was the only person who could kiss his own head: and proved it by kissing Gneisenau's brainy brow.

Born in 1760, Gneisenau commenced his career in the Austrian army, transferring to the Prussian army in 1786. Like Blücher, Gneisenau had fought against the French in 1806. Following Napoleon's defeat of Prussia in that year, Gneisenau helped the reformer General von Scharnhorst to remodel the outdated, professional Prussian army into a national, patriotic, motivated force. Gneisenau was strong, forceful and energetic. He was an impressive personality, not given to boasting or vanity and he exuded an air of wisdom and reliability.

Unlike Blücher, Gneisenau did not work well with allies. He disliked the Russians. From the outset, he suspected the honesty of Wellington. A copy of a secret treaty of January 1815 between Britain, Austria and royalist France aiming to check Prussian and Russian ambitions had been found in Paris by Napoleon on his return from exile. He had published it with glee. Wellington had stood by this treaty and consequently it was a maxim in Berlin that the Duke might be counted on to desert a friend.[12] Unlike Blücher, Gneisenau shared this view. He warned Baron Carl von Müffling, the Prussian liaison officer to Wellington's army, that the Duke had become a master of duplicity.[13]

Fortunately, Gneisenau's suspicions of Wellington's honesty did not immediately cause him to doubt his generalship. But following the Duke's tardiness in supporting the Prussians when the campaign opened, Gneisenau would come to doubt Wellington's resolution. It would take all Blücher's fierce loyalty to Wellington for Gneisenau's caution and distrust to be overcome. This would allow his better half – his undoubted organisational genius as Chief of Staff – to come to the fore.

Individually, both Blücher and Gneisenau were handicapped by serious flaws. Together, they made a formidable and brilliant command team.

The four Prussian corps commanders were Generals Ziethen, Pirch, Thielmann and Bülow. Count Hans von Ziethen, commander of I Corps, was a tough veteran of the 1813 and 1814 campaigns against the French. He had particularly distinguished himself at Leipzig, the great 'Battle of the Nations', in 1813. Now Ziethen was forty-five years old.

Georg von Pirch, at the head of II Corps, was a native of Magdeburg and was fifty-two years of age.

Baron Johann von Thielmann, fifty years old and commander of III Corps, was Saxon by birth. He had served in the French ranks, commanding a Saxon cavalry brigade in Napoleon's army at Borodino in 1812. But in 1813, Thielmann defected to the allies and carried out attacks on French lines of communication. Arrogant and tactless, Thielmann was nevertheless an experienced soldier and had the advantage of possessing a fine Chief of Staff in the person of Colonel Carl von Clausewitz. Clausewitz was destined to emerge after 1815 as the world's most famous military philosopher.

Friedrich von Bülow, the Count of Dennewitz, was sixty years of age and a seasoned veteran with several sucesses to his credit. In 1813, he had defeated Marshal Oudinot at Gross-Beeren and Marshal Ney at Dennewitz. Bülow had been present at Leipzig (1813) and Laon (1814) and in 1815 commanded IV Corps. Although Bülow's corps was not present at Ligny, it would form the main Prussian contribution at the Battle of Waterloo two days later.

With the exception of Bülow, none of these corps commanders belonged to the first rank of Prussian military leaders. Generals Tauenzien, Yorck and Count Frederick Kleist von Nollendorf were tried and tested commanders of genius, yet they were given commands outside Blücher's army. The reason for this was the outdated strict Prussian system of command by seniority. Baron Carl von Müffling wrote that 'Gneisenau really commanded the army, and ... Blücher merely acted as an example as the bravest in battle.'[14]

But Gneisenau was below Tauenzien, Yorck and Kleist in seniority. Gneisenau was essential to the Prussian army as Blücher's brains. Hence the only answer was to appoint younger generals to corps commands, even at the price of depriving the army of the services of better, yet senior, men. It was ridiculous, it was self-defeating but there was no choice. Of the four corps commanders, only Bülow was senior to Gneisenau, and so Bülow's IV Corps was expected to act as a reserve to Blücher's army. In the event, it would have to participate in the campaign and fight under Gneisenau's orders and this resulted in a misunderstanding that meant Bülow failed to arrive in time to participate in the Battle of Ligny.

All in all, the Prussian generals were reasonably able professionals with experience and valour, though they lacked the elan and flair enjoyed by the best of their French counterparts.

Field Marshal Arthur Wellesley the Duke of Wellington enters but briefly and indirectly into the story of the Battle of Ligny. However, as Blücher's ally and commander of the Anglo-Dutch-German army which tied down most of Marshal Ney's French forces at Quatre Bras and prevented them from outflanking Blücher at Ligny, Wellington's character demands analysis.

Although close friends and loyal allies, the Duke and Blücher were as different from each other as was possible. Wellington was an aloof, aristocratic egotist who carefully husbanded his resources. Always he was to be found at the danger spot, seeing to everything in person. In battle he inspired his troops by his own superb example in coolly disregarding the hail of musketry around him.

Wellington was an utterly dedicated professional, intolerant of incompetents, impatient of fools, determined, ruthless and successful. Formidably experienced after years of tough campaigning in India and the Peninsula, Wellington was a master of the art of timing. The Duke's true forte was a robust defence by well drilled, disciplined and trained troops placed in carefully chosen positions, but a daring and co-ordinated offensive was not beyond his talents – as he had demonstrated fully at Salamanca in 1812.

For all his genius, for all his well merited reputation as Britain's best commander after the Duke of Marlborough, Wellington was not on the same elevated plane as Napoleon. While Napoleon had dominated Europe both militarily and politically, the Duke conducted a mere sideshow in the Peninsula against a committee of quarrelsome French marshals. Wellington excelled at defensive tactics but was less sure at campaign strategy.

Moreover, he must be faulted for his failure to give sufficient praise and his innate inability to delegate responsibility. In the early years of the Peninsular War, the Duke had been able totally to control his small army himself and lacked subordinates of sufficiently high calibre to be entrusted with much independence. Yet the failure in subsequent years to encourage initiative and to delegate responsibility posed dangers if Wellington ever became a casualty. By contrast, the Prussian army continued to function when Blücher temporarily disappeared at the end of the Battle of Ligny; and Napoleon had groomed twenty-six marshals with the capacity for independent command.

Wellington's troops trusted and respected him, called him 'Hookey' after his nose and knew the care he took to keep casualties to a minimum. But Wellington never gained the intense, affectionate veneration enjoyed by Napoleon and Blücher. Blücher led by close personal contact with his troops and by his reputation as a hard fighting, hard drinking general. Napoleon led by a semi-deified aura of mystique. Owing to the nature of their leadership, Napoleon and Blücher were able to lead their men through, and beyond, disaster. Wellington led his soldiers by trust. They trusted him not to waste their lives. They trusted him to win. Wellington's ability to lead his men would last as long as he never lost a campaign. He never did.

The Battlefield Scenario

Although Napoleonic battles were chaotic, and the weapons used in them inaccurate, they were costly because they were cramped. Infantrymen had to be packed tightly together in order to fire dense volleys of lead musketballs. Cavalry manoeuvred in ordered ranks to furnish their charges with shock power while artillery guns were massed in order to pound enemy positions.

The main battlefield weapons were swords, lances, carbines and pistols for the cavalry, muskets and bayonets for the infantry and cannon and howitzers for the artillery. The muskets were flintlock muzzle-loaders, relying on the ignition of black powder by sparks resulting from a flint hitting steel when the trigger was pulled. Heavy rain would dampen the powder which would refuse to ignite. Even in dry weather muskets frequently misfired. The musket fired less than three rounds per minute and was, in battle conditions, accurate only up to 100 yards. Musketry was an extremely inefficient method of killing an enemy.[15] Certain allied units, most famously the British 95th Regiment, carried rifles which increased accuracy but took longer to load.

The artillery fired iron cannonballs and canister. The most powerful battlefield cannon, the 12-pounder, had a practical range for roundshot of up to 900 metres. Additional range could be achieved by ricochet fire, the bouncing of a cannonball along the ground. Ricochet fire was particularly effective when used against the whole length of an enemy formation. Nevertheless, artillery fire was most destructive at short range. This was particularly true of canister. Canister consisted of a tin can filled with lead balls. On firing the gun, the can burst, propelling a deadly swathe of lead into the enemy troops. The effect was like that of a particularly dense volley of musketry.

Howitzers also fired explosive shells – hollow iron spheres packed with explosive powder which was ignited by a fuse lit by the firing of the howitzer. The high trajectory of howitzers made them indispensable when the target was sheltered on the reverse slopes of a ridge. All guns were muzzle-loaders and slow firing – at most three rounds per minute. Firing produced dense clouds of smoke which soon hindered the aiming of the gun. The most effective way of neutralising an enemy gun was to hammer a spike into its touchhole. This rendered impossible the ignition of the powder charge inside the barrel.

The British had two artillery projectiles not employed by the other armies. The first was spherical case shot, more commonly known as shrapnel after its inventor. By bursting over a body of troops and showering it with musketballs, the shrapnel was able to reproduce the deadly burst of canister but at long range. Its effectiveness was reduced by the large number of premature explosions in flight. The second British invention was the Congreve rocket, which terrified horses but generally followed far too erratic a flight path to be one of the gunners' main weapons.

Cavalry firearms were unreliable except at almost point blank range and were difficult to reload on horseback. The most commonly used weapon was the sword, which came in various designs. Heavy cavalry wielded long, straight swords; light cavalry a lighter, curved sabre. The lance could be a deadly weapon in skilled hands, particularly against a scattered foe. But a compact and well-trained enemy cavalry formation would knock aside the lance points with swords and then have the luckless lancers at its mercy. The lance did have its advantages when used against formed infantry, for, unlike a sword, the long lance outreached a footsoldier's musket and bayonet.

Battlefield tactics relied on both physical and psychological effect. Massed guns would cause considerable enemy casualties, unless the foe was sheltered by the terrain, but would also shatter enemy nerves. Massed, ordered ranks of troops intimidated uncertain enemy conscripts before the firing even began and a bayonet charge would often cause an uncertain enemy to flee before the steel bayonets came into use. Magnificent, colourful uniforms increased the wearer's confidence, self-esteem and apparent size. Some French cavalry, the *cuirassiers*, wore breastplates, as much, perhaps, for the psychological impact on the foe as for physical protection. Although the gleaming breastplates deflected all sabre thrusts aimed at the chest and back, they offered no protection to the vulnerable neck and armpits. Moreover, they would never stop a cannonball and rarely a musket shot. They also added considerably to the wearer's weight and dismounted *cuirassiers* often found themselves quite helpless, sprawling on the ground. Nevertheless, *cuirassiers* enjoyed an awesome reputation and British infantry before the 1815 campaign widely believed the breastplates were impervious to musketry.

Battle formations were varied and troop manoeuvres complex. To maximise firepower, the infantry fought in lines of troops at least two ranks deep. Where shock power was required, soldiers were massed in dense assault columns which were easier than lines to manoeuvre. As the unprotected flanks and rear of infantry formations were particularly vulnerable to cavalry, the universal defence of footsoldiers against mounted attack was to form a hollow rectangle, known as a square even if the faces were not equal in length, bristling on all four sides with bayonets and musketry volleys. The infantry tended to fire at the horses rather than the riders so as to cause more confusion and hindrance to subsequent ranks. Squares, like columns, compressed large numbers of troops in a small area and thus were excellent artillery targets.

Swarms of skirmishers preceded the blocks of troops in order to pick off enemy officers and to shake up the opposing formations. Skirmishers acted in pairs, one soldier firing and reloading while the other kept an eye on enemy activities. Thus each pair of skirmishers had at least one loaded musket at all times. All armies possessed specialised companies of light troops trained for skirmishing tasks.

Cavalry wheeled and charged in both line and column. Charges were conducted at a brisk trot rather than at a gallop so as to preserve the cohesion of the formation. Horsemen bowled over the foe by their weight and skill as much as by their speed; maintenance of momentum was decisive. Heavy cavalry, such as *grenadiers à cheval* (horse grenadiers) and breastplated *cuirassiers*, were shock troops whose task was to crush the opposing mounted units and to crash through the enemy's front line. The heavy cavalry usually charged in column, as at Eylau in 1807 and Borodino in 1812 to inflict a series of shocks by successive squadrons. The leading ranks generally fell victim to enemy fire or became dispersed while cutting up enemy formations. Then the subsequent ranks would press forward. Such tactics were expensive as artillery fire plunged down the length of the column and often mounting casualties eventually formed an impassible barrier to further progress.

Light cavalry such as *Uhlans* or lancers, hussars and *chasseurs à cheval* mainly scouted, reconnoitred, pursued and supported the infantry. The versatile dragoons undertook the functions of both heavy and light cavalry.

Artillery came in different calibres. Lighter guns, such as the 6- or 8-pounders, were more manoeuvrable but possessed less range and hitting power. The heaviest guns on the battlefield were 12-pounders, for the primitive roads, wooden bridges and muddy fields did not readily bear greater burdens. The two categories of artillery were horse and foot batteries. Horse batteries were generally lighter and, with all the gunners mounted on either horses or limbers, able to keep up with cavalry. Foot batteries were heavier, slower and more adept at pounding a position than at supporting and keeping pace with an advance. The artillery pieces were hooked up to wheeled limbers drawn by teams of horses. Once the guns reached the designated firing position, they were unlimbered and formed up in a line facing the enemy. While firing was in progress, the limbers, horses and ammunition waggons were sent to the rear of the gun line.

Artillery concentrated its efforts against the massed enemy infantry and cavalry but did sometimes engage in counter-battery fire to distract enemy fire from friendly troops undertaking an attack. Counter-battery fire relied as much on killing the horses and men serving the guns as on scoring a lucky direct hit on the artillery pieces themselves. To support an assault, massed preparatory artillery fire was instrumental in softening up the enemy line. The French also excelled at integrating light guns with attacking formations to blast their way through. The classic example is the Battle of Friedland in 1807, in which thirty-eight French guns fired, then limbered up and advanced to a new firing position again and again right up to the enemy.

Medical services were primitive, where they existed. Amputations were performed without anaesthetics, which were yet to make their appearance in the domain of medicine, and the amputee had to make do with a swig of brandy and a staunch sense of honour which forbade him to cry out. Some amputees immediately went back to their regiments, such was their patriotism and devotion to duty. Medical officers relied heavily on bleeding, when today they would be giving blood transfusions; often a wounded soldier's best hope of survival was keeping out of the hands of the medics. Nevertheless, promise of future progress could be seen in the French army, where the remarkable Surgeon-General, Baron Dominique Larrey, had introduced fast, well-sprung, horse-drawn carriages to ensure the prompt evacuation of stretcher cases and had set high standards for the speed of operations.

All in all, a Napoleonic battle was a terrifying event. The senses of the soldiers were confused by the clouds of rolling smoke, by the continuous roar of cannon and musket, by the swiftly moving troops and fluctuating fortunes of battle. Bands played to drown the screams of wounded men and to transmit orders above the roar of battle. The troops were heavily laden by knapsacks, cartridge pouches, water canteens, greatcoats and blankets. All transport was non-mechanised and only the cavalry and artillerymen rode on horseback. The infantry had to march everywhere. Speed could be achieved only at the risk of exhaustion.

Generals commanding armies had to choose high ground from where they could observe as much of the battlefield as possible and where they could conduct the fight, attempting to impose order on chaos. Their orders had to be sent by galloping aides-de-camp and often reached their destination late, if at all. Similarly, intelligence reached the commander only at the speed of a horse. In these circumstances, battles were decided as much by the actions of sub-ordinate generals in the battle line and by chance as by the decisions of the commander. In the Napoleonic era, even more than in the present, a commander had to send clear, unambiguous orders and had to ensure his subordinates thoroughly understood his aim and method before they departed from his headquarters to their commands in the field.

Thus the generals laboured under serious limitations in commanding their armies. For this reason, the armies needed a robust and effective organisation.

The Rival Armies

The weapons employed by the two armies at Ligny were equally advanced in technological terms. The numbers of troops and guns were approximately equal. In these circumstances, what counted was how experienced the armies were and how they were organised, commanded and inspired. 'In war', propounded Napoleon, 'morale counts for seventy-five per cent; the balance of tangible strength counts for only the remaining twenty-five per cent.'

Napoleon's army of 1815 was a finely tuned structure. It had no weak links. It was highly flexible and articulate. It consisted of the I, II, III, IV, and VI Corps, plus a reserve of four cavalry corps and the elite Imperial Guard.

The Imperial Guard was a crack force composed of experienced veterans utterly dedicated to their Emperor. The Guard provided both an example to the ordinary units of the French army and a powerful, effective reserve which Napoleon habitually used to break through the enemy battle line towards the end of the combat. The Imperial Guard included twelve infantry and five cavalry regiments as well as sixteen artillery batteries. The Guard infantry was divided into the less experienced Young Guard and the formidably experienced Old Guard. Napoleon's Imperial Guard was truly the most magnificent fighting force of the Napoleonic Wars.

The four cavalry corps each contained two divisions of massed horsemen. One corps was of light cavalry, another of dragoons, the other two of heavy

THE FRENCH ARMY

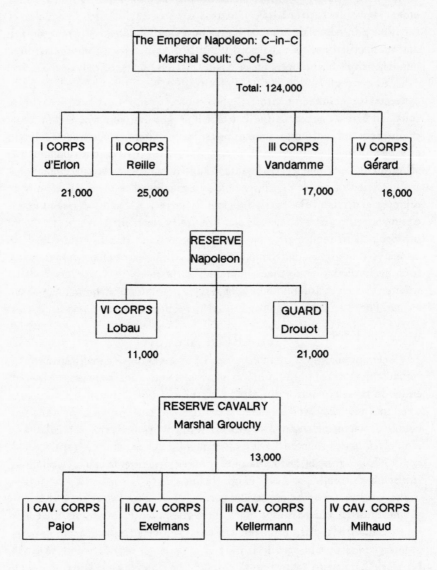

The Emperor Napoleon: C–in–C
Marshal Soult: C–of–S

Total: 124,000

I CORPS
d'Erlon

II CORPS
Reille

III CORPS
Vandamme

IV CORPS
Gérard

21,000   25,000   17,000   16,000

RESERVE
Napoleon

VI CORPS
Lobau

GUARD
Drouot

11,000   21,000

RESERVE CAVALRY
Marshal Grouchy

13,000

I CAV. CORPS
Pajol

II CAV. CORPS
Exelmans

III CAV. CORPS
Kellermann

IV CAV. CORPS
Milhaud

cavalry. These reserve cavalrymen could be used as reinforcements for front line troops or as a concentrated assault force to gain a breakthrough – often in conjunction with the Imperial Guard.

The basic building block of the rest of the French army was the army corps. This was a self-reliant body of troops, between ten and twenty thousand strong, containing three or four infantry divisions each of four regiments. Usually, one of these four regiments would be light infantry, the others being line. Each regiment possessed two or three battalions of six companies. Battalion strength varied but was about 500 men. The corps also included a light cavalry division and artillery units to support the infantry. One battery was attached to each division while a 12-pounder battery formed the corps reserve. The corps further included engineers and a well-organised staff to assist the corps commander.

The corps commander was a vital figure in the French army. Napoleon, who had risen straight from being a gunnery officer to being a general, was a master of gunnery tactics but never truly got to grips with infantry or cavalry tactics. He, unlike Wellington who personally inspected every detail, preferred to devise a plan of battle in broad, strategic terms, allowing the corps commanders much initiative in carrying out this plan. Their role was to keep control of the situation in their sector and then to send reports on progress back to Napoleon who thus kept an eye on the battle as a whole, co-ordinated the fighting and intervened when it was necessary to bolster the front line or to send in the Guard.

What, though, of the quality of the troops? The French Army of the North contained a remarkable proportion of experienced veterans. Even those who had fought in the 1814 campaign as 'Marie-Louises', raw teenaged recruits, possessed by 1815 considerable battle experience. Furthermore they had fought in one of Napoleon's finest military campaigns, they had fought in a relatively small force under the generalship of their Emperor in person, and they had fought next to the seasoned veterans of the Guard. All too many of Wellington and Blücher's troops had never fought before.

The loyalty and spirit of the French rank and file were remarkable. The veteran French General Count Maximilien Foy noted in his journal that 'the troops exhibit not patriotism, not enthusiasm, but an actual mania for the Emperor and against his enemies.'[16] Never, added Lieutenant Jacques Martin of the 45th Line, did an army march off more certain of victory.[17]

But the mood of the soldiers had its darker side. The army was feverish with irrational emotions. 'You are perfectly right as to the enthusiasm of the troops', wrote one of Napoleon's ADCs. 'I have never seen anything like it. They are like men possessed.'[18]

Troops wanted revenge for the humiliation of defeat and surrender in 1814. Former prisoners-of-war desired revenge on the English for the terrible prisoner-of-war hulks on which they had been held. Suspicion of high-ranking officers, fear of betrayal by royalist sympathisers, and jealousy thriving on the lack of supply administration were rife in the French army. One Frenchman moaned: 'no mutual confidence, no fraternity of arms, no interchange of generous feelings; pride, selfishness and thirst of prey, reigned throughout.'[19]

General Baron Etienne Radet, Napoleon's provost-marshal, found it impossible to prevent looting. The poorly equipped and supplied French Revolutionary armies had set a tradition of living off the land. This tradition made French soldiers expert looters and improvisers but by encouraging independence and self-sufficiency did terrible damage to discipline. The Imperial Guard itself pillaged and set an example that the rest of the army followed.

The French historian Henry Lachouque lamented the lack of cohesion resulting from the men not being familiar with their commanders and mistrusting their generals. The army, he considered, was capable of exuberant morale and, shortly afterwards, of gloomy depression.[20] The army lacked discipline; it was brilliant but unstable. Ultimately, the French army was held together only by a shared, fanatical loyalty to its Emperor. Troops attributed every mishap and delay to treason and if put under pressure were liable to panic.

As a consequence, the French soldier was a dangerous weapon. He was capable of magnificent feats of arms but also of failing his commander *in extremis*.

'My army is in the best of shape and its morale is all that can be wished for', insisted Blücher at the beginning of June 1815.[21]

Blücher's army consisted of four corps: Ziethen's I Corps, Pirch's II Corps, Thielmann's III Corps and Bülow's IV Corps. A corps contained four infantry brigades, each of which was approximately equal in numerical strength to a French division and contained two or three regiments. The regiment comprised three battalions of four companies each. One battalion in each regiment was formed of fusiliers, who were trained skirmishers and marksmen. The other two were ordinary musketeer battalions. Battalion strength was approximately 730 men. The Prussian infantry formations were large, and hence their brigades were not organised into divisions. The Prussian corps also contained sometimes two, sometimes three, cavalry brigades. In addition, each corps possessed its own artillery force of between six and twelve batteries of eight guns each. Each corps also contained a company of engineers.

Units ranged in quality from regulars, through reserve regiments newly brought into the line, to the militia, or *Landwehr*. No elite regiments were present with Blücher's army, for the Prussian Guards had been left at Berlin. This was a serious drawback, as was the absence of the Prussian *cuirassiers*. The Prussian cavalry was worse equipped, worse mounted and worse led than its French counterpart. Nevertheless, the cavalrymen themselves were as

THE PRUSSIAN ARMY

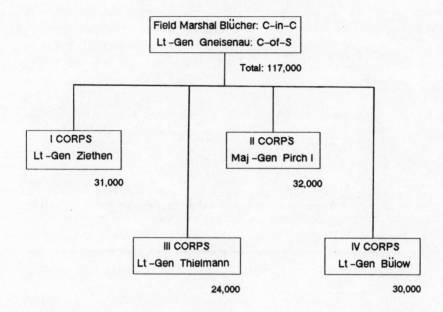

THE COMPOSITION OF THE THREE ARMIES

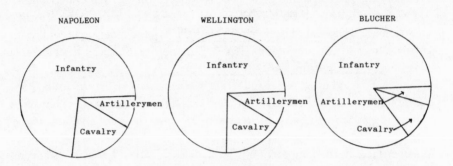

In stark contrast to Napoleon and Wellington's armies, Blücher's army was unbalanced. The Prussians had too small a proportion of cavalry and artillerymen to support their infantry. Battle would test the young Prussian infantrymen's endurance to the utmost.

courageous as the infantry and possessed more discipline than many British cavalry units. The Prussian artillery was of satisfactory quality.

Grave disadvantages attended the organisation of the Prussian army. Unlike Napoleon, Blücher had no centralised reserve whatsoever. There was no artillery or cavalry force in reserve, under the direct control of the Commander-in-Chief, that could be thrown into a dangerous sector. Each corps was a self-contained, self-sufficient force. This fact was reinforced by a tendency to group units from the same province in the same corps. For instance, I Corps showed a preponderance of formations from Westphalia and IV Corps a preponderance from Silesia.

In short, the Prussian army was an unsophisticated organisation. Its component blocks were held together relatively loosely. The primitive set-up of the Prussian army lacked the flexibility and sensitivity of the complex French army structure.

The Prussian staff was much smaller and less complex than the staff of the French army. Nevertheless, it was competent and contained some experts. Gneisenau was a good Chief of Staff and the Chief of Staff of Thielmann's III Corps, Colonel Carl von Clausewitz, possessed one of the finest intellects in Europe.

However, no one man directed the operations of the Prussian army. Blücher knew how to fight a battle, but had to rely on Gneisenau in order to formulate campaign strategy. In important decisions throughout the campaign, the Prussian headquarters would debate the issue, with Blücher the Commander-in-Chief, Gneisenau the Chief of Staff and General Karl von Grolmann the Quartermaster-General all having a say. Inefficiency and indecision could well emanate from Prussian headquarters if it were not for Blücher's fierce determination on basic principles.

The character of the Prussian soldiers of 1815 makes for a curious study. For the most part, the Prussian army that fought at Ligny was composed of untried, young, inexperienced troops. All too many of the units were *Landwehr* regiments. Prussia, moreover, lacked the economic strength of Britain or France. Impoverished by the long years of the Napoleonic Wars, burdened between 1806 and 1813 by French exactions to feed Napoleon's military machine, Prussia was unable to equip her soldiers with the best uniforms and weapons.

In stark contrast to the often magnificent, gaudy dress of the British and French, the Prussians opted for simple, cheap and practical clothing. Dull, drab, dark tunics, grey trousers, soft caps or shakos characterized the Prussian soldiers. Lack of uniformity was the most noticeable feature of Prussian uniforms.

The worst equipped units were the *Landwehr*: some formations marched in clogs and civilian clothes, others contained muskets of different calibres. The Prussian high command was careful to brigade *Landwehr* units with a highly trained and well equipped regular regiment of the line. Each brigade thus possessed a backbone on which less experienced units could rely.

The Prussian army, for all its weaknesses, had a soul. It breathed the fire of vengeance. It loathed Napoleon and the French, who had in the long years of the Napoleonic Wars occupied Prussian lands, looted Prussian homes and finally had caused a national Prussian spirit to be born. Blücher's was a national army. Before 2 May it had included a contingent of 14,000 Saxons. At the Congress of Vienna, Prussia had annexed part of Saxony. But the Saxons, resentful of their new masters and wistful for the days when they had served under Napoleon, never truly felt themselves to be part of the Prussian army. On 2 May, elements of them mutinied with shouts of 'Long live the King of Saxony. Long live Napoleon!' Blücher himself had to evacuate his headquarters at Liège, and after the ringleaders of the mutiny had been shot, the whole Saxon contingent was sensibly returned east of the Rhine. Thereafter, Blücher's army was a uniformly Prussian, national army.

However young and inexperienced, Blücher's soldiers in 1815 had morale. They were resilient. Unlike the French, the Prussian troops were not demoralised by reverses, but bounded back for another scrap. Blücher encouraged his adoring troops with guttural roars of 'Forwards!'. To them, he was 'Papa Blücher'; to him, they were his children.

The Prussian army reflected the character of its aged chief. Neither troops

THE ANGLO-DUTCH-GERMAN ARMY

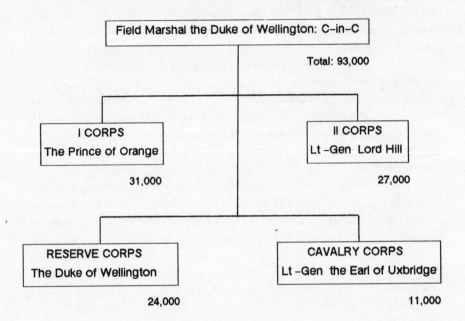

Field Marshal the Duke of Wellington: C–in–C

Total: 93,000

I CORPS
The Prince of Orange

31,000

II CORPS
Lt –Gen Lord Hill

27,000

RESERVE CORPS
The Duke of Wellington

24,000

CAVALRY CORPS
Lt –Gen the Earl of Uxbridge

11,000

nor commander knew how to economize their strength. Foreign to them was the British infantryman's robust and cool defence of a fixed position. Blücher's men defended a post by attacking in battalion columns with fixed bayonets, hurling back their enemy temporarily before falling back under renewed pressure until, having received reinforcements, they could advance once more.

In short, in this simple, national army quantity counted for more than quality. But it was an army whose simplicity afforded it – in contrast to the French – resilience and an irresistable, united spirit.

Wellington's army was an inexperienced composite force. It was but one-third British, and most of that contingent had never seen a battle before. Even so, the Duke could expect to be able to rely on his British infantry to put up a good fight. Wellington could also count on the superbly professional King's German Legion. Although the rest of his army performed well on occasion, its overall performance in battle was erratic. The cavalry lacked discipline and proper organisation. Many of the Dutch–Belgian contingent had served in former years in Napoleon's Grand Army; the troops from the German states of Hanover, Brunswick and Nassau were young and often unsteady. 'I have got an infamous army', Wellington complained, 'very weak and ill-equipped, and a very inexperienced staff.'[22]

Nevertheless, by placing poor brigades next to reliable ones and ensuring no part of his line consisted entirely of non-British troops, the Duke would be able to put up a tough fight at both Quatre Bras on 16 June and at Waterloo two days later. Unlike the Prussians, Wellington's army would fight better in defence than on the offensive.

Such were the two foes at the Battle of Ligny and their allies or auxiliary forces. The fatal course of events that was to bring these two inveterate enemies face to face across Ligny brook was already in motion.

Notes

1. Longford, *Wellington: Pillar of State*, p.78
2. Charras, *Histoire de la Campagne de 1815*, p.212
3. Brett-James, *The Hundred Days*, p.102
4. Damitz, *Histoire de la Campagne de 1815*, v.1, p.47
5. Chandler, *Napoleon's Marshals*, p.371
6. *Ibid*, p.LVII
7. It is sometimes asserted that General Alava, the Spanish liaison officer with Wellington's army, was the only man present at both Trafalgar and Waterloo. This is false, as Drouot was also present at both battles.
8. De Chaboulon, *Mémoires pour servir à l'histoire*, v.2, pp.151–2
9. Treitschke, *History of Germany in the 19th Century*, v.2, p.152
10. *Ibid*, v.2, p.154
11. Müffling, *Passages from My Life*, p.225
12. Acton, 'German Schools of History' in *English Historical Review* (Jan. 1886)
13. Müffling, *op. cit.*, p.212

14. *Ibid*, p.225
15. See Griffith, *Forward into Battle*
16. Foy, *Vie Militaire*, pp.269–70
17. Martin, *Souvenirs d'un ex-officier*, p.273
18. Kerry, *The First Napoleon*, p.114
19. Booth, *The Battle of Waterloo by a near observer*, p.101
20. Lachouque, *Waterloo*, p.48
21. Chalfont, *Waterloo: Battle of Three Armies*, p.53
22. Longford, *Wellington: The Years of the Sword*, p.402

3

THE CAMPAIGN OPENS

Prelude to Combat

Ever since Napoleon had regained the French throne in March 1815, the armies of Wellington and Blücher had been hastily preparing to meet, check and rout any French invasion of Belgium. Wellington was positioned in the west of the country, Blücher further east.

At the Tirlemont conference of 3 May the two allied commanders promised closer co-operation and to come to each other's aid in the event of a French attack. Liaison officers – Major-General Baron Carl von Müffling and Lieutenant-Colonel Sir Henry Hardinge – were exchanged to facilitate the passing on of intelligence between the allies concerning French movements.

Napoleon, if he invaded, had a number of lines of attack open to him. Possible offensives could strike Wellington's army at Mons or even nearer the English Channel at Tournai in an attempt to cut Wellington's army off from the Channel ports. But Napoleon correctly anticipated that the fire-breathing Blücher would rush immediately to support his beleaguered ally.[1] So Napoleon wanted his offensive to strike Prussian troops first. He judged that the more cautious and egotistical Wellington would be tardier in succouring Blücher than vice versa. Events would prove him right.

Nevertheless, an onslaught aimed at the heart of the Prussian army could drive Blücher back towards Wellington rather than away from him. Instead, Napoleon wanted to employ his old strategy of 'divide and rule'. First, he would smash Prussian units guarding the junction of the two allied armies. Then he would separate Wellington from Blücher and bowl them over one by one before they could concentrate their units and unite.

To drive a wedge between the two armies, Napoleon would have to storm northwards into Belgium and cross the River Sambre somewhere near Charleroi. In his path lay the western half of Ziethen's Prussian I Corps.

Ziethen was well aware that he guarded the junction of the two allied armies; he was also aware that his corps might well bear the brunt of a French offensive. On 2 May, the day before the Tirlemont Conference, he issued orders to his subordinate commanders which were to be acted upon in the event of a French attack. The orders covered possible lines of advance of the French in the Charleroi sector and detailed the concentration points of the Prussian units. A

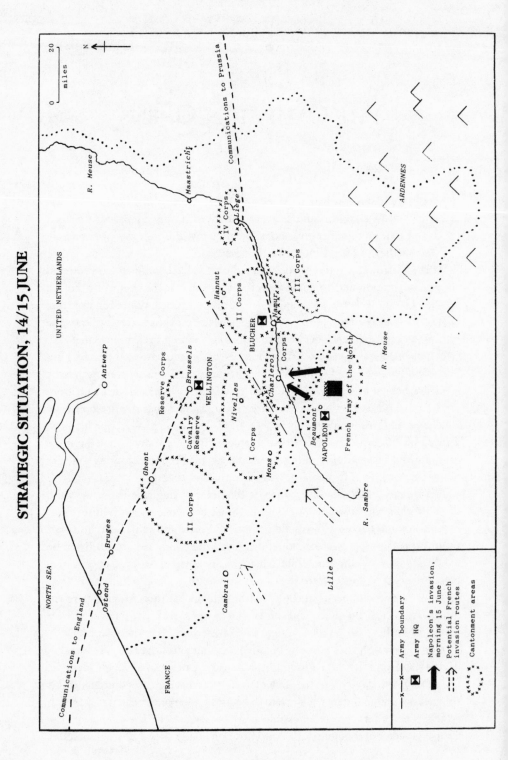

STRATEGIC SITUATION, 14/15 JUNE

stand was to be made by whichever brigade was attacked until all of the Prussian I Corps could assemble.[2]

Apart from these preparations and plans, there was little for the Prussian high command to do except wait. The Prussian soldiers on sentinel duty just to the north of the frontier were waiting too. One of these sentinels was Volunteer Henri Nieman, of the 6th Uhlans, who did not enjoy being on outpost duty.

'I found it very unpleasant to sit on my horse in a dark night facing the enemy and watching every sound. My horse was of a restless disposition, like its master, and I had trouble to keep him quiet to enable me to end in passing my two hours' post.' On one occasion Nieman was ordered to ride along the outpost line for several miles and in the course of this tiresome duty he came upon a sentry. 'Who is there?' he called, and back came the reply 'A sentinel.'

Nieman asked him for the password, only to receive the answer 'I forget it.'

'According to military custom,' Nieman related in his journal, 'having my pistol in my hand I should have shot him down, but being convinced he was one of my own regiment, I only put him in arrest.'[3]

Some weeks later, on the evening of Tuesday 13 June, reports began to filter in to Ziethen's headquarters at Charleroi from the outposts. Around Beaumont the night sky was orange with the reflected light of many bivouac fires. Was it the French army or merely a deception? No orders went out for a concentration of the Prussian army. Already there had been two false alarms and it was no easy task to obtain food for large numbers of soldiers concentrated in one area for any length of time. 'Scatter to live, concentrate to fight' was the military maxim of the day.

But on 14 June, some French deserters arrived with reports that Napoleon would attack early next morning, the 15th. Accordingly, towards midnight Gneisenau issued orders from the Prussian headquarters at Namur for II, III and IV Corps each to mass their regiments and to begin to move west. The precise concentration point of the army would be detailed once the French axis of advance became apparent. Meanwhile I Corps would remain in position to guard the River Sambre. But were the Prussians already too late? Blücher had been taken by surprise with only a few hours' warning of the impending attack. His army was disunited and dispersed in widespread billets. Wellington's army, too, was scattered in cantonments and unlike Blücher the Duke was oblivious to the imminent French onslaught.

North of the threatened frontier, the Prussian outposts watched and waited. The troopers of Nieman's unit were ordered not to undress, while it became generally known to the men of Ziethen's corps that the first three shots fired from heavy artillery pieces would signal the commencement of hostilities. The Prussians watched, tense and alert.

Napoleon had not been idle during these long weeks. Men had been mobilised,

Paris fortified, arms churned out and then the imperial eagles had marched. By nightfall on 14 June, the French Army of the North was massed in position just south of the Franco-Belgian border, distributed from Maubeuge in the west to Philippeville in the east.

Napoleon ordered his troops to light their campfires in hollows of the ground, but unknown to him the orange glow reflected on the clouds had been spotted by the Prussians the night before. The rain poured down while the French sheltered in their bivouacs and Napoleon in his headquarters at the Château of the Prince of Caraman-Chimay in the town of Beaumont.

Marching orders for the invasion of Belgium on 15 June had already been written. Light cavalry was to spearhead the drive into enemy-held territory. Scouting parties would push ahead in all directions. Local inhabitants were to be questioned, letters in post offices examined, enemy outposts to be removed.

Then would follow four lumbering columns, punching their way through the countryside up to the River Sambre and the town of Charleroi. Precise times were assigned to each corps for *réveille* and assembly. The columns were meant to wake up, stumble into shape and unwind like long snakes from the bivouacs. All the baggage, apart from some pontoons and ambulances, was to follow after the army; unauthorized waggons found in the midst of the columns were to be burnt to ensure greater mobility. Speed was all-important.

Small parties were to scout to the west and the east of the army to secure news of the enemy. In addition, communications were to be preserved between the columns to ensure they stayed level with each other.[4]

According to the French historian Henry Houssaye, 'this movement order is, with justice, regarded as a model. Never in the fortunate hours of Austerlitz and Friedland had Napoleon dictated a more studied or better devised marching system.'[5] It was a fine marching order, but unforeseeable delays could wreak havoc on its timetable, at a moment when everything was staked on speed, before the enemy could concentrate.

Napoleon, ever the man who knew how to electrify his soldiers, how to speak to their hearts, added one final touch to his invasion preparations: an Order of the Day.

Soldiers, today is the anniversary of Marengo and of Friedland, which on two occasions decided the destiny of Europe ... Soldiers! At Jena against these same Prussians, now so arrogant, you were one to two, and at Montmirail one to three ... Soldiers! we shall have to make some forced marches, fight some battles, run some risks, but with constancy victory will be ours. The rights, the honour and the happiness of the country will be reconquered. For every Frenchman who has courage, the moment has come to conquer or die![6]

Napoleon Attacks

At 2.30 am on 15 June, horsemen were riding north. French cavalry units were heading off into the curtain of darkness, mist and uncertainty. The invasion was under way. Half-an-hour later, the first of the columns was on the march. At about quarter-to-four the sun rose, but thick mist and light rain shrouded the countryside.

Soon afterwards the first shots were fired. French cavalrymen had brushed with the Prussian outposts, who retired. Meanwhile, three warning rounds were fired from Prussian cannon, signalling the start of hostilities.

But the French were already in difficulties. The officer bringing the orders of movement to the III Corps had, in the night, fallen from his horse and broken his leg. Consequently one of the columns was woefully behind time. In another column, the desertion of Lieutenant-General Louis de Bourmont the Count of Ghaines and five other officers had thrown the troops into confusion, anger and fear, resulting in delay.

Yet the other columns ploughed on. The morning sun was burning off the mists, revealing roads cut by trenches and barred by fallen trees – the work of the Prussians. The roads were little more than tracks; often they did not exist at all. Napoleon himself commented that 'from Beaumont to Charleroi there is no road to facilitate movement on the bad stretches, where defiles were encountered every few yards.'

Major Jean-Roch Coignet of the French staff wrote that the columns had to clear paths for themselves through the high rye. 'The front ranks could not advance. After being trodden down, it was only fit for straw, in which the cavalry stumbled. That was one of our misfortunes.'

An infantry officer complained that tracks that did exist were reserved for the artillery and cavalry. The footsoldiers had to trudge through soaked and muddy fields.[7]

Skirmishes flared up here and there as the leading French units clashed with Prussian outposts. When the French columns later passed the skirmish sites, the dead and wounded reminded Lieutenant Jacques Martin of former battles and caused his heart to beat faster in apprehensive anticipation.

At 11.00 am the Imperial Guard sappers and marines arrived at Charleroi, stormed the intact bridge over the River Sambre and dismantled the barricades. The Prussians had failed to destroy the bridges over the Sambre partly owing to uncertainty as to whether Napoleon would ever invade, and partly as they themselves needed the bridges to link the bulk of their army to their outposts who were south of the river and monitoring French activity. Prussian engineers were weak in numbers and experience, and unequal to the task of blowing the bridges at short notice. After the campaign, they would try to blow up the Bridge of Jena in Paris, but would succeed only in injuring one of their number and toppling another into the River Seine. So on 15 June the way was open for

French hussars to penetrate deep into the town. The Prussian defenders were already in retreat.

Soon the Belgian citizens of Charleroi were gleefully informing the French that the Prussian garrison of the town had been so surprised that some of the officers fled in a state of undress. Napoleon roared with laughter when he heard the story.[8] He himself was eating the lunch prepared for Ziethen at the Château Puissant on the south bank of the Sambre.

Now the Emperor crossed the river and rode through the town centre of Charleroi, acclaimed by the local Francophiles. Riding up the main road, Napoleon dismounted at a tavern. He sank into a chair and dozed, and not even the frenzied cheers of his soldiers passing by could rouse him.

From the Prussian viewpoint, the situation at noon on 15 June was critical but not beyond salvage. Blücher had learnt of the commencement of hostilities towards 9.00 am, and four hours later dashed off a note to his wife before leaving his headquarters at Namur: 'at this moment I have received the report that Bonaparte has engaged my whole outposts. I break up at once and take the field against the enemy. I will accept battle with pleasure.'[9]

Blücher was hurrying to concentrate his army around Sombreffe, eleven miles northeast of Charleroi. Prussian messengers were on their way to Brussels to inform Wellington of Napoleon's onslaught. Meanwhile, Ziethen's I Corps was performing a delaying action designed to cover the concentration of Blücher's army. Ziethen was in fighting retreat from Charleroi northeast towards Fleurus, three miles southwest of Sombreffe.

The French army, arriving at Charleroi, was splitting into two wings: one wing under Marshal Grouchy to pursue Ziethen to Fleurus, and another, under the famous Marshal Ney, who had just arrived to take up his command, to drive due north along the road to Brussels, to push back any troops of Wellington's army he might encounter and to try and occupy Quatre Bras.

Debate has raged ever since as to whether Napoleon specifically ordered Ney to seize the crossroads of Quatre Bras on 15 June. Napoleon must have realised the significance of the Nivelles–Namur road. This was the only lateral, cobbled route that linked the two allies south of Brussels. Napoleon had to seize the road as soon as possible to divide Wellington and Blücher.

However, Napoleon also realised the limits to what his overburdened troops could achieve. They were mere mortals after all. Hence while hoping if possible to cut the lateral road at Quatre Bras with his left wing and at Sombreffe with his right, Napoleon was realistic. His intention for 15 June was to penetrate as far north towards the lateral road as he could. Quatre Bras and Sombreffe were spurs or targets rather than fixed first day objectives.

According to this reasoning, Napoleon would have ordered Ney to charge up the Brussels road and to try to seize Quatre Bras. Ney can not be blamed for failing to seize the crossroads. His units were strung out and exhausted. They

THE FRENCH INVASION, 15 JUNE

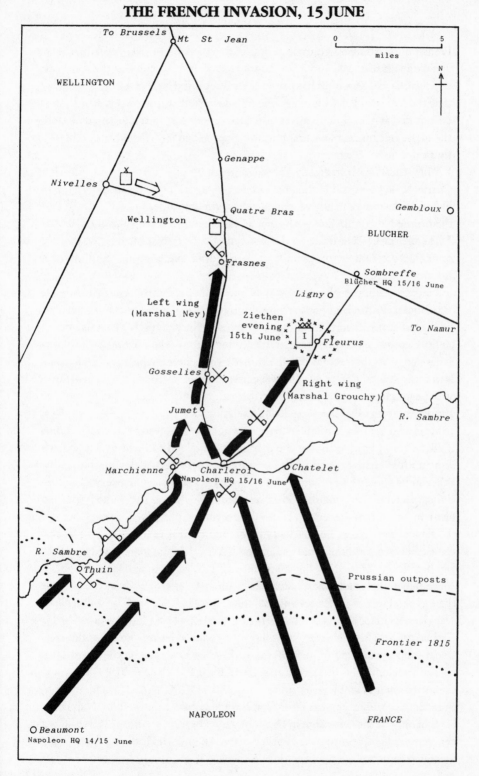

To Brussels

Mt St Jean

0   miles   5

N

WELLINGTON

Genappe

Nivelles

Wellington

Quatre Bras

Gembloux

BLUCHER

Frasnes

Left wing
(Marshal Ney)

Ligny

Sombreffe
Blücher HQ 15/16 June

To Namur

Ziethen
evening
15th June

I

Fleurus

Gosselies

Right wing
(Marshal Grouchy)

Jumet

R. Sambre

Marchienne

Charleroi
Napoleon HQ 15/16 June

Chatelet

R. Sambre

Thuin

Prussian outposts

Frontier 1815

NAPOLEON

FRANCE

Beaumont
Napoleon HQ 14/15 June

53

had been marching since early morning and needed to eat. Moreover, Ney would have heard the cannonfire from the French right wing to the southeast near Fleurus and so would have been wary of pushing too far north. If Ney had occupied Quatre Bras, his flanks would have been exposed (Quatre Bras is seven-and-a-half miles northwest of Fleurus). Ney had to relate his advance to that of the right wing to ensure mutual support. If either wing advanced slowly, it was the right.

Moreover, Napoleon had appointed Ney to command the left wing only that afternoon. Ney was still finding his feet. In the night, he would send his ADC to find out the strength and colonel of each regiment under his command.[10]

So while Ney did in fact push some of his lancers to within a cannon-shot of the hamlet of Quatre Bras, he did not bring forward his infantry to seize the strategic crossroads at this point from a brigade of Wellington's stout German infantry.

The occupation of these crossroads had been due to the German brigade commander, Prince Bernhard of Saxe-Weimar, acting on his own initiative. His move was immediately confirmed by the two local Dutch generals, Baron Henri-Georges de Perponcher-Sedlnitsky and Baron Jean-Victor de Constant-Rebecque, who soon reinforced the brigade with the remainder of its division. This was a commendable action with decisive implications for the future course of the campaign. On 16 June, the crossroads of Quatre Bras would be of the utmost value to both the French and the Allies.

Meanwhile, forces of the French right wing were involved in a fierce skirmish towards 5.30 pm at Gilly, on the road from Charleroi to Fleurus. The French drove a Prussian brigade off a ridge where it had prepared a delaying stand. One Prussian battalion was overrun and cut to pieces by French cavalry. The surviving battered and mauled Prussian formations hurriedly pulled back to Fleurus, where they joined the rest of Ziethen's I Corps. The leading troops of the French right wing bivouacked for the night a few miles south of Fleurus. Other units were as far behind as Charleroi. A few had not yet crossed the River Sambre.

Napoleon had made the Château Puissant at Charleroi his headquarters for the night. Fires were twinkling in the courtyard, for the 'grumblers' of Napoleon's Guard were cooking. Sergeant Hippolyte de Mauduit of the 2/1st Grenadiers recalled in later years how imperial aides-de-camp would continually dash in and out of the *château*. As they passed across the courtyard, they would occasionally knock over the stacked muskets of the Guard. This made the guardsmen grumble even more.

In spite of minor delays and mishaps, the day had gone well for Napoleon. He had opened the campaign in Belgium with a lightning strike. He had seized and now held the initiative. Neither of his enemies had all his forces concentrated in one place ready to offer battle.

Moreover, the confidence and morale of the French army was sustained by the gaining of an early success. 'We passed the night', reminisced a young hussar captain, 'lulled by the joyful singing of the soldiers celebrating the propitious beginning of the campaign.'[11] 15 June saw the first of Napoleon's military successes since the disastrous ending of the 1814 campaign. Morale and faith in the Emperor's 'magic touch' had needed to be restored. The Emperor therefore had a right to feel pleased with himself: 'all my manoeuvres had succeeded as I wished. I could now take the initiative of attacking the enemy armies, one by one.'[12]

Notes

1. Brett-James, *The Hundred Days*, p.31–2
2. Ziethen's orders are quoted in Siborne, *History of the Waterloo Campaign*, pp.543–5
3. *English Historical Review* (July 1888), p.48
4. The order is quoted in full by Siborne, *op. cit.*, pp.545–9
5. Houssaye, *Waterloo 1815*, p.110
6. *Ibid*, p.101
7. Martin, *Souvenirs d'un ex-officier*, p.274; Coignet, *The Notebooks of Captain Coignet*, p.273; Bonaparte, *Napoleon's Memoirs*, p.504
8. Pétiet, *Souvenirs Militaires*, p.190
9. Parkinson, *The Hussar General*, p.217; Ollech, *Geschichte des Feldzuges von 1815 nach archivalischen Quellen*, pp.96–9
10. For detailed evidence on the question of Quatre Bras on 15 June, see Charras, *Histoire de la Campagne de 1815*; Grouard, *Critique de la Campagne de 1815*; Saunders, *The Hundred Days*, and Houssaye, *Waterloo 1815*.
11. Captain de Vatry, quoted in Grouchy, *Mémoires du maréchal de Grouchy*, v.4, p.101
12. Bonaparte, *Napoleon's Memoirs*, p.507

4

APPROACH OF BATTLE

Night of 15/16 June: Wellington

Wellington first learnt of the French attack on Ziethen's Prussians at 3.00 pm on 15 June, at Brussels. One of Wellington's corps commanders, the Dutch Prince of Orange, had visited his outposts in the morning, before riding to Brussels to attend a Ball due to be held that evening. Owing to the heavy atmosphere, the Prince apparently had heard no gunfire at the front, but shortly after arriving at his house in Brussels, he received a message from Baron Behr, the Dutch commandant of Mons. The note stated that a Prussian brigade commander had informed Dutch outposts of a French attack in the Charleroi sector. The young and diligent prince took the news in person to Wellington's residence, which was in a neighbouring street round the corner of Brussels park.[1]

In spite of the intelligence brought by the Prince, Wellington failed to react. He did not deem the situation serious enough to order each of his divisions to assemble. This was the Duke's first blunder. When later information arrived, the Duke's army would be unable to march to meet the French until each division had drawn in its units from scattered cantonments.

Had Wellington at 3.00 pm commanded each of his divisions to muster, precious time would have been saved later on. Assembling each division in a different town would have placed the Anglo-Dutch-German army in an early state of readiness while still guarding all the possible invasion routes into Belgium.

The Prince of Orange and his Dutch generals had become so alarmed by the very indications of an imminent French attack which Wellington dismissed that as early as 9 June they commanded the units of the Dutch–Belgian contingent of Wellington's army to be ready to march at a moment's notice. Battalions were to mass each morning and only to return to their scattered billets at nightfall if everything were quiet. If Wellington had been as alert as his Dutch subordinates, his whole army would already have been ready to move.

But Wellington, unlike the Prussians, had totally discounted the possibility of a French offensive. On 13 June, the tutor to the Duke of Richmond's family wrote that 'though I have given some pretty good reasons for supposing that hostilities will soon commence, yet no one would suppose it, judging by the Duke of Wellington. He appears to be thinking of anything else in [the] world, gives a ball every week, attends every party, partakes of every amusement that offers.'[2] Thus, when the intelligence arrived of a French attack south of Charleroi, Wellington dismissed it as a mere clash of outposts. Yet his own liaison officer at Blücher's headquarters had written to him the night before stating that 'the prevalent opinion here seems to be that Bonaparte intends to commence offensive operations.'[3]

Only at 7.00 pm did Wellington order his divisions to muster at their assembly points. The immediate stimulus for the issuing of these assembly orders was the arrival of two Prussian messages. These came between 4.00 and 6.00 pm.[4] The first was written by General Ziethen at 9.00 am, from Charleroi, and the other despatched by Blücher from Namur at noon. These communications confirmed that a French attack had occurred in the Charleroi region. Blücher added that the Prussian army was concentrating at Sombreffe, northeast of Charleroi.[5]

Wellington now made his second crucial error. He expected, owing to false intelligence spread by Napoleon and to the inefficiency of his own intelligence service, that if the French attacked, their real thrust would come via Mons. 'It is supposed', one piece of faulty intelligence had read, that Napoleon 'would make a false attack on the Prussians, and a real one on the English army.'[6]

Baron Behr's letter, which the Prince of Orange had received at 3.00 pm, stated that 'the advanced posts before Mons are ... very quiet.' But this had been the situation early in the morning. Everything might have changed since then and so the Duke's 7.00 pm orders ensured that the disposition of his mustered divisions would cover the Mons area. But he omitted to cover the Charleroi–Brussels road, up which Marshal Ney was in fact thrusting.

Wellington's oversight is all the more serious in that he knew hostilities had occurred at Charleroi. He also knew that Blücher was concentrating at Sombreffe. If Wellington failed to block the Charleroi–Brussels road, the French would be able to advance along it to Quatre Bras and then swing east along the road to Sombreffe to outflank Blücher. If the French managed to do this, Napoleon would have achieved the separation of the two allies that was the essence of his plan.

Fortunately, two Dutch generals, Jean-Victor de Constant-Rebecque and Henri-Georges de Perponcher, would ignore Wellington's 7.00 pm orders to concentrate the 2nd Dutch–Belgian Division at Nivelles, six miles northwest of Quatre Bras. Instead, recognising the salient importance of the crossroads threatened by Marshal Ney, they would concentrate the division at Quatre Bras.[7]

'If Lieutenant-General de Perponcher had obeyed the Duke of Wellington's order,' wrote Gneisenau to the King of Prussia after the campaign, 'if he had

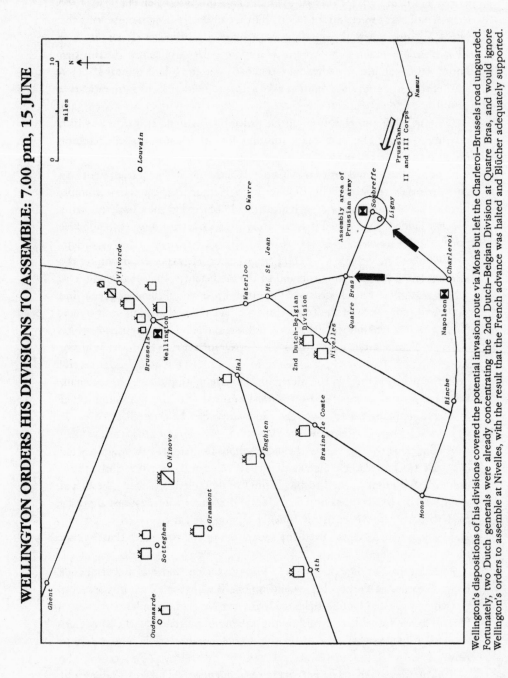

WELLINGTON ORDERS HIS DIVISIONS TO ASSEMBLE: 7.00 pm, 15 JUNE

Wellington's dispositions of his divisions covered the potential invasion route via Mons but left the Charleroi–Brussels road unguarded. Fortunately, two Dutch generals were already concentrating the 2nd Dutch–Belgian Division at Quatre Bras, and would ignore Wellington's orders to assemble at Nivelles, with the result that the French advance was halted and Blücher adequately supported.

marched on Nivelles and had not resisted so well, then Marshal Ney, having arrived at Quatre Bras, could have turned right and fallen on the rear of the army fighting at Ligny [on 16 June], thus totally destroying it.'

The Prussian king awarded Perponcher the Grand Cordon of the Order of the Red Eagle for saving the crossroads at Quatre Bras and, hence, the Prussian army.[8] Gneisenau did not recommend Wellington for a similar award.

Wellington received further intelligence at 10.00 pm. A communication arrived from Mons, from General Wilhelm von Dörnberg, a cavalry brigade commander temporarily detached from his unit on intelligence duties, which indicated that the French south of that city had marched to attack Charleroi, leaving only national guardsmen south of Mons.[9]

At 10.00 pm, having received this news from Mons, Wellington prescribed a march towards his inner flank, that is to say to support Blücher at Sombreffe. But this move was cautious and reluctant. Wellington failed to rush his army towards the vital, threatened point of Quatre Bras. Instead, he commanded his units to move one stage in that direction and then to await further orders. Instructions to continue towards Quatre Bras would be dispatched during the morning of 16 June when the strategic situation would be clearer.

This inevitably caused delay and confusion for often officers would not find those instructions after completing the first stage of their march. For instance, Captain Cavalié Mercer of the British artillery was ordered to march to Enghien and there an officer was to give him further orders. Needless to say, that officer was nowhere to be found at Enghien. The 16th Light Dragoons spent several hours waiting for orders at the same town. To take another example, Lieutenant Johnny Kincaid recorded that the Reserve Corps halted for at least four hours at Waterloo before continuing its march from Brussels to Quatre Bras.

It is clear that Wellington did not act in the spirit of co-operation with Blücher on which he had agreed at the Tirlemont Conference. Wellington acted on a selfish fear for his right flank and his communications with Ostend. He did nothing to aid or even support Blücher until informed by Dörnberg that all was quiet at Mons. Even thereafter, Wellington moved tardily towards the Prussians.

For even after receiving Dörnberg's intelligence at 10.00 pm indicating that the French had gone to attack Charleroi, Wellington was not wholly convinced. The possibility that Napoleon might have attacked Mons after Dörnberg's despatch had been sent from there at 9.30 am caused the Duke intense anxiety and hampered his freedom of action.

The other worry that was paralysing Wellington was that he had not yet heard from his trusted chief of Intelligence, Lieutenant-Colonel Colquhoun Grant. Grant had served Wellington extremely well in Spain during the Peninsular War and was now inside French territory, operating a network of contacts. Shortly before the outbreak of hostilities, Grant sent a message which, given his reliability, would certainly have convinced Wellington that Napoleon was going to attack: 'the roads are packed with troops and equipment; officers of all ranks boast that the big battle will be fought within three days.' The message may also have indicated that Charleroi would be the focus of the attack.[10]

The message went via Mons where Dörnberg, apparently questioning its contents or perhaps requesting further information, returned it to Grant.[11] Dörnberg may have passed a copy of the message on to Wellington but he certainly failed to mention that the message came from Grant, of whose mission and reliability he appears to have been unaware.[12] When Grant received his returned message, he rode in person to Belgium but would reach Wellington only on the morning of 18 June.

Dörnberg has become, unfairly, a scapegoat for historians anxious to explain the inactivity which pervaded Wellington's army for so long. Others have preferred to blame Wellington for relying too heavily on a single intelligence source, Grant. The intelligence fiasco should not be the subject of excessive recrimination; such confusions happen in war. The allocation of blame is a fruitless task when it is not coupled with an analysis of the lessons to be learnt.

First, intelligence must be centralised, with all information coming to one assessment centre, without being processed and fatally delayed by a series of assessment points. The central assessment centre requires full details of the source as well as of the contents of the intelligence, so as to enable it to distinguish reliable news.

Second, intelligence must be unified, to avoid the conflicts and confusion inherent in several intelligence services working in ignorance of the progress of the others. The root cause of Wellington's intelligence fiasco in 1815 was Dörnberg's ignorance of the reliability of Grant and his information.

Third, intelligence must come from a variety of sources, none of which should be relied on to the exclusion of the others. In 1815 Wellington relied too heavily on Grant and missed the indications present in other sources. A commander needs continually to reassess the intelligence situation and to keep a balanced, flexible mind. Wellington failed in this regard and laboured under the fixed ideas that Napoleon would not invade Belgium or that if he did, he would come via Mons.

By now, the most famous Ball of history had begun. The Duchess of Richmond was giving a splendid Brussels Ball and had invited an array of gallant officers and a host of fair ladies. Wellington himself went to the Ball. He has often been criticised for his presence, and unfairly so. The only reason for not attending would have been to obtain a good night's rest, and Wellington thrived on lack of sleep.

Moreover, he had already given his orders for the march of his army on the morrow. Many of his senior generals would be at the Ball and he could speak to them there. Failure to attend would cause alarm and encourage the Franco-philes among the inhabitants of Brussels.[13] Besides, the Ball was a mere 1000 metres from his headquarters. Further messages from the front could reach him at the Ball as easily as at his headquarters.

Wellington arrived late and the ballroom soon buzzed with rumours of imminent hostilities. Shortly after 11.30 pm, an aide-de-camp galloped up. Lights were blazing in the Richmonds' residence. The aide-de-camp jumped from his horse, threaded his way through the parked carriages in the street and into the building. He handed a despatch to the Prince of Orange, who in turn passed the news to Wellington.

It was from the Dutch General Constant-Rebecque. Rebecque stated that the French had already pushed up to Quatre Bras. Wellington received the alarming intelligence with admirable coolness. However, he remarked in private to the Duke of Richmond a little later that, 'Napoleon has humbugged me, by God! He has gained twenty-four hours' march on me.'[14]

Indeed Napoleon had. But Wellington did little to try and close the gap. Apart from ordering the Reserve Corps to leave Brussels two hours earlier than originally planned, he declared he had 'no new orders to give' and returned to his quarters to snatch a few hours' sleep. No orders went out for his army to march straight on Quatre Bras. Even the Reserve Corps would halt at Waterloo for four hours on 16 June before proceeding to Quatre Bras. Wellington, against all the evidence, still imagined there was a threat to Mons and still dawdled to contain the known threat to Quatre Bras. Significantly, on the back of the message from Constant-Rebecque stating that the French had pushed up to Quatre Bras, the Prince of Orange wrote that Wellington 'did not want to believe it.'[15]

In the early hours of 16 June, the Ball degenerated into tearful farewells and shuddering hearts. Officers left to rejoin their units; several would fight still in their ballroom dress, not having had time to change into campaign uniform. The streets of Brussels were alive with troops mustering for war. Bugles blared. The whole city was awake and humming with activity. At 4.00 am, the Reserve Corps marched out of Brussels and headed south.

Around 5.00 am, Dörnberg rode into Brussels from Mons and woke the Duke at his quarters to give him in person the latest news from the front. Dörnberg appears to have convinced Wellington that Mons was under no threat, for Dörnberg stated that the Duke sprang from his bed and said a battle would probably be fought at Quatre Bras.[16] Wellington's staff were soon hard at work despatching yet another set of orders, finally commanding practically the whole of his army to make for Quatre Bras.

As a consequence of the course of events of 15 June, Wellington's army would

STRENGTHS OF THE ARMIES, 16 JUNE

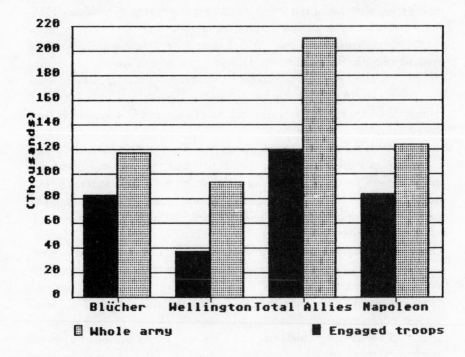

Napoleon's aim was to surprise the allies before they could mass their troops and bring their full numerical superiority of 86,000 to bear. He succeeded. Owing largely to Wellington's dilatoriness, just 57.1% of the allied troops would see action on 16 June. Thus the allies would enjoy a superiority of only 36,000 in the battles of that day. This would enable Napoleon to defeat the Prussians at Ligny.

fail to concentrate in time to lend direct assistance to the Prussians at Ligny the next day. Wellington would be able merely to contain Marshal Ney's wing of the French army at Quatre Bras. Wellington's troops would arrive at these crossroads only after 3.00 pm and only in a steady trickle. The Anglo-Dutch-German army would not finally be united until the evening of 17 June, on the battlefield of Waterloo (minus garrisons of towns and a detachment of 17,000 men at Hal to prevent the Waterloo position being outflanked).

Night of 15/16 June: Blücher

Unlike Wellington, Blücher and Gneisenau had been convinced on 14 June that a French attack was imminent. This allowed the Prussians precious extra hours in the concentration of their army.

A position immediately south of Sombreffe had been selected in May as a suitable spot for a battle against a French attack coming from Charleroi. Now, on 15 June, the Prussian plans were being transformed into reality. Sombreffe had been named as the concentration point. At noon Blücher had written to Müffling at Wellington's headquarters that 'the [Prussian] army will be concentrated tomorrow in the position of Sombreffe where I intend to give battle.'[17]

At the close of 15 June, Ziethen's I Corps was drawn up around Fleurus with vedettes further south. Ziethen's successful fighting retreat from his original position along the River Sambre had gained valuable time for the rest of Blücher's army to march towards Sombreffe.

Ziethen's men, chattering nervously about the expected battle on the morrow, were writing letters home to loved ones, using pale ink on coarse paper. The corps commander himself and his staff rested on a shallow mound called the Tombe de Ligny, just north of Fleurus. Ziethen's Chief of Staff, Lieutenant-Colonel Ludwig von Reiche, considered the present positions of the I Corps to be hazardous if the French attacked. With Ziethen's approval, Reiche rode over to Sombreffe where Blücher had established his headquarters in the village presbytery. Here, Reiche found Gneisenau and requested permission to withdraw the I Corps north of the Ligny brook, the natural obstacle which ran along the whole extent of the chosen position. Gneisenau refused Reiche's request, no doubt because he did not want to disturb the troops' sleep or to allow the French to approach the Ligny brook under cover of darkness.

Dawn broke around 4.00 am. Reiche returned a second time to Blücher's headquarters and this time Gneisenau agreed to Reiche's suggestion. At 5.00 am, I Corps began to retire to positions north of the Ligny brook. These troop movements were spotted from the French outpost lines by Marshal Grouchy's cavalry. Grouchy forthwith despatched a report to Napoleon at Charleroi, that strong Prussian columns were heading towards Brye and St Amand villages. A further note departed for Napoleon an hour later. The French had spotted Prussian troops massing around the Bussy windmill.

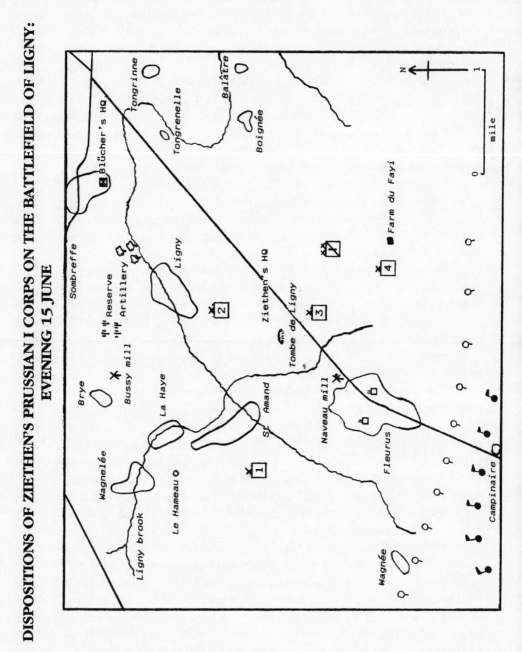

DISPOSITIONS OF ZIETHEN'S PRUSSIAN I CORPS ON THE BATTLEFIELD OF LIGNY:
EVENING 15 JUNE

The Prussian headquarters had spent an anxious night. At 10.00 pm, Blücher and Gneisenau had written to the Austrian commander, Field Marshal Prince Karl Schwarzenberg: 'the enemy has advanced by Charleroi and is now before Fleurus ... At this moment I am still without news from the Duke of Wellington but his left wing has been in action today and one can presume that the enemy intends to penetrate between the Duke's army and mine.'[18]

Clearly the Prussians were worried about the security of their western flank and wanted to know how soon they could expect support from Wellington.[19] Cause for further anxiety arrived at 1.00 am on the 16th. A messenger from General Bülow reported that as the general was not aware of any urgency, he would delay setting his IV Corps on the march westwards until the morning of the 16th, when the troops would be fresh. The implication of this startling message was horrendous: IV Corps was still fifty miles away at Liège and therefore would be unable to reach Sombreffe that day.

On 14 June, Gneisenau had ordered Bülow to march from Liège twenty miles westwards to Hannut, as a precaution against the anticipated French invasion. But Gneisenau, junior to Bülow in age and experience, had phrased the order in respectful terms:

> I have the honour humbly to request your Excellency to be kind enough to concentrate the IV Corps under your command tomorrow, the 15th, at Hannut, in close cantonments. Information received makes it more and more probable that the French army has concentrated against us and that we must expect from it an immediate change to the offensive ... Your Excellency had doubtless better make Hannut your headquarters.[20]

As Blücher had been asleep when this order was despatched, Gneisenau had been unable to have it signed by the Commander-in-Chief. Thus Bülow, burdened by a surfeit of Prussian pique at having to obey not Blücher but a Chief of Staff junior to himself, took the message as advisory not mandatory. Bülow failed to detect the need for haste. At any rate, that was one of his more plausible excuses afterwards for his failure to obey the order.

So Bülow delayed leaving Liège for Hannut until the morning of 16 June. Consequently, Bülow was not at Hannut to receive an urgent order, sent from Blücher in person at noon on 15 June, to continue his march westwards. Owing to Bülow's awkwardness, IV Corps would join the rest of the Prussian army only on 17 June.

Now Blücher could count on only three corps to defend the extensive position at Sombreffe. II Corps, originally quartered around Namur, would arrive at about 10.00 am on 16 June, followed by III Corps from the region of Dinant at 12.00 pm. Thus Ziethen's I Corps would be unsupported at Sombreffe for several hours and the Prussian headquarters must have doubted their ability to accept battle in their position along the Ligny brook. All depended on how soon the French would resume their advance. Irreverent Gallic graffiti still on the staircase of Blücher's headquarters in Sombreffe may have reminded him that French troops had successfully come this way before: twenty-one years previously during the Revolutionary Wars.[21]

Nevertheless, Blücher was spoiling for a fight. 'With my 120,000 Prussians', he had boasted in a letter to his wife, 'I would undertake the capture of Tripoli, Tunis and Algiers, if there wasn't any water to cross!'[22] Ziethen's men formed up in the hope that support would arrive before the French did. The villages lying along the marshy river valley were occupied and prepared for the expected fight. 4th brigade marched into Ligny while elements of the 3rd entered St Amand. Further back were the remaining infantry units, together with their attached bronze cannon.

North of St Amand was posted 1st brigade, while north of Ligny stood the remainder of 3rd brigade. 2nd brigade, already sorely tried in the skirmishes of 15 June, formed up around Bussy windmill. Between Fleurus and the Ligny brook, meanwhile, stood the I Corps' cavalry, with some advanced posts in front. Blücher himself had mounted his horse, left his headquarters at Sombreffe and was now at Bussy mill, his observation post for the coming battle.

Henri Nieman of the black-coated 6th Uhlans was one of the cavalrymen stationed north of Fleurus. As he recalled in later life, it was a beautiful morning. Looking down the line of cavalry formations, he saw a whole row of silver masses, as far as his eye could reach. Sharp sun rays blasted through an already fading morning mist and flashed off clumps of cavalry sabres, off serried lance tips and off gleaming bronze cannon mounted on their sky blue carriages. It would be a hot day.

For Captain von Reuter, one of Ziethen's battery commanders, however, dawn brought not so much a beautiful morning as a severe shock. Reuter had arrived with his 12-pounder battery on the south side of Fleurus on the previous evening. But unlike the rest of Ziethen's corps, he had stayed there until morning slowly broke, until the early gloom gradually faded and as the mist eventually dissipated. He was utterly alone. So far as he could determine, his eight bronze guns were isolated, without an escort, and under the very noses of the French outposts. Reuter reminisced in later years: 'during the night [at 5.00 am] the remainder of the troops had all received orders to retire; but I and my guns had been completely overlooked!'[23] Fortunately for the Prussian gunners, who hastily withdrew the solitary battery to Bussy windmill, the French picquets had not been at all adventurous.

Meanwhile, Ziethen's infantrymen in the villages along the Ligny brook were busy loopholing walls, constructing barricades, putting the stone, thatched houses and the farms in a state of defence. By 8.00 am Ziethen's corps had completed its dispositions on the battlefield. The other corps were on their way.

Morning, 16 June: Napoleon

On the morning of 16 June, Napoleon was ready to deal his enemies another blow. Napoleon believed his lightning stroke of 15 June had surprised and intimidated both his foes. Both Wellington and Blücher, he fondly imagined, would be in retreat along their respective, mutually divergent lines of communication, striving to put a safe distance between their hastily concentrating armies and the powerful, menacing French forces.

While Wellington had seriously underestimated Napoleon's ability to invade Belgium and had also misjudged where Napoleon would attack, Napoleon underestimated Wellington and Blücher's determination to fight. For reasons of strategy, prestige, morale and English politics, they had to fight south of Brussels to prevent that city falling into French hands. Napoleon wrongly judged that the two allies would fall back into Holland to unite and there await the arrival of the Russians and Austrians. Before the campaign had begun, he confidently had had proclamations printed, dated 17 June at the Laeken Palace of Brussels, calling on the liberated Belgians to join his army.[24]

Napoleon's goal was two-fold. Firstly, he intended to occupy Brussels and secure his seizure of Belgium. Secondly, he wished to inflict as much damage as possible on the two enemy armies during his march on Brussels.

The news that Brussels was in French hands would be a severe blow to the morale of Napoleon's numerous enemies. The political repercussions might well topple the English Government and cause its successor to sue for peace. With Brussels and Belgium in French hands and with Wellington and Blücher's armies either destroyed, mauled or evacuated, Napoleon would be in a much stronger position either to sue for peace or to prepare to meet the mighty Austrian and Russian commands descending on France's eastern frontiers.

Napoleon's plan on the morning of 16 June began with the French completing the division of Wellington from Blücher as part of the Napoleonic 'divide and rule' campaign strategy. This would entail seizing the vital Nivelles–Namur road along which lateral communications and movements of troops could pass between the two French wings at Quatre Bras and Sombreffe. In addition, the denial of this road to Napoleon's enemies meant Wellington and Blücher would experience great difficulty in uniting or in reinforcing each other. The Nivelles–Namur road was the only cobbled route, linking the two allies, south of Brussels.

Through his Chief of Staff, Marshal Soult, Napoleon issued orders to the commanders of the two wings, Marshals Ney and Grouchy, for the seizure of this road. Ney was to position the left wing beyond Quatre Bras, and Grouchy to push the right beyond Sombreffe. About 8.30 am, after these orders had been sent, Napoleon dictated two letters, to Ney and Grouchy, which repeated the orders just sent by Soult and expanded on Napoleon's plan.

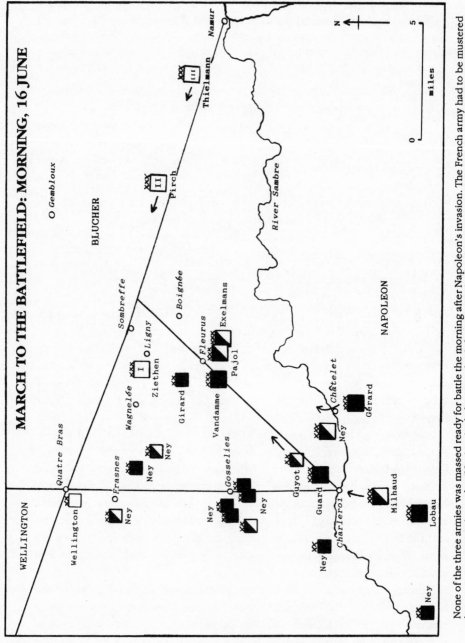

MARCH TO THE BATTLEFIELD: MORNING, 16 JUNE

None of the three armies was massed ready for battle the morning after Napoleon's invasion. The French army had to be mustered into two compact wings: the 'Ney' units belong to the left wing, and all other French units are part of the right wing under Napoleon's command. By the time the right wing was massed around Fleurus, three of Blücher's corps were concentrated at Ligny.

Napoleon told Grouchy he would come in person to Fleurus to join the French right wing:

> If the enemy [Prussians] are at Sombreffe, I want to attack them there; I also want to attack the enemy at Gembloux and take this position, my intention being, after I have occupied these two positions, to leave this same night and to move my left flank, under Marshal Ney's command, against the English.

In short, Napoleon would drive any Prussian rearguards well to the northeast away from the campaign area. Then, leaving the right wing to observe the retreating Prussian army, he would take his reserve along the lateral road from Sombreffe to Quatre Bras. At Quatre Bras Napoleon would join Ney and the French left wing, and with this wing, united with the reserve, he would march north throughout the night. Napoleon intended to arrive at Brussels at 7.00 am on 17 June. Such a sudden stroke would terrorize Europe.

Put simply, then, Napoleon's intention at this stage of the campaign was to seize Brussels in a single march, brushing aside any of Wellington's troops who stood in the way. Napoleon seems not to have anticipated a serious clash of arms, but if such a clash did occur, it would afford the French an opportunity of crushing the enemy troops as well as capturing Brussels.

In his letter to Marshal Ney, Napoleon spelled out the vital principle behind his strategy:

> For this campaign I have adopted the following general principle – to divide my army into two wings and a reserve ... The Guard will form the reserve, and I shall bring it into action on either wing as circumstances may dictate ... Also, according to circumstances, I shall draw troops from one wing to strengthen my reserve.

Between 6.30 and 8.00 am, Napoleon had received two messages from Marshal Grouchy indicating that massed Prussian troops were around Sombreffe. Nevertheless, Napoleon persisted in assuming that these troops were merely rearguards, that the bulk of the Prussian army was in retreat and concentrating far to the northeast. Napoleon believed that Blücher would never be so foolish as to try to concentrate his entire army as far forward as Sombreffe, within striking distance of the French.

However, if serious Prussian resistance was encountered either at Sombreffe or further northeast at Gembloux, then Napoleon's plan was flexible. As he explained to Ney, his Guard could be brought into action 'on either wing as circumstances may dictate.' A full-scale victory over the Prussians by the French right wing and reserve would delay, not cancel, the march by the left wing and reserve to Brussels.

It all depended on circumstances: 'depending on what happens, I will make my decision, possibly at 3.00 pm, possibly this evening', Napoleon informed Ney. 'My intention is that, immediately after I have made my decision, you will be ready to march on Brussels.'

On the morning of 16 June, French formations were strung out all over the countryside like crumbs on a table. Some of Ney's units of the left wing were grouped around Frasnes on the Brussels road; still others were further back. Of Marshal Grouchy's right wing, Pajol and Exelmans' cavalrymen together with Vandamme's III Corps were a few miles south of the town of Fleurus, while Gérard's IV Corps and Milhaud's *cuirassiers* had still not even crossed the River Sambre. The veteran Imperial Guard was massed around its Emperor and Charleroi. Napoleon was in the same predicament as Blücher: his forces were disunited and he needed time to mass them together.

At 9.30 am Napoleon departed. With the exception of Lobau's VI Corps left at Charleroi ready to march to help either Ney or Grouchy's wing, the French right wing and reserve were on the move. The cogs of the feared French military machine were in motion. Gérard's infantry slowly filed over the Sambre at Châtelet; shimmering *cuirassiers* clattered forward; the Guard assembled at Charleroi, and all converged on Fleurus as if to a magnet. The clash of arms drew near.

North of Fleurus, the Prussian cavalry outposts were still waiting. Between 10.00 and 11.00 am, Henri Nieman was ordered to enter Fleurus in search of food and fodder for his comrades in the 6th Uhlans. Unknown to him, Napoleon was at that moment arriving to the south of the town and soon French sharpshooters were ordered forward into the streets. As Nieman entered by one gate, the French came in by the other and, he remarked, 'of course I said "Goodbye" for the present.'

A short skirmish flared up to the north of Fleurus, the Prussian cavalry outposts slowly falling back after, in Napoleon's words, 'a few cannon-shots.'[25] Covered by the 5th Dragoons and Nieman's unit, the 6th Uhlans, together with two cannon, the remainder of I Corps' cavalry retired across the Ligny brook to take up a position southwest of Sombreffe. Nieman and the covering force remained for some time to the south of the brook.

French forces moved slowly forward. Outpost lines were in front, while further back and level with the northern outskirts of Fleurus were halted the massed ranks of troops. Girard's division, serving on detachment from Reille's II Corps of Marshal Ney's left wing, and Vandamme's III Corps were on the left. Two cavalry corps under Marshal Grouchy stood on the right.

Heading towards the south of the town were the Guard, Milhaud's *cuirassiers* and Gérard's IV Corps. The Emperor himself, in his legendary grey coat and black cocked hat, was in the northern sector of Fleurus, beside the Naveau mill.

Sappers laboured under a blistering sun to knock a hole in the roof and construct a wooden observation platform for Napoleon.

Major Coignet, Waggon-Master of the Imperial French Army, recalled that Napoleon sent officers in every direction to reconnoitre the Prussian positions. The officers returned shortly only to report, 'their position is concealed; we cannot see them.'[26]

A local surveyor, called Simon, briefed the Emperor on the area. Years later, the Emperor's nephew, Napoleon III, would award him the medal of the Legion of Honour. After consulting with Simon, Napoleon ascended the Naveau windmill to the platform the sappers had created. From there he looked out over the countryside. His legendary eagle-eye spotted the Prussians – at least a whole corps of them. Their left was at Sombreffe, their centre at Ligny, their right at St Amand. Reserves lined the heights around the village of Brye.

'The old fox will not stir out'[27] commented Napoleon drily about Blücher. The Prussians would stand and fight a defensive battle. 'They are going utterly to be smashed', Napoleon added.[28] And so he altered his original plan.

He would smash and hurl back the Prussians in a full scale battle at Ligny *before* turning on Wellington and marching on Brussels. Ney's would be a subsidiary role designed to hold off Wellington while Napoleon defeated the Prussians. Baron Müffling, Prussian liaison officer to Wellington's army, wrote later:

> Chance would have it that on the 16th June, the Prussian army stood on the defensive while the English was disposed for attack. Officers of any discernment {as to the respective characters of the two armies and their generals} could all have wished it the other way round, but nothing could be done about that.[29]

Napoleon had resolved to smash the Prussians at Ligny. All he needed to open battle was for his remaining formations to arrive.

The rolling plains had become an oven and thick columns of dust headed towards Fleurus along shimmering tracks of baked dirt. A band played and brass drums beat the line of march as Napoleon's veteran Guard passed by wearing their famous blue greatcoats, white crossbelts, and magnificent black bearskins that made them appear two feet taller – in height and in pride. The long blue column marched past the site of a skirmish of 15 June and the guardsmen saw the victims still awaiting burial.

Among the sweltering Frenchmen was Sergeant Hippolyte de Mauduit of the 1st Grenadiers, enveloped like the rest by the dense cloud of dust that made it hard to breathe. 'The heat was stifling', he recalled. 'There was no breeze to cool one's face and the sun was right overhead.'

Mauduit's comrade, Lieutenant Barral, later remembered that he was never so cold as in Russia, so hot as at Ligny and so drenched as on the eve of

Waterloo. Noon brought welcome relief after three harsh hours of marching, as the veterans of Napoleon's ultimate reserve escaped briefly from the furnace.

They had entered a wide and fertile plain just to the south of Fleurus where they stacked their arms and halted for about an hour to allow the other French formations time to arrive. The 'grumblers' of the Guard were veterans of Egypt and of Spain. They tied together dozens of handkerchiefs and suspended them over a ring of piled muskets to give themselves a little shade.

Beneath this welcome cover, those guardsmen who had fought in the same region during the Battle of Fleurus between the French Republic and Austria in 1794, lay down on the trampled rye and regaled their listeners with tales of unusual incidents of that battle, perhaps of the French observation balloon. And when one weathered grenadier produced a tattered map of Flanders, the guardsmen discussed the manoeuvres of 1794, as if they had been staff officers.[30]

Then Lieutenant-General Edouard Milhaud's armoured *cuirassiers*, their polished breastplates glittering in the burning noon sun, jingled up to the south of Fleurus to halt next to the Guard. But where was Lieutenant-General Maurice Gérard? Having arrived at Châtelet late the previous evening, he had only succeeded in pushing one division of his IV Corps over the Sambre. Now the other two had to file over the narrow bridge, then there was a long, hot march to the north.

It was just after noon. Blücher had received timely reinforcements in the shape of Pirch and Thielmann's corps now gathered around Sombreffe in dark, huddled masses.

Napoleon was undertaking a personal reconnaissance, accompanied by Marshal Grouchy and several other generals.[31] He surveyed the screen of Prussian cavalry picquets stationed temporarily south of the Ligny brook. 'With very few attendants', the Emperor later boasted, 'I toured the line of the outposts, climbed heights and windmills, and obtained a perfect reconnaissance of the enemy army.'[32]

Elsewhere on the plain, Gérard was looking for his Emperor. Having ridden on ahead of his marching IV Corps with a small escort, he was searching along the French outpost lines and now strayed too near an advanced post of the Prussian 6th Uhlans.

Suddenly the lancers charged. Gérard's Chief of Staff was pierced seven times by Prussian lances. Gérard's horse collapsed into a ditch and the general escaped only thanks to Marshal Grouchy's son heading a squadron of the 12th Chasseurs à cheval. Bruised and battered, Gérard eventually found the Emperor at Naveau mill about an hour or so later.

Colonel Auguste Pétiet of the staff witnessed the meeting. Pétiet was standing at the foot of the mill holding the bridle of his horse and conversing with a fellow officer when Gérard appeared. Gérard's protégé and subordinate, Lieutenant-General Louis de Bourmont, had deserted to the Prussians on 15 June, despite Gérard's earlier assurances to Napoleon that he would answer for Bourmont with his head.

'Well then, Gérard', Napoleon now called down from the top of the Naveau mill. 'You told me that you would answer for Bourmont with your head. Now see what he has done.'

'Sire', Gérard defended himself, 'General Bourmont had fought honourably under my eyes. He had shed his blood for your Majesty's cause. I had to believe he was irreproachable and devoted.'

'Bah!' snorted the Emperor, 'a man who has been white [royalist] will never become blue [Bonapartist] and a blue will never be white.'[33]

According to another account, Napoleon simply teased Gérard by asking, 'so I can have this head, can't I?' Napoleon tapped Gérard's cheek as he spoke. Then he added, 'but I need it too much.'[34] Indeed, Gérard was one of the Emperor's best generals. Now he asked for instructions, for his corps had at last arrived on the field. Major Jean-Roch Coignet, the army's Waggon-Master, recalled how the Emperor pointed towards Ligny church in the distance. 'You must go towards that steeple, and drive the Prussians in as far as you can. I will support you', he told Gérard.[35]

At 2.00 pm, countdown to the commencement of battle had entered its final hour. To the north of the Ligny brook, another important meeting had just finished.

The Meeting at Bussy Windmill and Final Preparations

At 1.00 pm on 16 June, Sir Henry Hardinge, the British liaison officer with the Prussian army, was at the Bussy mill with Blücher. Looking northwest towards Quatre Bras, Hardinge saw a group of horsemen. Judging from the short tails of their mounts that they were English, he set his swift horse at a gallop in their direction. If they should prove to be French, the swiftness of his horse would save him.

They were English: the Duke of Wellington no less, accompanied by his stout ADC Colonel Sir Alexander Gordon, several orderlies, an escort of hussars and Baron Müffling, the Prussian liaison officer attached to the Duke's army. Wellington, riding on ahead of his troops, had arrived at Quatre Bras from Brussels at 10.00 am on 16 June. He had found all quiet and Marshal Ney still inactive. Thus the Duke took the opportunity to ride over to meet Blücher at Ligny and to discuss allied strategy against Napoleon.

Wellington greeted Hardinge and inquired how the Prussian army was forming.

'In column, not in line', responded Hardinge. 'The Prussian soldier, Blücher says, will not stand in line.'

'Then the artillery will play upon them, and they will be beaten damnably', returned the Duke.[36]

Lieutenant-Colonel Ludwig von Reiche, Chief of Staff of Ziethen's I Corps, watched the Duke ride up to Bussy mill. Wellington was dressed, as was his custom, in a simple blue overcoat and an ordinary cocked hat with three cockades. So civilian was his dress, indeed, that none of the Prussian troops recognised him as the Anglo-Dutch-German Commander-in-Chief until Reiche told them. Then everyone nearby turned to gaze upon the man whom Reiche admiringly called 'the famous war hero'.[37]

The allied commanders met: the cool, unflappable Duke and the fiery, intense Field Marshal. From the hill they surveyed the battlefield and in the distance saw a French party. All with telescopes could identify Napoleon himself as he reconnoitred the Prussian position before his meeting with Gérard at Naveau mill. 'Perhaps', mused Reiche, 'perhaps the eyes of the three greatest commanders of the age had their eyes directed on one another.' Wellington turned his attention to the Prussian army on the slopes before him.

He greatly disapproved. In later years he told a friend how he found the Prussian battalions massed in columns and dotted along the forward slopes of the position, ready to be shattered by French artillery. 'I said that if I were in Blücher's place with English troops, I should withdraw all the columns I saw scattered about in front, and get more of the troops under shelter of the rising ground.'[38]

All that was needed out in front were some advanced battalions in the villages and skirmishers lining the banks of the Ligny brook which ran along the whole of the Prussian front line. The Prussians, however, thought they knew best. 'Our men like to see their enemy', responded Gneisenau.

The conversation was conducted in French; Wellington did not know German. After some discussion, the group at Bussy concluded that the main thrust of the French army was directed against the Prussians. Consequently, when the Duke demanded, 'what do you want me to do?', Gneisenau suggested that the Duke should concentrate his forces at Quatre Bras and then bring his troops eastwards to act as a reserve to the Prussians.

Müffling noted Wellington examine his map intently. The Duke spoke not a word. He disliked Gneisenau's suggestion since it would rob him of his customary independence. It would never do to have Prussian generals sending British battalions piecemeal into the front line to reinforce the Prussian units already there. Particularly Prussian generals who needlessly exposed their forces to an enemy artillery barrage. And Waterloo on 18 June would demonstrate the risks of 'friendly fire' incidents between the two allies mutually mistaking each other, in the heat of battle, for the French.[39]

Wellington preferred to concentrate at Quatre Bras, march south and sweep the French forces at Frasnes away, before turning east to link up with the

Prussian right and to outflank Napoleon. 'I will cut up whatever is in front of me at Frasnes', the Duke assured the Prussians. But Gneisenau argued that direct support by Wellington's army would be even better.

Blücher, whose understanding of strategy was minimal and knowledge of the French language almost non-existent, appears to have kept silent in this dispute which ended in a compromise. Until 4.00 pm, Wellington would act independently, attacking south towards Frasnes and threatening Napoleon's west flank at Ligny. The two allies hoped that this would cause Napoleon to fall back southwards, that his retreat would be blocked by the River Sambre, which could be crossed only slowly, and that thus he could be crushed. But if after 4.00 pm Wellington judged that Blücher's right wing required direct support, he would send forces to bolster the Prussian line.[40]

Accounts vary as to how the meeting ended. The Duke certainly under-estimated the time needed for his troops to arrive at Quatre Bras. The Prussians gained the false impression that Wellington would be able to take the offensive in strength and immediately. Wellington's parting remark was probably: 'well, I will come, if I am not attacked myself'. Then he turned to leave for Quatre Bras and one of the most confused and desperate battles he had ever fought.

To the Prussian high command, Wellington's promise of support was wel-come news. Gneisenau for one forgot or did not hear Wellington's condition '... if I am not attacked myself', and concluded that English help would be definitely forthcoming.[41] Since Napoleon clearly had most of his army with him south of the Ligny brook, it must have seemed highly unlikely to the Prussians that the Duke would be attacked in strength.

Blücher decided on the strength of his English friend's promise to accept a full-scale battle at Ligny rather than further north. Perhaps Blücher would have arrived at the same decision without the Duke's assurances of support, for the French south of the brook were no stronger than the three Prussian corps north of it. Furthermore, retreating to a different position would entail the aban-donment of the excellent supply route to Prussia along the River Meuse and also the lateral cobbled road from Namur to Nivelles which linked the two allies.

But Wellington's promise did reassure the Prussians, it did give them great hopes of victory and it did cause Blücher to take the formal decision to fight at Ligny. Captain von Reuter noticed General von Holtzendorff, the Prussian artillery commander, riding up to Reuter's battery, which was stationed near Bussy windmill, to order number one gun to fire a round. 'We were told at the time that this was a signal to our army corps that the Prince [Blücher] had made up his mind to accept battle.'[42]

As Wellington and his staff rode off from Bussy mill at 1.45 pm, Blücher accompanied them for a little way before turning back. 'What a fine fellow he is!' exclaimed the Duke to one of his officers.

And so Wellington took leave of his old friend Blücher. They would not see each other again for fifty-five hours. Although they would next meet in victorious circumstances, on the field of Waterloo, it was in a way neither could have anticipated. Wellington would not come to Blücher's support on 16 June, rather Blücher to Wellington's on the 18th. Moreover, victory would be gained only after a defeat, a severe fall from a horse, two retreats, and fifty thousand allied casualties.

On that hot June day, neither general foresaw the terrible path that lay ahead.

Soon after two o'clock, Prussian officers at Bussy windmill spotted French columns marching forward. Napoleon was completing his dispositions for battle. Originally, he had intended merely to hurl the Prussians back towards Gembloux before marching to Quatre Bras and thence to Brussels. But now Napoleon had realised he faced a large section of Blücher's army at Ligny, and thus he had decided to destroy rather than bowl over the Prussians.

Napoleon now wanted Ney to send elements of his command east from Quatre Bras to outflank Blücher's right wing. In addition, Napoleon altered the dispositions of his troops on the Ligny battlefield: the French centre was pushed forward. Gérard's IV Corps, minus Hulot's division which was attached to Grouchy's cavalry, now faced Ligny. Gérard would attack northwest through Ligny to link up with Ney's forces arriving from the west. Napoleon intended to support Gérard with his Guard at the moment a breakthrough at Ligny appeared likely. This pincer move would surround a large portion of the Prussians.

The French left flank, Vandamme's III Corps with Baron Jean-Baptiste Girard's detached division to the west, moved forward to within 1500 metres from St Amand. Vandamme's task was to attack St Amand in order to draw as many Prussian reserves as possible into the front line on the western wing. This would ensure large numbers of Prussians would be trapped around St Amand when the troops from Ney arrived.[43]

On the French right flank, Pajol and Exelmans' horsemen, under Marshal Grouchy's command and with Baron Etienne Hulot's infantry division attached, faced the Prussian left flank and the collection of villages and castles between Sombreffe and Balâtre.

Meanwhile, the Imperial Guard moved forward from its temporary halt south of Fleurus. General Baron Jean-Martin Petit, commander of the veteran 1st Grenadiers, remembered how a column was formed, how on arrival at the town of Fleurus it was broken up to get through the streets and how it was reformed on the other side, halting on the road.

The four infantry regiments of Guard *chasseurs* took up position next to the Naveau mill, while the *grenadier* infantry units formed up to their right. Behind

THE ALLIED AND FRENCH PLANS FOR THE BATTLE OF LIGNY, 16 JUNE

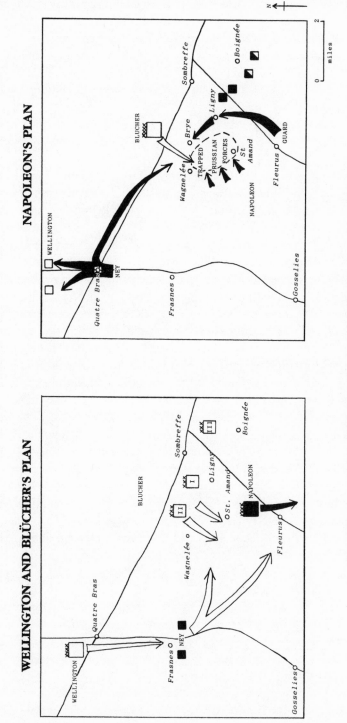

WELLINGTON AND BLÜCHER'S PLAN

NAPOLEON'S PLAN

Wellington planned to march south from Quatre Bras and then east to link up with Blücher, causing the French army to retreat to the River Sambre where the allies hoped to trap and destroy it. Napoleon planned to draw Blücher's forces into an attritional battle in the St Amand sector, and encircle the Prussian forces using the Guard and a detachment sent from Quatre Bras by Ney. Both plans underestimated the strength of the foe at Quatre Bras, and counted on the support of friendly forces sent from there. Neither became a reality.

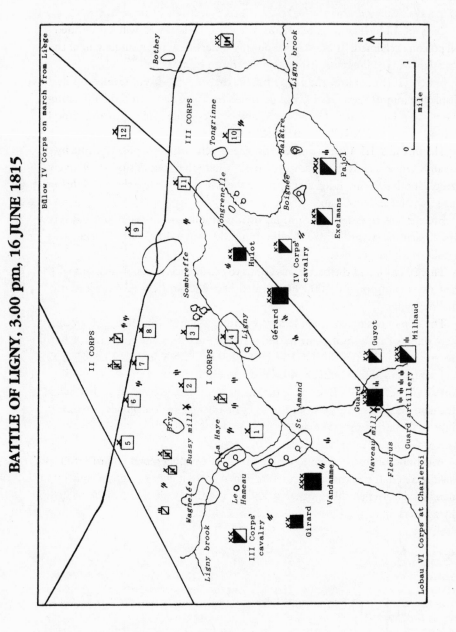

BATTLE OF LIGNY, 3.00 pm, 16 JUNE 1815

At 3.00 pm, the two massed foes confronted each other across the Ligny brook. Battle was about to begin.

the *grenadiers* stood the Guard artillery and Baron Claude Guyot's cavalry guardsmen. To the left of the *chasseurs* was the Young Guard infantry division. As always, the Guard had the post of honour and stood next to its Emperor. Milhaud's heavy *cuirassiers* were stationed to the east of Fleurus.

'It is possible that in three hours the issue of the war will be decided', Napoleon exclaimed. 'If Ney carries out my orders well, not a single gun of the Prussian army will escape; it is going utterly to be smashed'.[44]

On the north bank of the Ligny brook, the Prussians were formed up in a display of might. Ziethen's I Corps occupied the right flank, troops garrisoning the villages lying along the marshy Ligny brook, while Pirch's II Corps stood behind, along the Nivelles–Namur road in reserve.

Thielmann's III Corps formed Blücher's left wing, opposite Grouchy's cavalry. On this eastern sector of the field, where the ground sloped relatively steeply, both sides intended merely to tie the other down while the real fighting raged on the easier terrain to the west.

Blücher felt confident, both in his own positions and in the hope, however unfounded, of support from Wellington. Old rough and ready Blücher was wholly confident of victory.

Three o'clock and the battle was about to commence. 83,000 Prussians with 224 guns confronted 63,000 Frenchmen and 230 artillery pieces across the shallow valley.

The two opposing commanders were unmerciful foes who, like their troops, were filled with an implacable hatred for their enemy. Many times before had the two met in battle. Blücher had been present at both Jena and Leipzig and had commanded at several 1814 battles, urging his Russian and Austrian allies to Paris. The victor of Brienne and Vauchamps was pitted against that of La Rothière and Laon. Ligny would be a fight to the end – a bloody attritional fight with no quarter given or sought.

It was time to settle old scores.

A cannon boomed. Then again and a third time a French Guard artillery piece recoiled. It was the signal. Gérard's men heard it over at Ligny, Grouchy's men heard it over on the right wing, and over to the south of St Amand village, the soldiers of Vandamme heard the cannonshots.

Notes

1. De Bas, *La Campagne de 1815 aux Pays-Bas* v.1, pp.384– 92; Sweetman, *Raglan. From the Peninsula to the Crimea*, p.57; Ellesmere, *Personal recollections of the Duke of Wellington*; Siborne, *History of the Waterloo Campaign*, p.39; Thornton, *Your most obedient servant*, p.94; Henegan, *Seven Years' Campaigning*, p.282. The contents of Behr's despatch are quoted in Wellington's *Supplementary Despatches* v.10, p.481. A copy of Behr's letter was apparently sent direct to Lord Fitzroy Somerset, Wellington's military secretary, in the afternoon, from Braine-le-Comte, through which messages from Mons passed (see Berkeley's letter, *Supp. Desp.*, p.480).

2. Petrie, *Wellington. A Reassessment*, p.195

3. Chalfont, *Waterloo: Battle of Three Armies*, p.62

4. *United Service Magazine* (June 1841), p.172: 'towards six o'clock, sauntering about the walks [of Brussels park], I encountered two Prussian aides-de-camp, who had come from Blücher with intelligence of the advance of the French army ... We were instantly ordered to hold ourselves in readiness ... About seven o'clock, the orderlies were soon flying about.'

5. English historians have condemned the Prussian staff for the time both these important messages took to reach Wellington. The Duke himself declared, 'I cannot tell the world that Blücher picked the fattest man in his army to ride with an express to me, and that he took thirty hours to go thirty miles' (Siborne, *The Waterloo Letters*, p.2).

Wellington may have been correct about the corpulence of one of the Prussian messengers; he was wrong about his speed. Hamilton-Williams, *Waterloo: new perspectives*, p.374 has skilfully researched the communications network between and within the two allied armies. By the Duke's own order, all Ziethen's messages went via the intelligence centre at Mons and thence to Brussels, instead of proceeding directly north up the Charleroi–Brussels highroad. Thus Ziethen's messages had to travel an extra twenty-five miles. His messenger of 15 June moved at the praiseworthy rate of eight miles per hour. Blücher's messenger almost certainly would have travelled from Namur along the cobbled highroad to Quatre Bras and thence along the *chaussée* to Brussels. Dirt tracks did provide a direct link from Namur to Brussels but were less easy to ride on and would have shortened the ride by only five miles.

Thus Blücher's messenger rode at just over six miles per hour. This was a respectable pace by the standards of the day. One of Napoleon's ADCs took about 100 minutes to bring a letter from the Emperor at Charleroi to Ney at Frasnes on the morning of 16 June. Thus he moved at an average speed of eight miles per hour (Kerry, *The First Napoleon*, p.124). Ordinary French staff officers were not as well mounted or as fast as Napoleon's own ADCs. The best messengers were British and rode with a reckless disdain for danger and obstacles (see Müffling, *Passages from My Life*, p.214). Just after 11.30 pm on 15 June, a Lieutenant Webster reached Wellington from Braine-le-Comte, having covered the twenty miles to Brussels in about 100 minutes (twelve miles per hour), though admittedly he rode less than half the distance travelled by either of the Prussian messengers and changed horses halfway.

6. Wellington, *Supp. Desp.*, v.10, p.424. See also de Bas, *op. cit.*, v.1, p.347, for an example of French counter-intelligence stating that Mons was the real target. Since war had not been declared, peace technically prevailed until hostilities commenced. This prevented Wellington sending cavalry patrols into France to reconnoitre.

7. This enlightened disobedience saved Wellington's reputation as a great general. But such initiative was more than he had a right to expect for he had always demanded total obedience from his subordinates. In 1813 he arrested the famous artillery officer, Norman Ramsey, following the Battle of Vitoria. Ramsey had moved his battery from reserve, where Wellington had ordered him to remain, to the front line where the situation seemed critical. Wellington stated that he was making an example of Ramsey to ensure the strict obedience of orders by his subordinates. Luckily for the Duke, Perponcher and Constant-Rebecque still had Ramsey's spark of moral courage and initiative (Dalton, *The Waterloo Roll Call* (1978), p.218).

8. Navez, *Les Quatre Bras, Ligny, Waterloo et Wavre*, p.143; de Bas, *op. cit.*, v.1, p.443

9. Wellington, *Supp. Desp.*, v.10, p.481. Hamilton-Williams, *op. cit.*, p.174, believes that Dörnberg's letter reached Wellington at 5.00 pm. This is an error, for Müffling quotes Wellington as saying to him: 'I have a report from General Dörnberg at Mons that Napoleon has moved on Charleroi with all his force and that he, General Dörnberg, has nothing in his front' (*Supp. Desp.*, v.10, p.510). Müffling asserts that the Duke said this 'towards midnight'. It was the arrival of the news from Dörnberg that caused Wellington to issue his orders of 10.00 pm.

In his account of the campaign, quoted in Pflugk-Harttung, *Vorgeschichte der Schlacht bei Belle-Alliance – Wellington*, pp.291–3, Dörnberg stated that he was unable to comprehend why his message, which left Mons at 9.30 am, took twelve-and-a-half hours to reach Brussels. He could only suggest that it was delayed at the Prince of Orange's headquarters in Braine-le-Comte (Wellington had decreed that all intelligence from Mons should be sent to Brussels via Braine-le-Comte: Gurwood, *The Dispatches of the Duke of Wellington* v.12, p.363). Dörnberg was correct in his suspicion. When his message reached Braine-le-Comte, the Prince of Orange was absent, having gone to Brussels to dine with Wellington. The Prince of Orange's staff officers should have forwarded Dörnberg's message forthwith to Wellington. Instead, some of them seem to have held it up for hours in the mistaken belief that the Prince was about to return to Braine-le-Comte. See Lieutenant-Colonel Berkeley's letter, *Supp. Desp.*, v.10, p.480 and de Bas, *op. cit.*, v.1, p.392. Berkeley eventually sent on Dörnberg's message with this covering letter. Berkeley's letter is annotated '2.00 pm' but this may have been an attempt to cover up the delay. See also Lachouque, *Le Secret de Waterloo*, p.112, and especially Hamilton-Williams, *op. cit.*, p.374, whose detailed research on the intelligence network has greatly clarified the early stages of the campaign.

10. The story of Grant's mission is related in a memorandum by Lieutenant-General W. Napier, quoted in McGrigor, *Autobiography and Services*, pp.415–6. Napier saw the message but was quoting it from memory and wrote his memorandum as late as 1857. As an instance of his confusion, Napier asserted that Grant sent his message as late as 15 June, by which time it would have been too late to warn Wellington of Napoleon's impending invasion, as Napier claimed Grant's message would have done had it not been intercepted by Dörnberg.

Napier errs in criticising Dörnberg, who had probably received orders similar to those given to the Prince of Orange by Wellington: to evaluate messages arriving at his headquarters and only to send to Brussels those it was considered Wellington should see (Hamilton-Williams, *op. cit.*, p.374; Siborne, *History of the Waterloo Campaign*, p.107). Dörnberg was merely doing his duty. Pflugk-Harttung, *op. cit.*, pp.220–2, is rightly devastating in his criticism of General Napier's reliability as a witness and defends Dörnberg against Napier's slanders.

11. In his memorandum, Napier asserted that Dörnberg returned the message on the grounds that Dörnberg did not believe it. But this does not agree with Dörnberg's own account, in which he claimed he was convinced of an impending French attack. In support of Dörnberg, Wellington's *Dispatches* and *Supplementary Despatches* contain dozens of letters from Dörnberg to Brussels with news of French threatening moves. It is undeniable that Dörnberg did return Grant's message, but probably owing to a desire for further and more recent information, rather than stupidity, as Napier claimed.

12. Hamilton-Williams' hypothesis is that Dörnberg incorporated most of Grant's news into one of the intelligence reports he sent the Duke (see pp.149–50). This is probable but impossible to substantiate.

13. Among the critics of Wellington's attendance of the Ball is Field Marshal the Viscount Montgomery of Alamein. But Montgomery's style of command would not have been suitable for Wellington's era. Similarly, Wellington's reserved, disdainful attitude would not have appealed to the educated and questioning troops Montgomery led. At Alamein in 1942, Montgomery was able to concentrate on fighting the battle from his Tactical Headquarters near the front because General Alexander was at Cairo dealing with the public relations and political aspects. In 1815, Wellington had to undertake his own public relations, which is why he attended the Ball.

14. Longford, *Wellington: The Years of the Sword*, p.421

15. De Bas, *op. cit.*, v.1, p.429

16. Hamilton-Williams, *op. cit.*, p.178, places an ingenious but not wholly substantiated interpretation on Dörnberg's ride to Brussels. He suggests that Dörnberg suddenly realised the importance of Grant's message and rode through the night to explain to the Duke exactly who had sent it. This is reading too much into the evidence. In fact, Dörnberg was the commander of a cavalry brigade quartered at Malines, north of Brussels. In April, he had been detached from his unit to Mons on intelligence work and had been ordered to return to Brussels and his brigade as soon as hostilities commenced. Dörnberg did precisely this on the night of 15/16 June. When he arrived in Brussels, he insisted on seeing the Duke because he suspected, with reason, that the Duke might not be convinced that Napoleon was threatening Quatre Bras in force.

Dörnberg himself relates (Pflugk-Harttung, *op. cit.*, pp.291–3) how on 14 June he showed a message he had received from a royalist-sympathising French officer to the commander of the British 2nd Division. The divisional general read the intelligence that the French Army was assembling, that Napoleon was joining it and that hostilities were about to commence with an attack at the junction of the Allied armies. Then he announced: 'yes, I believe it now – but the

Duke, who is always very well informed, believes it not.' It may well have been this conversation which prompted Dörnberg to speak to the Duke in person on his return from Mons. No doubt Dörnberg also had more up-to-date intelligence to give him. Indeed, Siborne, *History of the Waterloo Campaign*, p.53, mentions that Wellington sent to Dörnberg on the afternoon of 15 June, requesting information on any French movements in the direction of Mons.

17. Ollech, *Geschichte des Feldzuges von 1815*, p.99

18. Treuenfeld, *Die Tage von Ligny und Belle-Alliance*, p.114

19. The Prussians were very much in the dark as to Wellington's intentions. From his own account (*Passages from My Life*, pp.229–30), Müffling appears to have drafted a message to Gneisenau only at 7.00 pm and to have completed and sent it 'towards midnight' (in fact, about 11.00 pm) on 15 June, after the Duke ordered the shift of his divisions eastwards, towards the Prussians. Müffling's message is quoted in Delbrück, *Das Leben des Feldmarschalls Grafen Neithardt von Gneisenau*, v.2, pp.170–1 and promises that Wellington will be around Nivelles on the 16th to support the Prussians. This communication must have reached Gneisenau at 3.00 am at the earliest.

20. Henderson, *Blücher and the Uprising of Prussia against Napoleon*, p.286

21. Lachouque, *Le Secret de Waterloo*, p.126

22. Houssaye, *Waterloo 1815*, p.141

23. *United Service Magazine* (Oct. 1891), pp.44–5

24. Saunders, *The Hundred Days*, pp.104 and 116

25. Bonaparte, *Napoleon's Memoirs*, p.508

26. Coignet, *The Notebooks of Captain Coignet*, pp.275–6

27. Houssaye, *Waterloo 1815*, p.156

28. Pétiet, *Souvenirs Militaires*, p.194. Literally: 'they are going to be caught red-handed.' ('Ils vont être pris en flagrant délit.') This was a phrase commonly used to mean the enemy would be smashed. Napoleon used the same phrase in an order to Marshal Grouchy on 18 June.

29. Müffling, quoted in Chalfont, *Waterloo: Battle of Three Armies*, p.63

30. Barral, *L'Epopée de Waterloo*, p.163; Brett-James, *The Hundred Days*, pp.69–70

31. Grouchy, *Mémoires du maréchal de Grouchy*, v.4, p.9

32. Bonaparte, *op. cit.*, p.509

33. Pétiet, *op. cit.*, p.195

34. Maxwell, *Life of Wellington*, v.2, pp.7–8

35. Coignet, *op. cit.*, p.276

36. Saunders, *The Hundred Days*, p.136

37. Brett-James, *The Hundred Days*, p.70

38. *Ibid*, p.71

39. Moreover, Damitz, *Histoire de la Campagne de 1815*, v.1, p.171, quotes a Prussian account as saying that 'more than one Prussian fell at Ligny to Prussian musketballs.'

40. This compromise is recorded by Damitz, *op. cit.*, v.1, p.92, who based his account on the documents of General Grolmann, the Prussian Quartermaster-General, who was at the conference.

41. The sources describing the meeting at Bussy mill are few, contradictory and subjective. Wellington's concluding remark is given by Müffling. Dörnberg's account quotes Wellington as saying merely: 'I will see what is in front of me [at Quatre Bras] and how much of my army has arrived, and act accordingly' (Pflugk-Harttung, *Vorgeschichte der Schlacht bei Belle-Alliance – Wellington*, pp.291–3). Several German historians have concluded that Wellington did not add the condition 'if I am not attacked myself.' The issue is uncertain, but I think Wellington did add the condition. It is noteworthy that he wrote in his Waterloo Despatch that 'I was not able to assist them [Prussians] as I wished, as I was attacked myself.' What is certain is that Gneisenau forgot or did not hear Wellington's condition; throughout the conference Wellington had clearly indicated that he did not expect to meet serious resistance at Quatre Bras.

42. Reuter's testimony (*United Service Magazine*, Oct. 1891, p.45) is confirmed by the Prussian Official Account, written by Gneisenau: 'Field Marshal Blücher resolved to give battle, Lord Wellington having already put in motion to support him a strong division of his army, as well as

his whole reserve stationed in the environs of Brussels' (Booth, *The Battle of Waterloo by a near observer*, p.175).

Reuter's evidence is further confirmed by some notes by Baron Müffling discovered in the British Museum: 'Wellington had an interview with Blücher at the mill of Brye [Bussy] and assured him that, most of his troops having been concentrated, he was going to set them in motion towards the attacked points. On his side, Blücher resolved in consequence to give battle' (de Bas, *La Campagne de 1815 aux Pays-Bas*, v.1, p.476). Damitz, *op. cit.*, v.1, p.92, basing his account on the documents of General Grolmann, agrees exactly with Müffling. According to Damitz, Wellington said: 'I am convinced that at 2.00 pm I will have enough troops massed to take the offensive immediately.' Damitz adds that after such a positive assurance, the Prussians decided to accept battle.

43. The heaviest French attacks were made on the Wagnelée–St Amand sector. Ligny was attacked by a mere two divisions of Gérard's corps. Napoleon clearly wanted to draw the Prussian reserves on to St Amand rather than Ligny, where the Guard would have to try and break through. In fact, the Prussians would conform perfectly with Napoleon's hopes. A mere twenty-five per cent of the Prussian II Corps entered Ligny; the rest joined the Wagnelée–St Amand sector. I am indebted to Patrick Maes for this observation.

44. Bonaparte, *Napoleon's Memoirs*, p.510

Face to Face Across Ligny Brook: The Balance of Forces

NAPOLEON	BLUCHER
Left flank	**Right flank**
* Girard's division (serving on detachment)	* Ziethen's I Corps
* Vandamme's III Corps	
Centre	
* Gérard's IV Corps (minus Hulot's infantry, and Maurin's cavalry, divisions)	
Right flank	**Left flank**
(Marshal Grouchy)	* Thielmann's III Corps
* Hulot's division	
* Maurin's division	
* Pajol's I Cavalry Corps	
* Exelmans' II Cavalry Corps	
Reserve	**Reserve**
* Guard (infantry and Guyot's heavy cavalry division)	* Pirch's II Corps
* Milhaud's IV Cavalry Corps	
* Lobau's VI Corps (at Charleroi)	* Bülow's IV Corps (coming from Liège)

Order of Battle of the Prussian Army at Ligny

Commander-in-Chief:	Field Marshal Blücher
Chief of Staff:	Lt-Gen Gneisenau
Quartermaster-General:	Maj-Gen Grolmann
Artillery Commander:	Maj-Gen Holtzendorff

I Corps (29,000 men)

Commander:	Lt-Gen Ziethen
Chief of Staff:	Lt-Col Reiche

I Corps Infantry
1st Brigade (Maj-Gen Steinmetz)
 12th and 24th Infantry; 1st Westphalian Landwehr; 1st and 3rd Silesian sharpshooter companies
2nd Brigade (Maj-Gen Pirch II)
 6th and 28th Infantry; 2nd Westphalian Landwehr
3rd Brigade (Maj-Gen Jägow)
 7th and 29th Infantry; 3rd Westphalian Landwehr
4th Brigade (Maj-Gen Henckel von Donnersmarck)
 19th Infantry; 4th Westphalian Landwehr; 2nd and 4th Silesian sharpshooter companies

I Corps Cavalry (Maj-Gen Röder)[1]
5th Dragoons; 4th Hussars; 1st Westphalian Landwehr Cavalry
Tresckow's Cavalry Brigade
 4th Uhlans; 1st Kurmark Landwehr Cavalry
Lützow's Cavalry Brigade
 2nd Dragoons; 6th Uhlans; 2nd Kurmark Landwehr Cavalry

I Corps Artillery (Lt-Col Lehmann)
Brigade artillery[2]

Foot artillery:	6-pounder batteries nos. 3; 7; 8; 15

Reserve Artillery

Foot artillery:	12-pounder batteries nos. 2; 6; 9
	6-pounder battery no. 1
	Howitzer battery no. 1
Horse artillery:	Batteries nos. 2; 7; 10

1st Engineer company

II Corps (31,000 men)

Commander:	Maj-Gen Pirch I
Chief of Staff:	Col Aster

II Corps Infantry
5th Brigade (Maj-Gen Tippelskirch)
 2nd and 25th Infantry; 5th Westphalian Landwehr
6th Brigade (Maj-Gen Krafft)
 9th and 26th Infantry; 1st Elbe Landwehr
7th Brigade (Maj-Gen Brause)
 14th and 22nd Infantry; 2nd Elbe Landwehr

8th Brigade (Col Langen)
   21st and 23rd Infantry; 3rd Elbe Landwehr

II Corps Cavalry (Maj-Gen Jürgass)
Brigade cavalry[3]
   5th Kurmark Landwehr Cavalry; Elbe Landwehr Cavalry
Thümen's Brigade
   6th Dragoons; 11th Hussars; 2nd Uhlans
Schulenburg's Brigade
   1st Dragoons; 4th Kurmark Landwehr Cavalry
Sohr's Brigade
   3rd Hussars; 5th Hussars

II Corps Artillery (Lt-Col Röhl)
Brigade Artillery	
Foot artillery:	6-pounder batteries nos. 5; 10; 12; 34
Reserve Artillery	
Foot artillery:	12-pounder batteries nos. 4; 8
	6-pounder battery no. 37
Horse artillery:	Batteries nos. 5; 6; 14
7th Engineer Company	

III CORPS (23,000 men)
Commander:	Lt-Gen Thielmann
Chief of Staff:	Col Clausewitz

III Corps Infantry
9th Brigade (Maj-Gen Borcke)
   8th and 30th Infantry; 1st Kurmark Landwehr
10th Brigade (Col Kemphen)
   27th Infantry; 2nd Kurmark Landwehr
11th Brigade (Col Luck)
   3rd and 4th Kurmark Landwehr
12th Brigade (Col Stülpnagel)
   31st Infantry; 5th and 6th Kurmark Landwehr

III Corps Cavalry (Maj-Gen Hobe)
Brigade Cavalry
   3rd and 6th Kurmark Landwehr Cavalry
Marwitz's Brigade
   7th and 8th Uhlans
Lottum's Brigade
   4th Dragoons; 5th Uhlans

III Corps Artillery (Col Mohnhaupt)
Brigade Artillery
    Foot artillery: 6-pounder batteries nos. 18; 35
Reserve Artillery
    Foot artillery: 12-pounder battery no. 7
    Horse artillery: Batteries nos. 18; 19; 20
5th Engineer Company

NOTE: The following units were absent from their parent corps on 16 June and were not present at the Battle of Ligny:
3rd battalion, 21st Infantry; 2nd battalion, 3rd Kurmark Landwehr; 9th Hussars; two squadrons of the 6th Dragoons; two squadrons of the 6th Kurmark Landwehr Cavalry.

Order of Battle of the French Army at the Battle of Ligny

Commander-in-chief: Emperor Napoleon
Chief of Staff: Marshal Soult
Artillery commander: Lt-Gen Count Ruty
Engineers commander: Lt-Gen Baron Rogniat

IMPERIAL GUARD (Lt-Gen Count Drouot) (17,000 men)

Guard Infantry
Two Old Guard divisions (Lt-Gens Counts Friant and Morand)
    1st, 2nd, 3rd and 4th Grenadiers
    1st, 2nd, 3rd and 4th Chasseurs
One Young Guard divison (Lt-Gen Count Duhesme)
    1st and 3rd Tirailleurs; 1st and 3rd Voltigeurs

Guard Cavalry[4]
Heavy Cavalry Division (Lt-Gen Count Guyot)
    Grenadiers à cheval; Empress' Dragoons; Gendarmerie d'élite

Guard Artillery (Lt-Gen Desvaux de Saint-Maurice)
    Horse artillery: 1 battery
    Foot artillery: 13 batteries
One company of engineers
One company of marines

III CORPS (17,000 men)
Commander: Lt-Gen Count Vandamme

Chief of Staff:	Brig-Gen Baron Revest

8th Division (Lt-Gen Baron Lefol)

Billiard's Brigade:	15th Light and 23rd Line Infantry
Corsin's Brigade:	37th and 64th Line Infantry

10th Division (Lt-Gen Baron Habert)

Gengoult's Brigade:	34th and 88th Line Infantry
Dupeyroux's Brigade:	22nd and 70th Line Infantry; 2nd Swiss Infantry

11th Division (Lt-Gen Baron Berthezène)

Dufour's Brigade:	12th and 56th Line Infantry
Lagarde's Brigade:	33rd and 86th Line Infantry

3rd Cavalry Division (Lt-Gen Baron Domon)

Dommanget's Brigade:	4th and 9th Chasseurs à cheval
Vinot's Brigade:	12th Chasseurs à cheval

Four foot and one horse artillery batteries

Two engineer companies

7TH INFANTRY DIVISION (detached from II Corps) (5000 men)

Commander:	Lt-Gen Baron Girard
De Villiers' Brigade:	11th Light and 82nd Line Infantry
Piat's Brigade:	12th Light and 4th Line Infantry

One foot artillery battery

IV CORPS (16,000 men)

Commander:	Lt-Gen Count Gérard
Chief of Staff:	Brig-Gen Saint-Rémy

12th Division (Lt-Gen Baron Pêcheux)

Rome's Brigade:	30th and 96th Line Infantry
Schoeffer's Brigade:	6th Light and 63rd Line Infantry

13th Division (Lt-Gen Baron Vichery)

Le Capitaine's Brigade:	59th and 76th Line Infantry
Desprez's Brigade:	48th and 69th Line Infantry

14th Division (Brig-Gen Baron Hulot)

Brigade:	9th Light and 111th Line Infantry
Toussaint's Brigade:	44th and 50th Line Infantry

7th Cavalry Division (Lt-Gen Baron Maurin)

Vallin's Brigade:	6th Hussars and 8th Chasseurs à cheval
Berruyer's Brigade:	6th and 16th Dragoons

Four foot and one horse artillery batteries

Three engineer companies

RESERVE CAVALRY

Commander:	Marshal Grouchy
Chief of Staff:	Brig-Gen Baron Le Sénécal

I Cavalry Corps (2000 men)

Commander: Lt-Gen Count Pajol

4th Cavalry Division (Lt-Gen Baron Soult)[5]
    4th and 5th Hussars

5th Cavalry Division (Lt-Gen Baron Subervie)
    De Colbert's Brigade: 1st and 2nd Lancers
    De Douai's Brigade: 11th Chasseurs à cheval

Two horse artillery batteries

II Cavalry Corps (3000 men)

Commander: Lt-Gen Count Exelmans

9th Cavalry Division (Lt-Gen Baron Strolz)
    Burthe's Brigade: 5th and 13th Dragoons
    Vincent's Brigade: 15th and 20th Dragoons

10th Cavalry Division (Lt-Gen Baron Chastel)
    Bonnemains's Brigade: 4th and 12th Dragoons
    Berton's Brigade: 14th and 17th Dragoons

Two horse artillery batteries

IV Cavalry Corps (3000 men)

Commander: Lt-Gen Count Milhaud

13th Cavalry Division (Lt-Gen Wathier, Count de Saint-Alphonse)
    Dubois' Brigade: 1st and 4th Cuirassiers
    Travers' Brigade: 7th and 12th Cuirassiers

14th Cavalry Division (Lt-Gen Baron Delort)
    Vial's Brigade: 5th and 10th Cuirassiers
    Farine's Brigade: 6th and 9th Cuirassiers

Two horse artillery batteries

Notes

1. The command structure of I Corps' cavalry at the Battle of Ligny was unusual. Officially, in the 1815 campaign, Lützow commanded the 6th Uhlans and the 1st and 2nd Kurmark Landwehr Cavalry. Tresckow was at the head of the 2nd and 5th Dragoons and the 4th Uhlans. The other two regiments, the 4th Hussars and the 1st Westphalian Landwehr Cavalry, were divided up and assigned to the four infantry brigades as cavalry scouts. However, at Ligny, the I Corps' cavalry was organised as shown in the order of battle. Lützow and Tresckow did not command their usual regiments. The 1st Westphalian Landwehr Cavalry alone was attached to the infantry (to 2nd brigade). The 4th Hussars was covering the extreme western flank of Blücher's army. The sources do not state where the 5th Dragoons were.

2. Brigade artillery were batteries attached to specific infantry brigades. The remaining batteries formed the corps' reserve artillery.

3. Brigade cavalry were regiments split up and attached to specific infantry brigades. In general, two squadrons accompanied each brigade. The brigade cavalry was used to scout for, and support, the infantry. The other cavalry regiments formed the corps' reserve cavalry.

4. The Guard Light Cavalry Division was attached to Marshal Ney's wing. It was accompanied by two Guard horse artillery batteries (Bonaparte, *Napoleon's Memoirs*, p.505), leaving the remaining one at the Battle of Ligny. Sources differ on the number of batteries in the Guard. I

have followed Houssaye, *Waterloo 1815*, p.104, who quotes from a document in the War Archives signed by a Guard officer and setting out the composition of the Guard on 16 June.
5. The 1st Hussars, which also belonged to this division, had become caught up in the French left wing during 15 June and remained with Marshal Ney on 16 June (*Pajol, Général en chef*, v.3, p.205).

5

BATTLE OF LIGNY

Phase One: St Amand and Ligny Come under Fire

The first moves were made. French forces attacked to draw the Prussian reserves into an exhausting attritional fight in the villages along the Ligny brook. South of St Amand the band of the French 23rd Line infantry struck up, playing a tune that haunted old fields of glory: *La Victoire en Chantant*. Men stood up from where they had been resting in the wheatfields. Battalions formed up.

One of Vandamme's three infantry divisions rolled forward to the attack. The divisional general, Baron Etienne Lefol, had formed his men in a large square around him and then had harangued them into a fever pitch. They demanded to be allowed to march against the Prussians. As the 15th Light infantry spread out into swarms of skirmishers, the remaining three regiments of Lefol's division each formed a dense assault column and followed close behind.

The men, bearing heavy packs and sweltering in grey greatcoats, trampled slowly through fields of tall wheat. Just then the Prussian guns opened up. The slopes north of the Ligny brook erupted in fire and smoke as Blücher's artillery discharged a salvo. The first round fell right in the midst of a French company and killed eight men. Cannonballs smashed into the French columns, which closed ranks to push on. Bloodied and broken bodies marked the advance of the columns.

In St Amand three Prussian battalions of 3rd brigade lay in wait. Some soldiers were in the houses, some around the church, still others crouched within walled gardens and behind the bushy hedges of orchards.

Fifty metres from the first enclosures of St Amand, the French skirmishers rushed forward. Under a hail of Prussian musketry they forced their enemy back. Corpses already littered the streets. Then the French columns, following their skirmishers, thrust their way into the assaulted village, and after fifteen minutes' fighting the Prussians poured out of the north face of St Amand to rally on the far side of Ligny brook.

French forces tried to debouch from St Amand, only to be crushed by a hail of canister shot from Prussian cannon. General Holtzendorff, Blücher's artillery

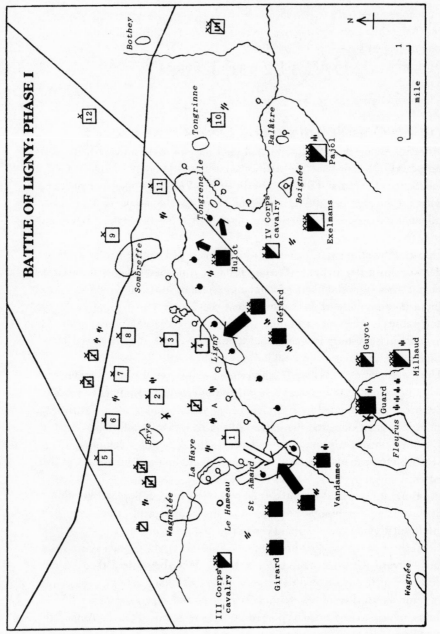

BATTLE OF LIGNY: PHASE I

Phase One of the battle saw French infantry attacks on St Amand and Ligny as well as probing operations by Grouchy's cavalry in the eastern sector. The French captured St Amand but were soon checked by the fire of the massed Prussian battery (A) north of the village. Then the Prussian 1st brigade retook St Amand. The French secured but a foothold in Ligny.

commander, had lined up a formidable array of I Corps guns north of St Amand and leading round to the southwest of Ligny. This powerful line of forty massed guns totally checked the French advance. 'When our columns', wrote one French general, 'sought to debouch on to the plain [to the north of St Amand], they were halted by very superior forces, crushed by a formidable battery and forced to retreat back into the village.'[1]

Meanwhile, the French artillery commenced firing. Howitzer shells and cannonshot smote the ground. Prussian guns returned the compliment; a thunderous bombardment was building up. The very earth trembled with the terrific concussion of the awesome barrage. Guns spat fire and death.

One Prussian battery pounded the French troops inside St Amand, causing fires to break out at several points. Then came the Prussian counter-attack. Four infantry battalions of 1st brigade swept down in compact columns preceded by the customary wave of skirmishers. The charging Prussians screamed war cries as they rushed into St Amand and expelled the French in short order, despite an obstinate resistance around the church.

Fifteen minutes after the attack had first opened on St Amand, Ligny also came under fire. 'In a few moments', wrote Colonel Auguste Pétiet of the French staff, 'the fighting became general and a heavy cannonade gradually increased in intensity and made itself heard all along the line.'[2] The opposing artillery built up to a crescendo of explosions, a fog of smoke, and a harvest of death. In Ligny village itself stood the Prussian 4th infantry brigade. The troops cowered behind whatever shelter they could find – banks, walls, hedges and trees.

Much of the French artillery fire, however, was directed against the opposing guns and the Prussian reserves beyond Ligny. 'By what we could judge', wrote one French eyewitness, 'our artillery did considerable mischief among the great body of Prussian troops that were posted in mass on the heights and slopes.'[3]

Wellington had evaluated only too well the faulty Prussian dispositions, and the French gunners, on slightly higher terrain than their opponents, were now taking full advantage of it. Napoleon's own forces, better protected by undulating ground, were less exposed, but the Prussian cannon kept firing away.

Then, under the cover of this thunderous bombardment, Lieutenant-General Baron Marc Pêcheux's division from Gérard's IV Corps advanced on the village with drums beating, spirits high and muskets loaded. The French troops advanced noisily, cheering loudly to intimidate their foe and to boost each other's morale. Heavy lines of skirmishers led the attack to pick off enemy officers and to infiltrate into the Prussian defences. They were followed by three columns, which set off in succession along a broad front so that the leading column would distract Prussian fire from the other two, thus giving them a greater chance of success.

Shots followed flashes from behind the outermost gardens and the first

Frenchmen fell. Prussian skirmishers reloaded to fire again and again. Losses built up; bodies slumped to the ground. The psychological impact of these losses caused the French columns to slow and then to halt. But soon they were advancing once more into the deadly hail of lead musketballs.[4] Two of the three shaken French infantry columns were forced by Prussian fire to retire, but elements of the 30th Line infantry managed to penetrate down a banked track leading into Ligny.

Captain Charles François of this regiment later recalled how the Prussians had barricaded this hollow lane with timber, carts and ploughs. François and his comrades negotiated this obstacle under fire from Prussian troops concealed behind thick hedges. A veritable fort, the Farm d'en Haut, stood firmly at the end of the lane, but the soldiers of the 30th passed it and ran across a street to enter the square surrounding the church. They could go no further. Prussians sniped at François and the French from the windows of houses, from behind ruined walls and from rooftops.

Confusion reigned supreme. 'No one', François bitterly remembered, 'no one was in command. No generals, no staff officers, no aides-de-camp were in sight'. François was so angry at witnessing a fight so poorly controlled that he raged and fumed and sought to get himself killed. He cursed his very existence to see French troops thrown into such disorder by Prussian fire. Neither reinforcements nor orders arrived and so François and the 30th Regiment were forced to retreat. The wounded had to be abandoned and disorder prevailed.[5]

East of Ligny, more French guns came up to the artillery firing positions. Round after round blasted off. Some newly arrived French Guard batteries shelled Ligny village, while Gérard's corps artillery hit the slopes further back with a deluge of iron. Several gunners rammed the charges down the bronze gun barrels, then others applied the slowmatches to the touchholes. A pause preceded mighty explosions and a deafening roar as the guns were flung back; clouds of obscuring smoke were blown out of the muzzles as the blue-coated gunners went forward to reload.

A fresh wave of French infantry attackers went in. A line of skirmishers, strengthened by the troops of whole battalions to achieve superior firepower, crept unperceived through the tall corn to seize the outermost hedges and gardens of Ligny. Smitten by this new onslaught, the Prussians yielded, but rallied and repulsed their foe. Hard-hit by casualties as the French were, their morale was still high. They attacked again and again. Four attacks were needed just to establish a hold on the outlying gardens and hedges. But once the French secured these meagre posts, they were able to use them as a basis for the long, expensive process of infiltrating into the surrounding area and expanding their hold.

French swarms reached the church square once more, being desperately counter-attacked by Prussian troops sheltering behind the church itself. The small square was crammed full with fighting troops. Men were not just shot, they were crushed, trampled and hacked to death.

The heat was stifling and the heavily laden troops were tortured by thirst. Some men fell through exhaustion alone. The soldiers became caked in a layer of blood, dirt, sweat and mud. The distinctive colours of the tattered and torn uniforms were unrecognizable. Drums beating the charge, the flash and pungent smell of exploding powder, the burning shells of ravaged houses, the rival shouts of 'vorwärts!' and 'vive l'Empereur!' all mingled with the screams of wounded men burnt alive.

On both sides, whole battalions had dissolved into ragged lines of skirmishers or often simply into a frenzied mob of uncontrolled savages. Drilled and disciplined troops had turned into wild animals. For walls blocked retreat, narrow streets created torrents of enraged soldiers and the traditional enmity between France and Prussia played its destructive hand. No mercy was given or sought, one French eyewitness recalling that 'the combat was maintained on both sides with equal obstinacy; each soldier seemed to meet his adversary with personal rancour, and each had resolved, it is evident, to give no quarter'.[6] Corpses lay in sombre pools of blood in the shattered village of Ligny, while the fight raged on around.

By now, it was four o'clock and the battle had been under way for an hour. During this time the eastern sector of the battlefield had been relatively quiet. Brigadier-General Jean-Baptiste Berton, commanding a French dragoon brigade of Exelmans' II Cavalry Corps on this wing, wrote that here, Napoleon 'wanted only to contain the Prussians.'[7] Thus antagonism was limited to the ritual of two sides trying to tie each other down: skirmishing and mutual observance.

Marshal Grouchy's French cavalry manoeuvred well and seemed to threaten to outflank the east flank of the Prussian III Corps. Nevertheless, without infantry support the French horsemen were unable to expel a battalion of the 2nd Kurmark Landwehr occupying the villages of Boignée and Balâtre. Hulot's infantry division, detached from Gérard and under Grouchy's orders, was tied up further west. Hulot was skirmishing with units of Thielmann's III Corps that were posted in front of Sombreffe and in Tongrenelle village.

In the centre of III Corps' position stood a certain Prussian officer. In later years he would emerge as one of the world's foremost military thinkers, but for the moment he was simply Chief of Staff to Thielmann's III Corps. He was Clausewitz. Colonel Carl von Clausewitz had witnessed the terrific fight raging in the western sector of the battlefield. Such was the dense concentration of smoke and flame at Ligny that Clausewitz thought everyone inside must surely be dead.[8]

III Corps, like many Prussian units on the battlefield, was exposed to French cannonfire. The soldiers suffered severely. Reinforcements from the corps reserves stationed on the heights around the village of Tongrinne marched to join their comrades of the advanced battalions stationed along the Ligny brook. Here the skirmishing went on against Grouchy's Frenchmen.

Thus the first phase of the Battle of Ligny came to a close. French forces had made contact with the Prussians at Ligny and St Amand, fighting there being well developed. Grouchy was successfully tying down Thielmann's III Corps in the eastern sector of the battlefield.

It was now time for Napoleon to extend the battle line to the west, in order to step up the conflict, to suck in the Prussian reserves and also to further communications with Marshal Ney, the commander of the French left wing at that moment engaged with Wellington's forces at Quatre Bras.

Phase Two: The Combat Escalates

Extending the battle line began with Lieutenant-General Baron Jean-Baptiste Girard's 5000 men storming Le Hameau. His division, attached to Vandamme's corps, hurled back the Prussian defenders before bursting into La Haye to threaten the right flank of the Prussian units in St Amand village.

From the Bussy windmill Blücher spotted this new threat and sent the 2nd infantry brigade from reserve into a spirited counter-attack. Further troops, the 5th infantry brigade from II Corps, moved from reserve on the village of Wagnelée to the west to second the operations of the 2nd brigade. The whole of the II Corps' cavalry and Tresckow's two regiments from I Corps' cavalry, a total of ten-and-a-half regiments, advanced in support of both these infantry brigades. At about the same time, III Corps' cavalry was ordered to transfer Marwitz's brigade from the eastern sector of the field to reinforce the massed cavalry in the west.

The Prussian 2nd brigade surged forward under a hail of murderous artillery and musketry fire. The unit was drawn up in classic Prussian brigade deployment for attack. First came the fusilier battalions, one from each of the brigade's three regiments. These fusiliers were marksmen and attacked in skirmish order backed up by support platoons in ordered ranks. Three hundred paces behind charged the first of two waves of dense assault columns. These columns, each formed from an ordinary musketeer battalion, were about forty men wide and eighteen deep. The second wave followed two hundred paces after the first, its columns being placed behind the intervals of the battalions of the first wave. This resulted in a chequered formation of battalion columns. It was a highly flexible tactical organisation. Artillery and cavalry acted in close support, particularly on the flanks.

The Prussian skirmishers plunged into La Haye and smote Girard's men with a continuous fusillade. The supporting fusilier platoons arrived to swell the skirmisher line and to boost its firepower. Then the first wave of assault

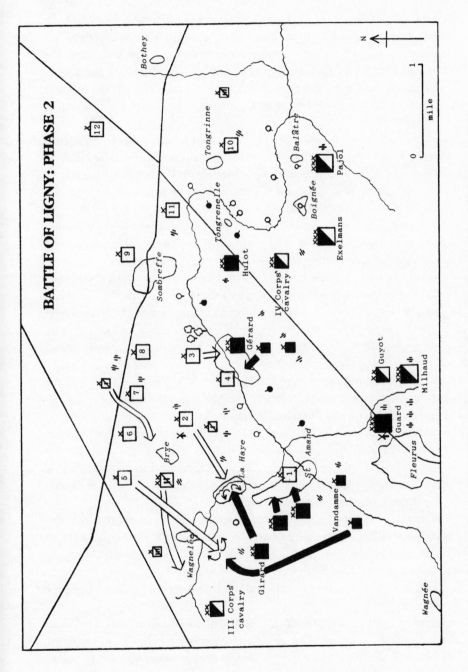

BATTLE OF LIGNY: PHASE 2

Bothey

Tongrinne

Balâtre

Tongrenelle

10

12

Pajol

Boignée

Sombreffe

Exelmans

Hulot

9

11

IV Corps'
cavalry

Gérard

3

8

4

7

Guyot

2

6

Brye

Milhaud

La Haye

Guard

5

St Amand

Fleurus

Wagnelée

1

Vandamme

Girard

III Corps'
cavalry

Wagnée

N

mile

0   1

Phase Two saw the battle intensify and extend. More units, both French and Prussian, were
sucked into Ligny and St Amand. Further troops surged into Le Hameau, La Haye and Wagnelée.

97

columns crashed into the already shaken French regiments. Battered by the succession of ferocious Prussian onslaughts, the French abandoned half of the beleaguered La Haye. But the French retained the formidable bastion of the Farm La Haye, which checked the Prussian momentum. The 1st battalion, 6th Regiment advanced from the second wave of assault columns to increase the pressure exerted by the first, but in vain.[9] The balance tilted back once more. The Prussians could press on no further. They had expended their shock power and reserve columns, while the street fighting had disordered the cohesion of the brigade.

Steadfast as always, Girard was rallying his four depleted French regiments. Suddenly, he was struck by several shots, one of which penetrated his lung. At the same time his horse, maddened by a head wound, threw him violently to the ground.[10] But even as Girard fell mortally wounded, his men gradually expelled the exhausted Prussians on to the north bank of the Ligny brook.

Once more the French threatened, once more Blücher rose to the occasion. Rallying the reeling Prussian units, he addressed them as no other commander could. 'Now children, behave well! Do not allow the great nation to rule over you again!' Yelling his famed battle cry 'vorwärts, vorwärts in Gottes Nahmen', Blücher flung his exuberant troops back into the contested village of La Haye.

Reculer pour mieux sauter, to step back in order to leap forward better, is one of the most underrated military maxims. By falling back out of La Haye once its first attack had been checked, the 2nd brigade had been able to replenish its order, cohesion and shock power. Now Girard's depleted division had to bear a second assault and it proved too much. His men broke. They had witnessed the fall of their remarkable leader, and both their brigadiers were out of action. So the French fell back to Le Hameau. While the Prussian 28th Regiment seized the formidable Farm of La Haye, the 6th Regiment, drunk with sudden success, sallied forth from La Haye, to be restrained by its officers with difficulty. The third regiment of 2nd brigade, the 2nd Westphalian Landwehr, stood in reserve. For Prussian commanders usually relied more heavily on their experienced regular units than on the *Landwehr*.

Further to the west, the Prussian 5th brigade advanced through the ungarrisoned village of Wagnelée in support of its comrades attacking La Haye. The Prussians debouched from the south of Wagnelée without even deigning to scout ahead. But in their path, General Vandamme had hidden two battalions as skirmishers amid the cornfields, backed up by a brigade of General Habert's division.

Surprised by a sudden fusillade, the Prussians fell into confusion while attempting to form line in order to have the firepower with which to reply to Vandamme's men. The Prussians were largely unaccustomed to fighting in line and in this action the end of one of the battalions of the 25th Regiment deployed in front of the wing of another.[11] The French compounded this confusion by charging home with the bayonet. The 25th Regiment simply dissolved.

Yet the French did not pursue too far; the shaken Prussian infantry rallied at the outskirts of Wagnelée, covered by supporting artillery fire. To the west, Vandamme's light cavalry division, under Lieutenant-General Baron Jean-Simon Domon, had contained the opposing Prussian squadrons during the infantry clash. At about this time, Domon received welcome reinforcements in the shape of Subervie's division, detached from Pajol in the eastern sector of the battlefield.

Thus the Prussians now controlled Wagnelée, La Haye, and St Amand, yet the French had established themselves in Le Hameau and were still launching attacks on the Prussian-held villages. General Vandamme brought into action his last unengaged unit, Colonel Stoffel's 2nd Swiss regiment, whose valorous soldiers were uniformed in their traditional red wool jackets. Invincible heroes of many a dramatic fight in the service of the French Empire, justly renowned for their defence of the River Beresina crossing in 1812, the Swiss now fought in Napoleon's last military victory.

As every battle progresses, the combatants lose track of time. Events become muddled while only particularly horrific yet minor incidents stick in their minds. Battle raged continously around the contested buildings and gardens of the villages along the Ligny brook.

The Prussian garrison of St Amand was eventually expelled and its mauled battalions retired to Brye. Even so, Ziethen's 12-pounder batteries concentrated their fire and kept the French from debouching from St Amand. Several Prussian battalions from the II Corps in reserve were being sucked into a long, intermittent stream into the battle zone.

Even the fiercely energetic Blücher was feeling the pressure of battle. 'The old marshal', wrote the German historian Carl von Ollech, 'seemed very pre-occupied by the effects of the terrible heat and by the weight of this long and indecisive fight.'[12]

Utter carnage met the eye at Ligny. Flames crackled in the burning houses. Dense smoke drifted into the sky. The intense heat was like that of a volcanic eruption. Reinforcements from both sides entered the fray; battalions melted like lumps of gold in a crucible. From the east, Gérard flung in the fresh 59th and 76th Line infantry from Lieutenant-General Baron Louis Vichery's division; from the west came four more Prussian battalions from 3rd brigade.

The fortunes of war swung back and forth. For an advance drove the foe back on his reinforcements while exhausting the attacker's strength and increasing the extent of ground to be held. On one occasion, the Prussians gradually gained ground, pushing past the small corpse-strewn square around the stone church and driving towards the eastern outskirts. Then a rumour spread that French troops had surrounded them and were entrenched in the churchyard.

Some soldiers in the vicinity panicked, firing their muskets at an imaginary threat. Further away, around the easternmost gardens and hedges, Prussian troops heard the shooting behind them and beat a retreat.

A dash by a daring group of French skirmishers for the flag of the 2nd battalion of the 7th Regiment was beaten off, but still the cries of 'Vive l'Empereur!' moved inexorably forward. They advanced until pinned down by fire from loopholes in the houses of the west bank of the brook. The butcher's bill in Ligny by now included several senior officers, including a French brigade commander, Lieutenant-General Baron Le Capitaine.

At one stage, the French even brought two cannon with them into the cemetery surrounding the church. Guns were rarely brought into contested villages lest fire from burning houses ignite the ammunition and annihilate the crews. At Ligny, the French clearly considered this risk to be outweighed by the tactical advantage offered by the added firepower. The 1st battalion, 3rd Westphalian Landwehr undertook three desperate attempts to seize the churchyard but failed each time. A subsequent attempt by the same battalion to outflank the post foundered when it came up against French reinforcements.

North and south of the ravaged village, the opposing artillery retired to refit. Other batteries thundered up to take their place and strove to drown the opposing cannon by sheer weight of fire. The battle was building up to a monstrous climax. Everywhere could be heard the ceaseless hammering of gunfire, everywhere the explosions of shells, everywhere the screaming and the cheering.

Inside Ligny, soldiers sniped from behind trees, adding to the dense billows of smoke. Overhead a storm was building up; the atmosphere was oppressive and hot, made hotter by the furnace that the shattered village had become. All this added up to what Gneisenau termed one of the most obstinate combats ever recorded in history. To observers from afar, the smoke and flames arising from the contested villages all along the Ligny brook gave the impression not merely of a mist-filled valley but also of a fiery river in hell.

Phase Three: French Hesitation and Prussian Counter-attacks

By 5.30 pm the second phase of the battle was drawing to a close. The Prussian reserves were being increasingly drawn into the long seven-mile stretch of contested villages along the winding Ligny brook. Soon Napoleon would deal the final death blow to this Prussian army which was rapidly expending its strength. In preparation for this *coup de grâce* the Emperor was waiting for reinforcements from Marshal Ney.

For Napoleon intended to defeat the Prussian army at Ligny with Marshal Ney's detachment first capturing Quatre Bras and containing Wellington's mustering forces, then marching eastwards to envelop the Prussian right wing on the Ligny battlefield. Accordingly, at 2.00 pm, Chief of Staff Soult had written to Ney: 'His Majesty's intention is that you will attack whatever force is before you, and after having vigorously driven it back, you will turn in our direction, so as to bring about the envelopment of those enemy troops whom I have just mentioned to you ...'

At 3.15 pm the battle was fiercely engaged at Ligny: Prussian resistance was stout, and French losses high, and so Soult sent a more imperious, even anxious order to Ney.

> An hour ago I wrote to you that the Emperor was about to attack the enemy in the position he has taken up between St Amand and Brye, and now the engagement has become very decided. His Majesty charges me to tell you, that you are to manoeuvre immediately, so as to surround the enemy's right, and fall upon his rear; the army in our front is lost if you act with energy. The fate of France is in your hands. Thus do not hesitate even for a moment to carry out the move ordered by the Emperor and direct your advance on the heights of Brye and St Amand so as to co-operate in a victory that may well turn out to be decisive ...

Just before this order was sent, a report reached the Imperial headquarters at Fleurus with the sobering news that 'the bravest of the brave' was confronted by 20,000 of Wellington's troops. Consequently, Napoleon had decided that it would be possible for Ney to send only d'Erlon's I Corps to surround the Prussian flank at Ligny. Colonel Forbin-Janson had been despatched with a pencil message ordering d'Erlon to make for the Battle of Ligny.

To compensate for the reduced numbers of reinforcements coming from Ney, Lobau's VI Corps had been summoned to Fleurus from Charleroi, where it had been left and then forgotten.

Napoleon calculated at 5.30 pm that d'Erlon would arrive in approximately half-an-hour. His Mameluke servant, Ali, recalled how the glasses of Napoleon's suite were constantly trained towards the west. 'We expected at any moment to see Count d'Erlon's corps, which we were awaiting impatiently, arrive.'[13] Napoleon prepared to throw in his reserve – the Guard together with Milhaud's heavy, breastplated *cuirassiers* – and these units began their approach march towards Ligny. This reserve, breaking through the Prussian line, would cut Blücher's army in two. The western forces would then be encircled and destroyed between the bayonets of Vandamme's III Corps, the reserve and the arriving d'Erlon. No wonder Napoleon had declared four hours earlier, 'if Ney carries out my orders well, not a single gun of the Prussian army will escape; it is going utterly to be smashed.'

Blücher would be wiped off the face of the earth. On the morrow Wellington would follow.

Then came devastating news. An unidentified column of troops, perhaps

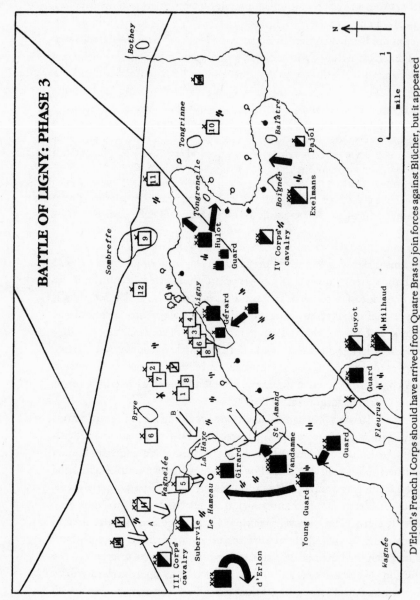

BATTLE OF LIGNY: PHASE 3

D'Erlon's French I Corps should have arrived from Quatre Bras to join forces against Blücher, but it appeared too far south and panicked Vandamme's III Corps before marching back towards its starting point. A Prussian onslaught (A) smashed into St Amand, Le Hameau and La Haye. The French Young Guard from reserve and Subervie's light cavalry division from Pajol were sent in to redress the balance in the western sector, with three Old Guard *chasseur* regiments following in support. The last French brigade entered Ligny. In the east, the 3rd and 4th Grenadiers of the Guard backed up Hulot's and Grouchy's attacks on the Prussian III Corps. Blücher's final offensive in the western sector (B) was repelled, and when Napoleon ordered his reserve to break into Blücher's army at Ligny village, the Prussians had no reserve left.

20,000 or 30,000 strong, was heading eastwards, straight for Fleurus. Girard's depleted division, commanded now by Colonel Matis of the 82nd Line infantry, had fallen back and abandoned La Haye, while Vandamme reported that unless the reserve was sent to help, he would soon be forced to relinquish St Amand.

The French troops were nervous, losses had been high and their lurking fear of treachery could not altogether be separated from this formidable, possibly hostile column approaching their left rear.

But what was this column? D'Erlon's troops had been ordered to head for Brye, not Fleurus, and, if Ney had captured Quatre Bras as commanded, would be moving down the Nivelles–Namur highroad. So was it an enemy column? English forces which had cut between Marshal Ney and Napoleon? A reliable ADC was sent to investigate.

For the moment, the reserve's attack had been postponed, the troops recalled to Fleurus, and part of the Guard hurried to support Vandamme's corps. Lieutenant-General Count Philibert Duhesme advanced with his Young Guard division to the area, followed by the 2nd and 4th Chasseurs of the Old Guard in support. The 3rd Chasseurs and Milhaud's IV Cavalry Corps marched to observe the unidentified column that had terrified Vandamme's men.[14]

At the same time, the 3rd and 4th Grenadiers were despatched to help General Hulot, who was now heavily engaged inside Tongrenelle village, to tie down the Prussian III Corps in the eastern sector of the field. If anything could restore morale to French troops, it would be the presence of the 'immortals' of the Guard.

Meanwhile the situation on the west flank had gone from bad to worse. Blücher had just launched a ferocious counter-attack, for the confusion among Vandamme's battle-tried men had caused Prussian observers to inform Blücher that Napoleon was retreating. Blücher ordered an assault.

A little after 5.30 pm, Prussian reserve batteries thundered into position to prepare the assault. Accompanying them was Captain Reuter advancing with four guns from his 12-pounder battery. Reuter traded shots with the French artillery to the south of St Amand village. A steady stream of French shells burst around Reuter and inflicted heavy losses on the Prussian gunners, but then Blücher sent forward his infantrymen.

Gathering some fresh battalions from the II Corps, inspiring some decimated I Corps troops, Blücher flung them all into the French-held St Amand. Battalion clashed against battalion, company against company, soldier against soldier. Fighting was hand to hand and bitter, yet the French still feared the unidentified column approaching from the west. Vandamme's men abandoned the northern sector of St Amand, some of the troops fleeing so frantically that their own cannon had to be turned on them to bring them to a halt.

To the northwest, the Prussian 5th infantry brigade debouched from Wagnelée to attack Le Hameau and La Haye. Major Witzleben led two battalions of the brigade to threaten the rear of the garrison of La Haye by assaulting Le Hameau with vigour. The 11th Hussars and 2nd Uhlans under Colonel Thümen protected 5th brigade's right flank while two foot batteries provided close supporting fire. Prussian infantry skirmishers blazed away so quickly that they ran out of ammunition. They were restocked by the neighbouring 11th Hussars who ran over to empty their own cartridge boxes.

Blücher himself, sword in hand and mounted on his magnificent black charger, was in the thick of the fighting. He joined the 3rd battalion, 2nd Regiment to capture Le Hameau, in spite of a bitter defence. Wagnelée, Le Hameau, La Haye and the northern sector of St Amand were all now in Prussian hands.

The acuteness of this crisis has never been recognised.[15] Napoleon's left wing was in tatters and apparently about to be crushed by a strong enemy column. Defeat loomed large. The Emperor had despatched two staff officers to rally the shocked French units. One of these officers, General Count Charles de La Bédoyère, called out: 'Soldiers, are you not ashamed to fall back before these same men whom you have beaten so many times, who begged for mercy while throwing their weapons at your feet at Austerlitz, Jena and Friedland? Attack, and you will see them once more flee and recognise you as their conquerors!'[16]

But the fight went on. Casualties rose. A cannon shot carried off the head of Colonel Thümen, whose hussars and *Uhlans* also suffered severely from the French fire.

Then the French Young Guard of the famed General Duhesme came up at the double to the carnage, with cheers of 'Long live the Emperor!' and its bands playing the *Chant du Départ*. At the arrival of the Young Guard, Vandamme's exhausted men burst into acclamations.

While the French light cavalry held opposing Prussian squadrons in check, the fresh guardsmen forced back the infantry. Girard's troops rallied to expel the Prussians from Le Hameau; Vandamme's men took heart to drive their enemy out of St Amand. 'What soldiers!' exclaimed one amazed eyewitness. 'These are no longer the spiritless wrecks of Arcis-sur-Aube. They are either a legion of heroes or of devils.'[17]

It was now six o'clock. The Young Guard, Girard's division, and Vandamme had checked the Prussians on the west flank, yet Napoleon's ADC, sent to reconnoitre the unidentified column that had appeared on the western horizon, had not yet reported back. Elsewhere on the extended battlefield, the fight went on. Grouchy stepped up his efforts on the right wing. Hulot skirmished with spirit and detached a battalion of the 50th Line infantry to bolster Pajol's cavalry and, presently, to clear Boignée and Balâtre of Prussian troops.

In Ligny, meanwhile, slaughter continued unabated. From afar, it seemed that the village had become a solid mass of fire. But closer inspection showed

Prussian troops fighting amidst the inferno and the shattered ruins, keeping their French foes at bay. Flames crackled in the Château des Comtes de Looz where embattled Prussian companies fought on against the French.

Captain Charles François and a fellow captain together rallied the tattered remnants of the French 30th Line infantry regiment. His troops entreated François to lead them once more back into Ligny village. François was flattered by the trust that his men showed in him. 'Long live the Emperor and Captain François!' they cheered.

Proud when his general complimented him on his soldiers' devotion, François led them back to the sunken lane running into the village past the Farm d'en Haut. François led the way with 100 men of the 30th, while the 96th Regiment followed in support. He ordered the men to keep silent. Suddenly, Prussian infantry appeared through the smoke. French and Prussians showed mutual astonishment at finding themselves so close to their enemy.

Then François struck his general's horse on the nose to make it get out of the line of fire of his unit. Out in front of his men, François himself ducked and shouted, 'Fire!' The Prussians likewise pressed their triggers. Several casualties slumped to the ground, but François escaped with a contusion on the chest, causing him to spit blood for several days thereafter. Then he was on his feet, crying out for a bayonet charge.

Frightful was the carnage that then ensued. François's sword broke; he toppled over in the crush; assorted feet trampled him underfoot. Then the French 96th Regiment advanced and the Prussians fled. Stunned and bruised, François rejoined the debris of his unit, which was still under Prussian fire.[18]

Some of the mauled Prussian units garrisoning Ligny were relieved and pulled back into reserve. The 4th infantry brigade had, in Ligny, lost 2500 men out of 4721. A captain in the *Landwehr* cavalry watched 4th brigade's shattered battalions retire. He noted the 4th Westphalian Landwehr regiment, which presented a sorry sight. The men were exhausted wrecks. Their faces were begrimed with sweat, mud and burnt powder. Their uniforms were dirty rags. Dark blood stained clumsily-applied bandages. Torn and unbuttoned coats revealed grubby shirts or chests.

Fresh Prussian battalions entered Ligny and joined the embattled troops inside the village. The 1st battalion, 23rd Regiment scored a tactical success by forming two columns and storming across the Ligny brook into the streets of the east bank. The left column battered down the gates of a farmhouse with hatchets and secured this post. This distracted the French skirmishers and protected the advance of the right column.

Yet the French attacks were becoming unendurable and Gérard's last reserve, the second brigade of Vichery's division, had just entered the fray. A desperate plea for help reached Gneisenau for reinforcements. 'Hold on for one half-hour longer', came the reply. 'The English army is drawing near.'

Wellington, though, had enough on his plate at Quatre Bras; a message from Müffling informed Blücher that no help could be despatched. This was indeed unpleasant news.[19]

Blücher, though, still clung to the idea of winning the battle by himself. He would attack. Perhaps it was a bad decision, to use up precious strength in offensive tactics when there was no hope of support. As Müffling had informed Wellington before the campaign opened, 'our infantry does not possess the same bodily strength as yours. The greater mass of our troops are too young and inexperienced: we cannot reckon on their obstinately continuing a fight from morning to evening. To economize their strength is a thing quite unknown to our men. Led by their officers, they expend in *one* hour what might have taken four to consume.'[20]

But Blücher and his Prussians fought best in attack. Theirs was not the dogged, iron defence of Wellington's British infantry, theirs was a ferocious battering ram of an assault. 'Papa Blücher' gathered up a few of his wrecked formations from the second line, collected the last fresh battalions from II Corps, rallied other units and ordered an attack. 'My men have fired off all their cartridges and also emptied the pouches of the dead', remonstrated one brigade commander. 'They cannot fire a single shot more.'

But Blücher would have none of it. 'Fix bayonets and forward!' he yelled. Galvanised by the battle cry, the electrified Prussian columns swept into Le Hameau and flowed out of the other side to break like surf on three immoveable rocks.

Stationed to the west of St Amand, the 2nd, 3rd and 4th Chasseurs of the Old Guard repelled the spent Prussian units with ease. The French tide flooded back into the villages from which it had been expelled.

The vibrating roar of the bronze-barrelled guns raged on. Pounding the French artillery positions from the north of the ravaged village of St Amand were Captain Reuter and four cannon of his Prussian battery. Reuter noted two substantial lines of skirmishers, apparently in retreat, emerge from St Amand. They began to work their way steadily towards Reuter's cannon. Ignoring them, Reuter continued to exchange gunfire with the vigorous French artillery but suddenly a sharp shout from the battery's surgeon alerted him to the red shako tufts of the skirmishers in front. They were French.

'With canister on the skirmishers!' roared Reuter. The French infantry peppered their Prussian foes with a salvo of musketry and promptly ducked to the ground to escape the murderous hail of artillery fire which came in reply. Reuter desperately tried to remove horses from an ammunition waggon to replace ones from a gun team smitten by the French volley. All the while, his guns were methodically loading and firing canister, constantly pinning down the French troops in front.

Desperately exhorting his feverish gunners, the hard-pressed Reuter was caught unawares by a sudden swirl of fifty French horsemen which swept in from the east led by an exuberant officer shouting triumphantly in German, 'Surrender, gunners, for you are all prisoners!'

The mutual and unrelieved hatred between French and Prussians seems to have resulted in considerable ignorance of how to proceed on the formalities of taking prisoners. The French officer went about it simply by aiming a vindictive sabre cut at a Prussian artilleryman. The gunner promptly dived from his horse for cover and the French sabre embedded itself in the recently vacated saddle. The frustrated French officer struggled in vain to extract the sabre, whereupon Gunner Sieberg seized a metal handspike and with the contemptuous words 'I'll soon show him how to take prisoners!' broke the French officer's skull.

The officer's corpse toppled from his bewildered grey horse. Followed instinctively by the mounts of the other fifty Frenchmen, the riderless animal charged straight into the French skirmishers in front of Reuter's guns. Under the timely cover of the consequent chaos and confusion among the French lines, Reuter seized his chance and limbered up three of his guns to their teams of horses. The cannon thundered back to refit north of Bussy mill.

Left isolated and immobile owing to insufficient horses to draw it, the fourth gun could not escape. From afar, Reuter sadly watched French troops overwhelm the gun crew and capture the cannon. Reuter's impassioned pleas to a couple of I Corps' cavalry regiments to recapture his lost gun all came to naught.

Around this stage of the action, the French 22nd and 70th Line infantry regiments of Habert's division from Vandamme's Corps tramped through St Amand and deployed to the north. More audacious now than when Reuter addressed them, the Prussian cavalry headed menacingly in the direction of the French. Forthwith, Colonel Louis Fantin des Odoards, commander of the 22nd Regiment, ordered his unit to form a hollow square, bristling with sharp steel bayonets all round – impervious to horsemen however much they raged and fumed and swirled round the formation, seeking a way in that did not exist. The 70th Regiment likewise hurried into square, forming to the northwest of the 22nd. This arrangement allowed the two squares to support each other with their volleys. If the squares had stood side by side, musketry might have struck French troops of the other square as well as Prussian riders in between. But by forming along a diagonal axis, the squares could set up a deadly crossfire with volleys from the north face of the 22nd merging with musketry from the eastern ranks of the 70th.

The Prussian cavalry commanders must have realised this and seem to have advanced on the vulnerable northwestern corner of the 70th. Prussian tactical doctrine prescribed that cavalry progressively pick up pace. The gallop commenced three hundred paces from the French square, followed by the all-out charge at just eighty paces. If the infantry stood firm, the Prussian riders and horses would shy away from the musketry and bayonets to sweep vainly past the flanks of the square. But often the cavalry's implacable progression to full speed caused the infantry to panic and in this case the horsemen would charge home without mercy.

The soldiers of the 70th were young, inexperienced troops. They panicked. Under the Prussian cavalry's advance, the terrified 70th broke ranks, disintegrated and fled. Sharp Prussian sabres swirled, cruelly hacked down and rose again stained an ominous dark red. French fugitives ran like sheep to shelter behind the 22nd Regiment.

Briskly firing accurate volleys, Colonel Fantin's men brought down swathes of riders and mounts. Other Prussian cavalry units charged repeatedly, to receive a drubbing again and again. The baffled and mauled horsemen retired to be replaced by two artillery pieces which blazed away with canister. Squares were particularly vulnerable to firepower, as unlike thin, extensive lines they packed large numbers of troops into a small formation several ranks deep. The presence of the Prussian cavalry prevented the French from forming line and by this combination of artillery fire and the threat of mounted attack, the Prussians inflicted heavy casualties. Nevertheless, Colonel Fantin managed to maintain his position.[21]

From the Naveau mill, Napoleon had observed Colonel Fantin des Odoards repelling the Prussian cavalry. Now, at 6.30 pm, the Emperor's ADC returned to inform him that the unidentified column heading towards Fleurus was, after all, d'Erlon's corps. But why was d'Erlon so far off course? Moreover, the column had now turned round towards Quatre Bras, leaving behind only a cavalry, and an infantry, division as a rearguard. D'Erlon had, in fact, been recalled to Quatre Bras by a desperate message from Marshal Ney.

And so, caught up in that fog of war, in that faulty staff-work and in that inexplicable machinery of chance that plagues most armies, d'Erlon's corps disappeared into the distance. Yet its intervention in the Battle of Ligny would have had a profound impact on the outcome of the campaign. Napoleon sent an officer to order d'Erlon to attack the Prussians at Wagnelée but it was too late now to call d'Erlon back. Already, the chaos caused by d'Erlon's transitory appearance had wasted an hour. At least Napoleon's left wing was no longer threatened. He was free to send in his Guard.

At Ligny fires burned red, as, overhead, ominous dark thunderclouds accumulated. Major Coignet had arrived at Ligny village from Naveau mill. Sent by Napoleon to find General Gérard, he picked his way around gardens and hedges, searching for the general. 'This was not a battle', thought Coignet who had already seen close on fifty actions, 'it was a butchery.'

Everywhere the drums were beating the charge, everywhere the soldiers were shouting 'forwards!', everywhere lay the dead. Gérard himself was covered in mud and had been fighting hand to hand. He told Coignet to ask Napoleon for reinforcements. 'Tell him that I have lost half my soldiers, but that, if I am supported, the victory is assured.'[22]

The end was approaching fast.

Phase Four: The Imperial Guard Attack and the End of the Battle

By 7.30 pm the sky consisted of the dense inky blackness of a storm. Raindrops pelted down. Peals of thunder rumbled overhead, suddenly to be drowned by an increased cannonade near Ligny. It was the herald of the *coup de grâce*. Several French Guard batteries had rapidly advanced to open a devastating, concentrated fire on the Prussian positions, ready for the last attack.

'It is the artillery of my Guard which decides my battles,' Napoleon had once declared, 'for, as I have it always at hand, I can bring it to bear wherever it becomes necessary.' Now it was pounding Blücher's army with a destructive crossfire launched from batteries south of St Amand and from others east of Ligny.

The Emperor had left Naveau mill to move over towards Ligny with his Guard – the 1st Chasseurs and the 1st and 2nd Grenadiers – as well as the cavalry of Guyot and Milhaud. The 3rd and 4th Grenadiers, sent earlier to support Hulot, now rejoined their sister regiments, ready to storm Ligny village. Around the same time, Lobau's VI Corps rolled up at Fleurus from Charleroi, but was too late to join the attack.

Now, from the south of Ligny, Napoleon surveyed the Prussian positions. Observing the relatively unoccupied space to the north of the village, he triumphantly exclaimed to Gérard: 'they are lost: they have no reserve remaining!'

The Prussian position was indeed critical. Blücher had squandered his reserves in wild counter-attacks in the Wagnelée–St Amand sector, exactly as Napoleon had hoped. At Ligny, a mere sixteen-and-a-half battered battalions of the Prussian I and II Corps were pitted against the mauled units of the French IV Corps.

And then the 'immortals' of the Guard went in. Columns of Guardsmen marched in formation past their Emperor and, roaring 'no quarter!', burst suddenly through the rolling screen of artillery smoke.

Through the centre of Ligny tramped the 2nd, 3rd and 4th Grenadiers together with an artillery battery. Circling the village to the north were the 'oldest of the old' – the 1st Grenadiers and 1st Chasseurs – accompanied by the Guard sappers and marines and followed by Milhaud's armoured *cuirassiers*; to the south were Guyot's Guard heavy cavalry. Napoleon, guarded by four service squadrons, watched the attack from the Tombe de Ligny, a mound south of the village.

'Tell the *grenadiers*', threatened Lieutenant-General François Roguet, their

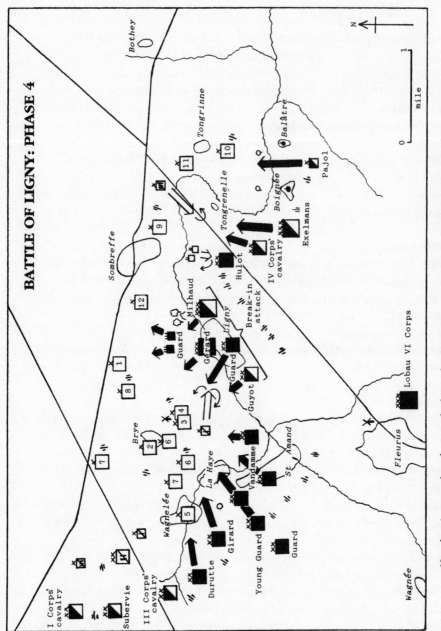

BATTLE OF LIGNY: PHASE 4

Napoleon's *coup de grâce* punched into the Prussian army at Ligny village. More French forces fought across the Ligny brook between St Amand and Wagnelée. Grouchy's men and the Prussian III Corps fought fiercely in the east, and the daring advance of two Prussian battalions from Sombreffe to the south bank of the brook intimidated the French, preventing a push too far north.

second-in-command, 'that the first man to bring me a Prussian prisoner will be shot.' And the Guard crashed into the Prussian defences.

Inside Ligny itself, the Prussians buckled but did not break. The few remaining battalions left in rear of the village desperately counter-attacked. Rifleman Franz Lieber of the 9th Regiment was burning for action. 'Now at last', he wrote, 'now at last was all to be realised for which we had ... so ardently longed.'

Lieber and his comrades were young soldiers and ran wildly forward in skirmish order. Fired upon by guard *grenadiers*, they surged on, driving the French veterans back, past houses on fire, through streets choked with corpses, littered with wounded and soaked in blood. Lieber himself forgot to fire, forgot all his past training and instructions. Seizing the red plume from a *grenadier*'s bearskin, he waved it in triumph to his comrades.

By now the Prussians had arrived at the corner of a house. Lieber's old sergeant-major managed to sober his battle-drunk soldiers, and was convinced the French were just round the corner. Nevertheless, the rash Lieber could not resist stepping round. Barely ten metres away was a French *grenadier*. Both levelled their muskets and the Frenchman fired. A musketball whizzed past Lieber's head. Then the unfortunate *grenadier* toppled to the ground, struck in the face. Lieber had fired his first shot in anger.[23]

But soon the Prussians were hurled back. Lieutenant Barral of the French *grenadiers* charged through Ligny, along a street paved with corpses. His feet did not touch the ground itself once. Behind him followed a French battery which trampled and galloped over the crushed bodies. The merciless passage of heavy hooves and wheels caused corpses seemingly to spring to life again by a freak of elasticity. Lieutenant Barral found it horrible to contemplate.

In the centre of Ligny, Gérard and three regiments of *grenadiers* captured the Farm d'en Bas and debouched from the pulverised village. Further guardsmen battled forward on the left and the right. The French halted for a moment to reform after the disorder caused by the street fighting and then they pushed on, forward from Ligny up the slopes towards Brye and the heart of the Prussian position.

In support of the infantry rode the massed column of Milhaud's *cuirassiers*. These heavy cavalrymen were coming into their own and were acting as a mighty battering ram of flesh and metal. As at Eylau in 1807 and Borodino in 1812, though on a far smaller scale, waves of horsemen charged into the enemy position. Once the first ranks had expended their strength and cohesion, the subsequent lines would crash into the hostile units. Napoleon's servant, Mameluke Ali, was awestruck at the sight and recalled how squadrons rapidly followed one after the other. All the *cuirassiers* shouted 'Long live the Emperor!' with the full force of their lungs to intimidate the foe. Ali himself heard the battle cry resound from far off.

The *cuirassiers* also overawed the Prussians with their visual impact. Mameluke Ali remarked that 'the appearance of this column, in the midst of the flashes and booms of gunfire, was a magnificent spectacle. Brave *cuirassiers*! I seem to see you still galloping into action with your swords high. How fine you were!'[24]

Suddenly the Prussian line cracked. Writing to Marshal Davout the next day, Chief of Staff Soult commented that 'it was like a scene on the stage.'[25] The French had broken into the Prussian position at Ligny.

Desperately, those Prussian units in the rear of Ligny attempted to secure an orderly retreat for the defenders. The 21st Regiment advanced but was then charged in the left flank by Milhaud's *cuirassiers*. Two squadrons of *Landwehr* cavalry attacked, only to receive a volley at a range of twenty paces. The 9th Regiment, Lieber's unit, fought its way through a mass of French cavalry and everywhere the Prussian infantry retreated from Ligny in squares. The French artillery battery which had traversed Ligny now opened up, with great effect.

Blücher galloped up from his right flank. The rain ceased and the wind gradually dispersed the straggling clouds, dispelling the darkness of the storm. The last rays of the setting sun flooded the ghastly scene and in the clear atmosphere glittering masses of French *cuirassiers* trotted forward. Here French guardsmen advanced, there the debris of a shattered Prussian brigade fell back.

Blücher saw only one way of halting the steady, powerful advance of the French. He had to meet it head-on with a ferocious counter-attack. He summoned the only reserve he had at hand: a brigade of I Corps' cavalry, already depleted by the French artillery bombardment and by earlier charges on French infantry debouching from St Amand. While the Horse Battery no. 2 fired in support into the left flank of the French advance, the cavalry brigade commander, Lieutenant-Colonel Baron Ludwig von Lützow, charged at the head of the 6th Uhlans. He headed for a motley collection of troops formed in square, no doubt thinking he was dealing with raw recruits. Some wore shakos, some bearskins, scarcely twenty were uniformed alike.

In fact, it was the 4th Grenadiers of the Guard. Two crisp musketry volleys from the 4th Grenadiers at a range of just twenty metres dispersed the luckless Prussians, leaving Lützow a prisoner and more than eighty of his *Uhlans* lying on the ground. Lützow would be conducted to Napoleon for interrogation.

Now the second wave of Prussian cavalry came on, composed of dragoons and of *Landwehr* cavalry. A sunken lane directly in the path of the Prussians drastically decelerated their charge, and as they attempted to get across they were struck by two artillery salvos. Next, a division of *cuirassiers* under Lieutenant-General Baron Jacques Delort fell on the flank of the luckless Prussian cavalry and dispersed it.

Finally, almost all of the Prussian squadrons attacked, in perhaps one, perhaps two, charges to meet with a similar fate. The French Guard cavalry advanced through the intervals between its infantry compatriots to enter the fray. At Ligny, French co-ordination between the three arms was superb.

Blücher lacked the advantage of surprise, he lacked time to organise and co-ordinate his units. But his energy and inspiring leadership compensated in large measure. In the midst of the cavalry charges, Blücher had attacked with the 6th Uhlans. His horse had been mortally wounded. The charger slowed; Blücher spurred. Staggering forward a few steps, the mount finally fell, with its aged rider crying out to an ADC, 'Nostitz, now I am lost!'

The Prussian commander was both unconscious and trapped beneath the dead horse, a superb, pure-blooded black beast with a large white star on its forehead.[26] Worse, French cavalry were approaching fast. Lieutenant-Colonel Count von Nostitz quickly dismounted, drew his sword and waited. The 9th Cuirassiers thundered past. One French cavalryman actually brushed against Nostitz's horse, which he was holding by the bridle. Unrecognized in the gathering gloom, Blücher lay still.

'The French *cuirassiers*', recalled Henri Nieman of the 6th Uhlans, 'drove us before them, but we soon rallied and drove them back. At this moment Blücher was yet lying under his horse. Nostitz, his aide-de-camp, had covered him with his cloak; after the French, driven before us, had passed, Nostitz sprang forward.'

NCO Schneider of Nieman's unit dismounted from his charger and Blücher, rescued by five or six powerful men who raised his dead horse, was placed on the saddle. Just as the tide of the skirmish swung back from the Prussians and just as French forces started to return, the small party reached the nearest Prussian infantry column which then retired to safety.

French forces pushed on, from St Amand in the south and from Ligny in the east. Baron Louis Vichery's depleted division of IV Corps and Count Pierre Wathier's *cuirassier* division had turned from Ligny to the north and now attacked towards Sombreffe, driving back squares formed by the Prussian 12th brigade and by the remains of the 1st brigade.

In the sombre shadow of Death, chaos and confusion roamed the gloomy, smoke-shrouded battlefield. French cavalry swarmed around a couple of Prussian batteries. The Horse Battery no. 2 charged straight ahead, and escaped to Brye with the gunners fighting off French dragoons as the heavy guns thundered along. The French tried in vain to cut the traces of the horses pulling the guns. The 6-pounder Foot Battery no. 3 was not so fortunate and lost a gun.

Units were mauled. Soldiers went missing only to turn up elsewhere, some lost Prussian dragoons attaching themselves to a regiment of *Landwehr* cavalry. Casualties continued to mount, not just among the rank and file but also among the senior officers. General Jürgass, commander of the II Corps' cavalry, was hit in the shoulder. Colonel Langen, in charge of 8th infantry brigade of the same corps, was first wounded and then driven over by a gun team.

But efforts were being made to halt the rot. Much initiative and defiance of the French was shown by all ranks. A Prussian battalion of Westphalian troops fired at some of General Delort's *cuirassiers* and then roared with laughter to see the fallen cavalrymen struggling to extricate themselves from under their dead horses and remove their heavy breastplates before fleeing on foot.[27]

On the outskirts of Sombreffe, the Prussian 6th Kurmark Landwehr Cavalry counter-attacked other *cuirassiers* from Wathier's division, only to have their wooden lance poles shatter as the metal lance points hit the Frenchmen's breastplates. Held at bay by the remains of the lance shafts, the *cuirassiers* were driven off when Prussian infantry arrived on the scene.

General Grolmann, Quartermaster-General of the Prussian army, was active in encouraging the troops to form a defensive line just south of Brye to halt the French advance. Grolmann also led two battalions of the 9th Regiment to extricate a 12-pounder cannon which had become stuck in a sunken lane southwest of Sombreffe. Grolmann successfully saved the gun within view of the French.

Another Prussian officer to demonstrate initiative that evening was Captain von Reuter, who withdrew his battery to take up an advantageous position northwest of Brye. A fiery Prussian general exploded with wrath, mistaking Reuter's retrograde movement for flight. But Reuter calmed him by explaining, 'truly, sir, matters are not looking very rosy, but the 12-pounder battery, No. 6, has simply come here to get into a position whence it thinks it may be able to check the enemy's advance.'

The general, satisfied, rallied some infantry on the battery: 'Soldiers, there stand your guns; are you not Prussians?' More and more troops came up and rallied. Reuter even opened fire on, and drove off, some French cavalry that was advancing on his battery.

In the eastern sector of the battlefield, General Thielmann's intact Prussian III Corps strove to aid its hard-pressed I and II Corps comrades further to the west. Just before the French Imperial Guard attacked Ligny village, III Corps switched from the defensive to a more offensive stance. Thielmann hoped thereby to relieve the pressure on the embattled Prussian units on the western sector of the field.

Clausewitz, Thielmann's Chief of Staff, despatched Colonel Count Lottum's cavalry brigade and the Horse Battery no. 19.[28] This force clattered down the Sombreffe–Fleurus highroad and across the bridge spanning the Ligny brook. Those French skirmishers in its path reeled back.

Then the 5th and 13th Regiments of green-coated French dragoons executed a decisive counter-stroke, dispersing the Prussian cavalry and seizing five cannon.[29] Onwards the French advanced. Prussian infantry units adjusted their positions. Shots cracked out. Prussian artillery fire added to the musketry. The French dragoons retired.

The senior officers of III Corps were at a loss to know how the fight was faring at Ligny when Napoleon's Guard went in. The light was failing. Dense clouds of murky smoke drifted over the ravaged battlefield. Nevertheless, Thielmann was determined to aid I and II Corps with some offensive moves of his own.

Two battered battalions of the 30th Regiment boldly advanced from Sombreffe, negotiated the Ligny brook and marched into a sea of confusion and darkness. French dragoons swarmed forward and were repulsed. The 30th Regiment charged up a slope to form on the top and repulse yet more French cavalry. French infantry also received a drubbing, but returned in over-whelming numbers.

The fierce, stabbing flashes of Prussian muskets so far advanced flared up in the night scenario. They encouraged the Prussian I and II Corps units and intimidated the French. Having accomplished its aim, the 30th Regiment retired back over to the north bank of the Ligny brook.

Hulot's French infantry had just seized the bridge over the Ligny brook on the Fleurus–Sombreffe highroad. Lieutenant-General Antoine Maurin now led his French cavalry division, detached from Gérard's corps, forward up this road, across the bridge deep into the Prussian position. Colonel Clausewitz was caught up in the mêlée until Prussian resistance intensified. The French 6th Hussars and 8th Chasseurs à cheval were brought to a halt near Sombreffe while Maurin himself was seriously wounded in a final charge. In 1860 an old woman living at an inn near Sombreffe still recalled seeing the inn packed with wounded Prussians, and French horsemen passing nearby through the corn in the twilight.[30]

Thielmann's III Corps was somewhat confused and abandoned its positions on the heights of Tongrinne. Thielmann sought to establish a coherent defence line. He occupied Sombreffe with a strong force and linked up with other Prussian forces further to the west. A Prussian rearguard line stabilised, from Brye to Sombreffe. Grouchy's French cavalry pressed forward to occupy Tongrinne but could advance no further.[31]

North of its rearguard line, the Prussian army was disunited and confused. Officers strove to halt and form up the scattered troops, trying to unite companies, battalions, regiments and brigades. Dispersion was chronic. Yet morale remained high and everywhere soldiers were looking for comrades, officers, someone to tell them what to do, where to go. Order gradually emerged from chaos.

Blücher's headquarters had no idea whether he were dead, a prisoner, or safe. Command of the Prussian army devolved upon the Chief of Staff, Gneisenau. A hurried consultation by the last of the twilight with various Prussian officers produced the decision to retreat thirteen miles northwards, and to rally the army at the town of Wavre.

The reasons for this decision were as follows. Firstly, retreating I and II Corps troops were already streaming away to the north. Gneisenau's orders merely recognised and confirmed this.

Secondly, the Prussians could not retreat along their lines of communication eastwards via Namur and Liège, as many troops had moved back north of the Nivelles–Namur road. Also, a Prussian movement to Liège would mean the abandonment of the campaign, their ally Wellington and all chances of an early defeat of Napoleon. To abandon Wellington would be to disobey the Prussian King, who had ordered Gneisenau on 29 March 1815 to co-operate with Wellington and to act in agreement with him in everything.[32]

Thirdly, the Prussians could not move west to link up with Wellington at Quatre Bras as this would abandon Bülow's Prussian IV Corps which had not yet joined the army. Also, Gneisenau did not know the outcome of Quatre Bras.[33] By retreating north, the Prussian troops who had fought at Ligny would be able to link up with Bülow's IV Corps and then either join Wellington or retreat to Prussia, according to circumstances.

Fourthly, originally, Gneisenau ordered the Prussian army to rally at Tilly, two-and-a-half miles north of the battlefield. But Tilly was not marked on all the maps, and many troops had drifted further north than this village. Following the suggestion of von Reiche, Chief of Staff to I Corps, Wavre, a town further north and marked on all the maps, was named as the rallying point.

Fifthly, Gneisenau had seen a report by a British staff officer, Basil Jackson, who before the campaign had reconnoitred much of the Belgian countryside. Jackson's report concerned the route from Ligny to Wavre and ensured a retreat to Wavre was not a march in or to unknown countryside.[34]

I and II Corps units would move in a direct line through Tilly to Wavre. Thielmann's intact III Corps on the eastern sector of the field was to retreat by a separate route, towards Gembloux. At Gembloux, Thielmann would join Bülow's fresh IV Corps which had arrived there from Liège. Together, the two corps would continue, from Gembloux, to retreat to Wavre.

Gneisenau eventually discovered Blücher at Mellery, three miles north of the battlefield. 'We have taken a few knocks and shall have to hammer out the dents!' Blücher exclaimed on seeing his trusted comrade. Bruised and battered, Blücher had been borne half-conscious from the fight. Vigorous rubbing with brandy had revived the aged warrior and he promptly demanded some of the medicine for internal application. The surgeon turned down the request but had to agree on a bottle of champagne. This soon put the spirit back into Blücher and he was now resting on a pile of straw, sipping some milk. Gneisenau was busy writing orders by candlelight while seated on a barrel of pickled cabbage.

In another room, the British liaison officer, Hardinge, was lying on a pile of straw, recovering from the amputation of his hand. He later pronounced himself not quite satisfied with the skill of the Prussian surgeons. Nevertheless, he would recover fully and years later would tell Wellington about a curious council of war held in the Prussian headquarters that night of 16/17 June.

The Prussian council of war was not so much an argument or a battle of wills as a reasoned discussion of the next move. All the Prussian generals were resolute and patriotic men not to be deterred by a single defeat. But Gneisenau was desperately anxious, and with reason.

With the exception of Blücher, who was ready to fight anywhere, the Prussian generals had always disliked the idea of defending the United Netherlands, where no Prussian interests were at stake. The Dutch authorities were obstructive and reluctant to grant the Prussians billets and supplies.[35] Placing the Prussian army in the forward position of the Netherlands, unsupported until mid-July by the vast Russian and Austrian armies, was a risky undertaking, as Ligny had shown.

The ideal situation in Gneisenau's eyes was for Wellington alone to defend the United Netherlands, while Blücher and the Austrians attacked across the Rhine closely suported by the powerful Russian army.[36] The Russians and Austrians were Gneisenau's allies of 1813–4 and he seems to have disliked the English more than other foreigners.

The real reason that the Prussians were in the Netherlands was their reliance on British subsidies. Prussia was a poor country and needed financial assistance to maintain her war effort. 'We are in such financial straits here that the Field Marshal almost had to pawn his whiskers', joked Gneisenau on 25 May.[37] In return for the vital subsidies, the Prussians complied with British wishes. Traditional British strategy dictated that France be denied both the trade and the coastline of the United Netherlands. Britain feared invasion and whoever controlled the coast from Brest to Emden was a threat.

Wellington's tardy concentration on 15 June and his failure directly to support the Prussians on the 16th apparently led Gneisenau to suspect Wellington was sparing British lives by using the Prussians to take the brunt of a campaign intended to further British interests. 'The Duke of Wellington had promised to fall on the enemy's rear but he did not come because his army, Heaven knows why, could not concentrate', complained Gneisenau after the campaign.[38] Would it not be safer, given Wellington's lack-lustre performance so far, to retreat east of the Rhine, to unite with the Russians and Austrians and then to crush Napoleon with the aid of surer allies?

But Blücher, dosed with gin and rhubarb and smelling like it too, and the Quartermaster-General, Grolmann, overcame Gneisenau's reservations. As Blücher announced the following morning to Hardinge, his British liaison officer, 'Gneisenau has given way! We are going to join the Duke.'

In years to come, British historians would portray this conference of Prussian generals as a triumph for Blücher over a recalcitrant and paranoid Gneisenau determined to abandon Wellington. In fact, it was nothing of the sort.

Hardinge, who is the sole primary source to mention this council of war, was both British and a close friend of the Duke. Yet he stated merely that Gneisenau had 'great doubts as to whether they ought not to fall back [to Prussia].'[39] That was all.

With the weight of the responsibilities on his shoulders, Gneisenau needed Blücher's optimism to convince him all would be well. Quite apart from the question of Wellington's reliability, the Prussian army was badly mauled. Units needed reorganising. If Napoleon launched a whirlwind pursuit early the next morning, the Prussians would come off badly. 'Our ammunition was expended and our reserve munitions nowhere to be found', Gneisenau wrote to a friend six days later. 'It was a dreadful situation and we were almost unable to come to help the Duke of Wellington. You can imagine my feelings ...'[40]

Thus the fate of the campaign was still in the balance, and with it, the fate of Europe. But the Prussian high command had together reached a crucial decision which would shortly begin to tilt the equilibrium in the allies' favour: 'we are going to join the Duke.' It was an historic moment.

At 5.00 am on 17 June, fourteen hours had elapsed since the first shots had been fired and all the Prussian units, including the rearguard line, had evacuated the field of combat and retreated northwards. The battlefield was totally in the hands of Napoleon. No more sudden flashes of fire, no more rattling musketry disturbed the calm. All clamour of strife had gradually faded away hours before. Now there was nothing but the sobering sight of dead soldiers, the piteous cries of the wounded, and the furtive movements of the looters. Red flames flickered in the ravaged and now oppressively silent villages. Troops, exhausted, wounded, or dead, littered the slaughter ground.

French bivouacs encumbered the battlefield. Vandamme's III Corps and the Young Guard rested north of St Amand. North of Ligny were the IV and VI Corps together with the Guard cavalry and Milhaud's *cuirassiers*. The *grenadiers à pied* and the 1st Chasseurs à pied were also north of Ligny, bivouacking in square three ranks deep and without camp fires, so fearful were they of a surprise Prussian night attack. The first two ranks stood guard with muskets ready while the third rank slept. Nerves became frayed by the suspense and in the VI Corps, the French 75th Regiment of line infantry had fired on the 11th Line regiment. French outposts exchanged the passwords: 'Adrien, Arles, Attention.[41]

Earlier, the band of the 1st Grenadiers had struck up *La Victoire est à nous*. The victory is ours. But it was only half a victory. Although the French had broken into the Prussian position through Ligny village, they never broke out of it into open country. Their advance was steady and ponderous and ground to a halt in the face of counter-attacks, casualties and fatigue. The Prussian rear-guard line had halted the French advance before slipping away to the north, unpursued. For most of the French army, including Napoleon, was too exhausted to march another step or fire another shot. The strong Prussian rearguard line would have necessitated tough, night fighting if an immediate pursuit had been launched.[42]

So it was only Pajol's relatively fresh French hussars on the far right wing that heard sounds of the Prussian rearguards leaving the battlefield in the course of the night and bothered to investigate. The hussars moved off in the early hours of 17 June. As luck would have it, they went the wrong way, going east instead of north, following not Blücher's army but fugitives and deserters.

Napoleon, exhausted, had returned to Fleurus between 10.00 and 11.00 pm; he spent the night at his quarters at the Château de la Paix, surrounded by his faithful escort of the Imperial Guard: the 2nd, 3rd and 4th Chasseurs à pied.

Notes

1. Berthezène, *Souvenirs Militaires*, v.2, p.363
2. Pétiet, *Souvenirs Militaires*, p.196
3. Booth, *The Battle of Waterloo by a near observer*, p.110
4. Charras, *Histoire de la Campagne de 1815*, p.147
5. François, *Journal du Capitaine François*, v.2, p.880
6. Booth, *op. cit.*, p.108
7. Berton, *Précis historique, militaire et critique des batailles de Fleurus et de Waterloo*, p.29
8. Parkinson, *Clausewitz*, p.255
9. Siborne, *History of the Waterloo Campaign*, p.124
10. Beauchamp, *Histoire des Campagnes de 1814 et de 1815*, v.2, p.272
11. Siborne, *History of the Waterloo Campaign*, p.126
12. Ollech, *Geschichte des Feldzuges von 1815 nach archivalischen Quellen*, p.153
13. Ali, *Souvenirs du Mameluck Ali sur l'Empereur Napoléon*, p.105
14. Pétiet, *Souvenirs Militaires*, p.197; Lachouque, *Le Secret de Waterloo*, p.145
15. Except by Fuller, *The Decisive Battles of the Western World*, p.179
16. Pétiet, *op. cit.*, p.198
17. Arcis-sur-Aube was a notable battle of Napoleon's 1814 campaign in defence of France. Many of the French soldiers were raw conscripts, nicknamed 'Marie-Louises'. By the time of Ligny, they had gained much in terms of experience and fighting qualities.
18. François, *Journal du Capitaine François*, v.2, p.881
19. Damitz, *Histoire de la Campagne de 1815*, v.1, p.126
20. Müffling, *Passages from My Life*, pp.216–7
21. Brett-James, *The Hundred Days*, pp.76–7; 71–2
22. Coignet, *The Notebooks of Captain Coignet*, p.276
23. Brett-James, *The Hundred Days*, p.75
24. Ali, *Souvenirs du Mameluck Ali sur l'Empereur Napoléon*, p.106
25. Lachouque, *Le Secret de Waterloo*, p.165
26. Garros, *Le champ de bataille de Waterloo*. Other sources insist Blücher rode a white horse which was a present from England's Prince Regent.
27. Treitschke, *History of Germany in the 19th Century*, v.2, p.174
28. Parkinson, *Clausewitz*, p.258
29. Berton, *Précis historique, militaire et critique des batailles de Fleurus et de Waterloo*, p.29
30. Hamley, *Wellington's career*, p.80
31. Pajol, *Pajol, Général en chef*, v.3, pp.206–7
32. Ollech, *Geschichte des Feldzuges von 1815 nach archivalischen Quellen*, p.14
33. Navez, *Les Quatre Bras, Ligny, Waterloo et Wavre*, p.131

34. Jackson, *Notes and reminiscences of a staff officer*, pp.vi, 5 and 97–8

35. Damitz, *Histoire de la Campagne de 1815*, v.1, pp.30 and 37

36. Pflugk-Harttung, *Vorgeschichte der Schlacht bei Belle-Alliance – Wellington*, p.209

37. Parkinson, *The Hussar General*, p.210

38. Delbrück, *Das Leben des Feldmarschalls Grafen Neithardt von Gneisenau*, v.2, pp.218–9

39. Brett-James, *op. cit.*, pp.82–3. Historians have often asserted that the council of war occurred on the night of 17/18 June, at Wavre. This is the result of Hardinge telling his anecdote twenty-two years later and asserting that Blücher 'had gone back as far as Wavre.' Nevertheless, it is clear from the anecdote as a whole that Hardinge is talking about the night after the Battle of Ligny, immediately after undergoing his amputation. Of course, further discussion may have occurred in the Prussian headquarters twenty-four hours later given Gneisenau's continuing anxiety.

40. Delbrück, *op. cit.*, v.2, p.219

41. Lachouque, *Napoleon's Battles*, p.430

42. Rarely are victories crowned by dynamic pursuits. The defeated foe is usually able to put up strong resistance, unless he has used up all his resources (as Napoleon had at Waterloo). A frontal attack exhausts the victorious army. Often the defeated foe will sacrifice a rearguard to gain sufficient time to enable the bulk of the army to escape (Rommel appropriated the Italians' transport at Alamein to escape with his German troops). David Chandler points out that only after Rivoli, Austerlitz, Jena and Eckmühl did Napoleon manage to pursue a beaten foe with the ruthless, unrelenting vigour necessary for complete success.

6

THE BATTLE OF QUATRE BRAS

David Chandler, the author of *The Campaigns of Napoleon*, classified Napoleon's battles into various types. One of these was the 'double battle'. This was two separate actions fought by two wings of Napoleon's French army against two allied enemy armies, and where the success of one action often both influenced and was influenced by the other.

16 June 1815 is a classic example. Two actions were fought. The main one, at Ligny, was a victory for Napoleon and the French right wing. The subsidiary action was Marshal Ney's fierce struggle, with the French left wing, against the Duke of Wellington at Quatre Bras, ending in a stalemate.

The outcome of Ligny was profoundly influenced by that of Quatre Bras, and vice versa. Although Wellington maintained his ground at Quatre Bras on 16 June, he was forced to retreat on the 17th owing to the defeat and withdrawal of the Prussians at Ligny. On the other hand, Wellington's resolute stand at Quatre Bras on the 16th prevented Ney from gaining the strategic crossroads and moving troops down the lateral road east to outflank Blücher and help Napoleon strike a truly knock-out blow at Ligny.

Owing to the close and complex interrelation between the two battles, any account of the Battle of Ligny must contain some description and analysis of Quatre Bras. Yet Quatre Bras was a subsidiary action and the English historian Archibald Becke has argued that it was hardly a real battle at all in its own right.

Instead of following the fighting step by step in detail as is appropriate in the case of Ligny, it is most useful to examine Quatre Bras as it appeared through Marshal Ney's eyes. Thus it will become apparent why Ney failed to seize the crossroads of Quatre Bras and to send reinforcements to Napoleon at Ligny.

Marshal Ney passed the night of 15/16 June at the Maison Dumont in the town of Gosselies, seven-and-a-half miles south of Quatre Bras. Contrary to statements by some historians, Ney apparently did not ride back to Charleroi for a consultation with Napoleon.[1]

Ney has often been criticised for his lethargy on the morning of 16 June. His formations were strung out after the long marches of 15 June and required

FRENCH COMMAND STRUCTURE, 16 JUNE

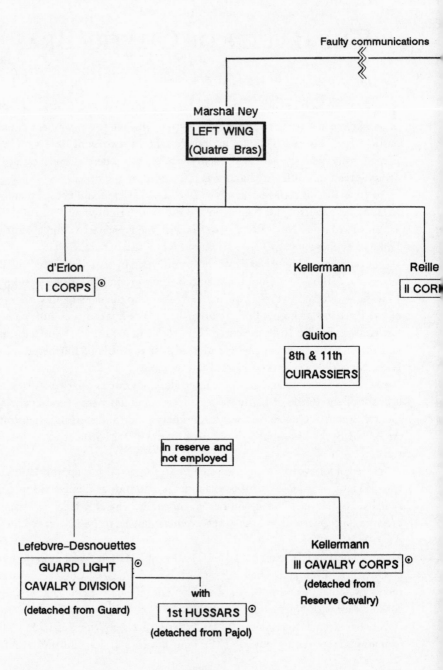

Faulty communications

Marshal Ney
LEFT WING
(Quatre Bras)

d'Erlon
I CORPS ◎

Kellermann

Reille
II COR...

Guiton
8th & 11th
CUIRASSIERS

In reserve and
not employed

Lefebvre–Desnouettes
GUARD LIGHT
CAVALRY DIVISION ◎
(detached from Guard)

with
1st HUSSARS ◎
(detached from Pajol)

Kellermann
III CAVALRY CORPS ◎
(detached from
Reserve Cavalry)

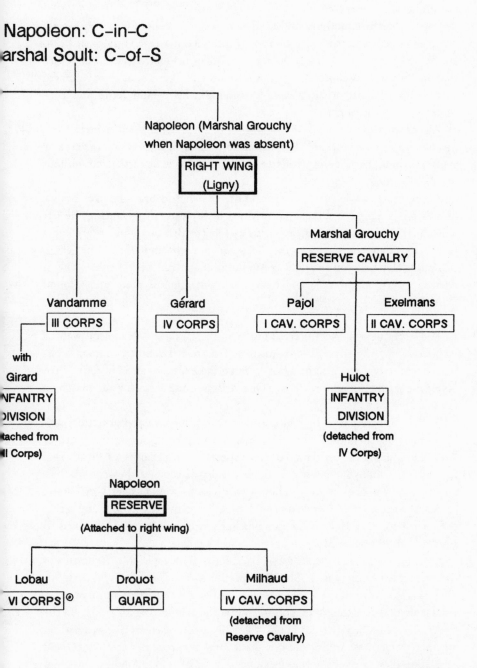

Napoleon: C–in–C

Marshal Soult: C–of–S

Napoleon (Marshal Grouchy
when Napoleon was absent)

**RIGHT WING
(Ligny)**

Marshal Grouchy

RESERVE CAVALRY

Vandamme

III CORPS

with

Girard

INFANTRY
DIVISION

(attached from
III Corps)

Gérard

IV CORPS

Pajol

I CAV. CORPS

Exelmans

II CAV. CORPS

Hulot

INFANTRY
DIVISION

(detached from
IV Corps)

Napoleon

RESERVE

(Attached to right wing)

Lobau

VI CORPS ⊚

Drouot

GUARD

Milhaud

IV CAV. CORPS

(detached from
Reserve Cavalry)

⊚ – unengaged

123

concentration. In fact, the rearmost divisions of I Corps were closing up. But Ney did not order II Corps to get under arms so as to be ready to march once the Emperor's orders arrived.

In Ney's defence, nothing indicated to him the necessity for speedy action. Napoleon's orders for the operations of 16 June did not reach him until 11.00 am. When Ney rode north at 7.00 am to reconnoitre Quatre Bras, he could see that only a few of Wellington's troops were present. Ney seems to have shared Napoleon's optimism that Wellington and Blücher would retire and concentrate far to the north.

'All information to hand', he would write to Marshal Soult a little later, 'tends to show that there are 3000 hostile infantry at Quatre Bras and very few cavalry. I think that the Emperor's arrangements . . . will be carried out without great difficulty.'

Furthermore, while Ney possessed more brawn and bravado than brains, he was an experienced soldier. He was justifiably wary of advancing the left wing of the French army as far north as Quatre Bras without orders lest a potentially dangerous gap open between himself and the right wing. Although Ney believed the bulk of Wellington and Blücher's armies to be in retreat, clearly some of their forces were at Quatre Bras and around Sombreffe.

At last, at 11.00 am, Ney received orders from Napoleon.[2] Napoleon wanted Ney to occupy the strategic crossroads of Quatre Bras and to contain Wellington while the French right wing defeated the Prussians at Sombreffe. Then Napoleon would bring his reserve to Quatre Bras, unite with Ney and march on Brussels.

Forthwith, Ney issued marching orders to his units, in conformation with Napoleon's instructions. Reille's II Corps was to take up a position north of Quatre Bras along the main road to Genappe. D'Erlon's I Corps was to advance to Frasnes, pushing one infantry and one cavalry division northeast to Marbais on the Nivelles–Namur road. These two divisions would cover Ney's flank against the Prussians at Ligny and could be called on by Napoleon in any action between the French right wing and Blücher's Prussians. Ney's cavalry was to station itself in reserve between Frasnes and Liberchies.

These orders would never be carried out, for fatal delays in the movements of the French left wing would allow Wellington to reinforce, and maintain, his initially weak hold on the vital crossroads of Quatre Bras. One cause of delay was General Reille's excessive caution and tardiness in setting his troops on the march. This cost two precious hours' delay. Even after Reille's II Corps had set off, the cumbersome troop columns made slow progress. Between 12.00 and 12.30 pm, Ney received another message from Chief of Staff Soult, urging him to hasten:

STRATEGIC SITUATION: 2.30 pm, 16 JUNE

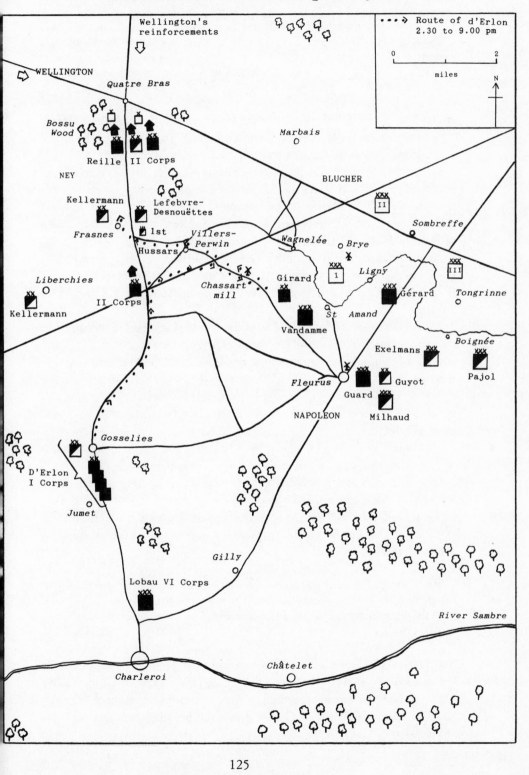

Group the corps of Counts Reille and d'Erlon with that of the Count of Valmy [Kellermann's III Cavalry Corps] ... With these forces, you must beat and destroy all the enemy corps which may present themselves. Blücher was in Namur yesterday and it is not likely that he will have moved troops towards Quatre Bras. So you have to deal only with what comes from Brussels.

At 1.30 pm, Reille's II Corps at last arrived at Frasnes. General Reille himself rode on ahead to meet Marshal Ney, who exclaimed: 'There is practically no one in the Bossu Wood. We must take that immediately.'

Once more this day did Reille's inherent caution hinder Ney. 'This could well be a battle as in Spain where the English only showed themselves when it was time', he warned the Marshal, refering to Wellington's habit of concealing and sheltering his troops on the reverse slopes of ridges. 'It would be sensible to wait before attacking until all our troops are massed here.'[3]

'We will finish off this handful of Germans that was cut up yesterday', Ney replied in exasperation. Nevertheless, Ney waited until more French troops of II Corps had deployed before beginning a general advance northwards at 2.00 pm.

Although the French troops had an overwhelming numerical superiority over their 7000 Dutch, Belgian and German foes, the advance was slow. Farms and woods had to be cleared. Enough time was gained for Wellington to return at 2.20 pm from his meeting with Blücher at the Bussy mill and to assume command of his forces at Quatre Bras. Just after his arrival, Wellington distinctly heard an ebullient roar from the French side: 'the Emperor will reward whoever advances.'

'That must be Ney going down the line', commented the Duke. 'I know what that means: we shall be attacked within five minutes.'[4]

Indeed, French forces now menaced the crossroads at Quatre Bras. They would have captured them had it not been for the reliable British 5th Division, which arrived just then from Brussels and launched a spirited counter-attack.

At about 3.00 pm Ney had just received a note in the Emperor's atrocious handwriting:

Monsieur the Prince of the Moskowa – I am surprised at your great delay in executing my orders – there is no more time to waste. Attack everything in front of you with the greatest impetuosity. The fate of the fatherland is in your hands.
1.00 pm   Napoleon[5]

But the two-hour lapse between the issue and reception of this order made it, like so many of Napoleon's orders to Ney throughout 16 June, meaningless. By 3.00 pm, Ney was already attacking 'with the greatest impetuosity.' Indeed, Ney had begun the Battle of Quatre Bras a full hour before Napoleon commenced that of Ligny.

The British 28th Foot repelling French cavalry at Quatre Bras.

A gradual stream of reinforcements was joining Wellington at Quatre Bras. 'Everywhere, the enemy put up a remarkable resistance', reminisced a French aide-de-camp. 'The interval between his firing and ours enabled us to hear perfectly the swiftly successive detonations of the cannon from Fleurus.'[6]

Now French light cavalry came into action, repelling some Dutch–Belgian horsemen and nearly capturing Wellington himself. The Duke had to gallop for safety and to jump his horse over a ditch lined by the redoubtable 92nd (Gordon) Highlanders.

At 4.00 pm, Ney received an order from Marshal Soult, written at 2.00 pm:

> The Emperor instructs me to inform you that the enemy has united a corps of troops between Sombreffe and Brye and that at 2.30 pm Marshal Grouchy will attack it with the III and IV Corps.
>
> His Majesty's intention is that you will attack whatever force is before you, and after having vigorously driven it back, you will turn in our direction, so as to bring about the envelopment of those enemy troops whom I have already mentioned to you. If the latter is overthrown first, then His Majesty will manoeuvre in your direction so as to assist your operations in the same way.
>
> Inform the Emperor immediately of your dispositions and of what is happening on your front.

But Napoleon's message had failed to make clear to Ney that the Emperor had altered his original plan. Napoleon, faced unexpectedly with a large proportion of the Prussian army at Ligny, now wanted to annihilate Blücher before marching on Brussels with Ney. The centre of attention on 16 June had now shifted to the French right wing at Ligny. But Napoleon did not inform Ney of this. Nor did he state categorically that Ney was to march to Ligny and outflank Blücher. To Ney, the penultimate sentence of this 2.00 pm order seems to have confirmed merely that Napoleon would march to Quatre Bras, help Ney defeat Wellington and then march to Brussels. Ney utterly failed to grasp that Napoleon had altered his original plan. Even as late as 26 June, Ney was writing:

> By what fatality . . . did the Emperor, instead of directing all his forces against Lord Wellington, . . . regard this attack as secondary? . . . Had he . . . left a corps of observation to hold the Prussians in check, and marched with his most powerful masses to support me, the English army would undoubtedly have been destroyed between Quatre Bras and Genappe. And once this position, which separated the two allied armies, was in our power, it would have opened for the Emperor the opportunity of outflanking the right of the Prussians and crushing them in their turn.

Nevertheless, the arrival of Napoleon's 2.00 pm order, with the command to attack and vigorously to drive back Wellington's troops, spurred Ney into

1. Napoleon in 1815.

2. and 3. The Prussian command team.
Prince Blücher (*above left*) and Count Gneisenau (*above right*).

4. and 5. The foes at Quatre Bras on 16 June.
The Duke of Wellington (*below left*) and Marshal Ney (*below right*).

6. (*above*) One of the tracks used by advancing French infantrymen. This example, an old Roman road south of Thuin, was one of the better quality routes in 1815.

7. (*below*) French infantrymen marching into Belgium during Napoleon's invasion of 15 June.

8. The Farm d'en Bas in Ligny village today.

9. (*above*) General view of the closing stages of the Battle of Ligny, seen from the French position. St Amand village is in the right foreground. Ligny village is in the centre of the picture, in flames. The church of Brye, not visible here, lies further left. Vandamme's troops advance in the foreground preceded by skirmishers. North of the brook, Prussian infantry retire in disorder up the gentle slopes.

10. (*below*) The Farm d'en Bas during the battle. Prussian infantry in the foreground charge over the brook to attack French troops on the far bank. The entrance gateway of the farm no longer exists but the walls behind it survive.

11. St Amand village today, from the French position.

12. (*above*) Napoleon's observation post, the mill of Naveau at Fleurus. The sails have disappeared. In the foreground stands the monument to the three French victories won in the vicinity of Fleurus.

13. (*below*) The view from Blücher's command post. Bussy mill used to stand in the foreground. Amidst the trees to the right of centre in the middle distance lies St Amand. The trees on the left cover a huge tip of waste from the local quarries. This wooded tip, created after the battle, hides Fleurus from view.

135

14. The eastern sector of the battlefield of Ligny. The view is from the French side of the valley looking towards the village of Tongrinne, whose church is on the horizon in the centre. Around Tongrinne stood the Prussian III Corps. At the bottom of the valley the Ligny brook flows past the houses of Boignée. Note the relatively steep slopes on this sector of the field; Napoleon concentrated his attacks on the easier terrain of the western sector.

15. Ligny village. The Farm d'en Haut and the post-1815 church. When they attacked Ligny, Captain Charles François and his comrades of the French 30th Line infantry charged down the road in the foreground.

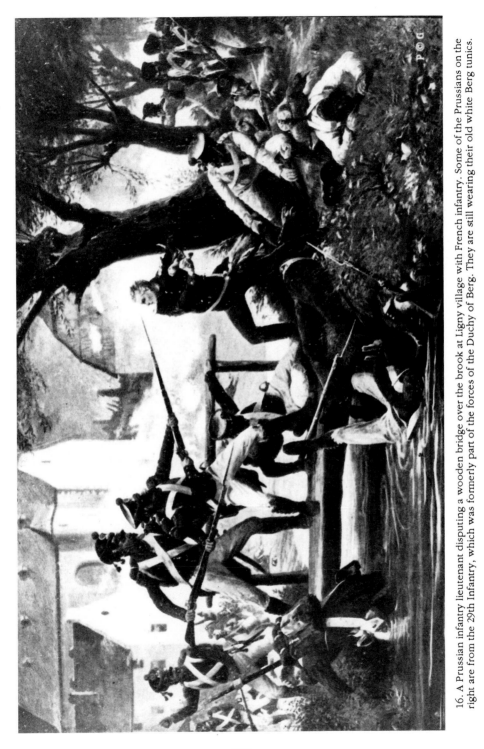

16. A Prussian infantry lieutenant disputing a wooden bridge over the brook at Ligny village with French infantry. Some of the Prussians on the right are from the 29th Infantry, which was formerly part of the forces of the Duchy of Berg. They are still wearing their old white Berg tunics.

17. Blücher trapped beneath his horse at the end of the Battle of Ligny.

18. Farm of La Haye, with a memorial plaque on the wall
to the French General Girard.

19. Gemioncourt farm on the battlefield of Quatré Bras.

20. Looking west along the Roman road used by d'Erlon's French I Corps on its march towards the Battle of Ligny. This section of the road is still as it was in 1815.

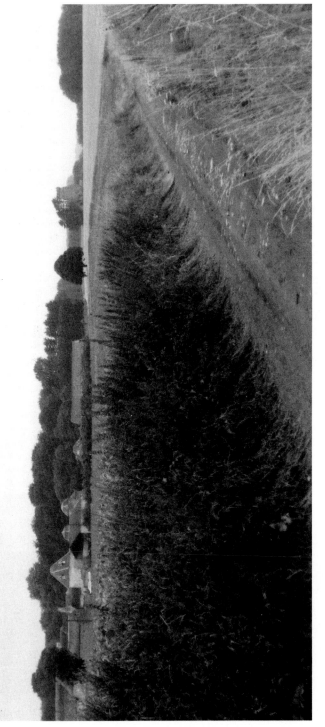

21. After leaving the Roman road, d'Erlon's troops marched along this dirt track past the Chassart farms (on the left of the photograph). Chassart mill is to the right of centre. A few hundred metres behind the camera's position, d'Erlon received a recall from Marshal Ney and marched back the way he had come.

22. (*left*) Château des Caraman-Chimay at Beaumont, Napoleon's quarters on the night of 14/15 June. The facade has been modified slightly since 1815.

23. (*below*) The north side of the Château de la Paix, now Fleurus Town Hall. Napoleon rested here on the night following the Battle of Ligny. His room was on the first floor of the central building of the *château*, third window from the left.

24. (*above*) The presbytery at Sombreffe, Blücher's headquarters for the night of 15/16 June. The two plane trees in the foreground are as old as the house.

25. (*below*) The house in the rue Royale, Brussels, in which Wellington resided in June 1815. After the Duchess of Richmond's Ball he snatched a couple of hours' sleep here before riding to Quatre Bras on the morning of 16 June.

26. (*above*) Inn of the King of Spain, at Genappe: Wellington's quarters on the night after the Battle of Quatre Bras. At 11.30 pm on 18 June Blücher arrived at this inn from Waterloo and rested until dawn. On the ground floor he discovered the grievously wounded French General Duhesme who died on 20 June in spite of care by Blücher's surgeon.

27. (*below*) Wellington's headquarters at the town of Waterloo, $2^{3}/_{4}$ miles north of the battlefield. The Duke slept here on the night of 17/18 June and returned to pass the night after the battle. On the morning of 19 June he wrote his famous Waterloo Despatch here to announce the victory to the British War Minister.

launching a new offensive at Quatre Bras. Reille's infantry columns advanced on all fronts with cavalry and artillery in support.

The Brunswick contingent of Wellington's army, raised from one of the many German states and uniformed in black to mourn the loss of a duke killed at Jena-Auerstädt in 1806, clashed with the French advance. The Brunswick infantry fell back in disorder. While leading a spirited charge by his hussars and *Uhlans* against the French 1st Light infantry regiment, Duke Friedrich Wilhelm of Brunswick was mortally wounded by a French musketshot. He was the son of the Duke killed at Auerstädt.[7]

French lancers and light cavalry swarmed after the routed Brunswickers, sweeping round to fall on British infantry which hurried into square formations. It was a desperate fight. When the 42nd Highlanders formed square, they caught a party of French cavalrymen inside and bayoneted them all. Elsewhere, the French 6th Lancers all but destroyed a Hanoverian *Landwehr* battalion they had surprised in line formation.

Marshal Ney was elated. 'We advanced towards the enemy with an enthusiasm difficult to be described', he related afterwards. 'Nothing resisted our impetuosity ... Victory was no longer doubtful.' Ney now intended to order d'Erlon's I Corps up to the front line to lend overwhelming weight to a steam-roller advance that would crush Wellington and capture Quatre Bras.

Then Tragedy crushed all Ney's hopes to dust. At 5.00 pm, up came General Baron Victor-Joseph Delcambre, Chief of Staff of I Corps, to inform the startled Ney that d'Erlon had marched off to the battlefield of Ligny by Napoleon's direct order. Napoleon had not even advised Ney of this move, let alone consulted him. And why, Ney raged, should d'Erlon presume to march away without Ney's permission? After all, in Napoleon's letter to Ney received at 11.00 am, the Emperor had stated that 'the Chief of Staff [Marshal Soult] will give strict instructions to ensure that no difficulties arise over your orders being obeyed after you have been detached; corps commanders will have to take orders direct from me when I am present.'

But Napoleon was not present, so why had he sent a direct order to d'Erlon? Ney understandably was furious that d'Erlon had departed without Ney's agreement. To crown it all, more troops, units of the British 3rd Division, were now arriving at Quatre Bras.

Ney feared that with his forces suddenly diminished, with d'Erlon's departure, by 20,000 men, he might well be overwhelmed by Wellington's steadily increasing army. Ney still, moreover, had not yet been disillusioned in his belief that Quatre Bras, not Ligny, was the important point of 16 June. So Ney sent Delcambre rushing back to d'Erlon to recall I Corps to Quatre Bras.

Half an hour later, at 5.30 pm, up came a staff officer, Colonel Laurent, bearing another order from Marshal Soult, despatched at 3.30 pm:

... His Majesty charges me to tell you that you are to manoeuvre immediately so as to surround the enemy's [Blücher's] right and fall upon his rear; the army in our front [the Prussians] is lost if you act with energy. The fate of France is in your hands. Thus do not hesitate even for a moment to carry out the move ordered by the Emperor, and direct your advance on the heights of Brye and St Amand so as to co-operate in a victory that might well turn out to be decisive ...

Furthermore, Laurent mentioned that the Emperor had already directly ordered d'Erlon to head for the heights of St Amand.[8]

Now at last the wool was lifted from Ney's gallant but slow-witted eyes. For the first time Napoleon had made it clear to Ney that he had altered his original plan and that Ney was to come to Ligny rather than Napoleon to Quatre Bras. Here, too, was official notification from Napoleon that he had ordered d'Erlon to the Battle of Ligny.

Now, under heavy fire from an enemy battery, with shells exploding either side, amidst whizzing cannonballs, Ney stormed in wretched despair. 'Oh, how I wish these English cannonballs would all bury themselves in my stomach!' he raged in frenzied abstraction.[9]

Ney quite overlooked the obvious step of cancelling his recall of d'Erlon's corps. In any case, Delcambre had departed a full thirty minutes before to summon d'Erlon back. Ney, moreover, was in no mood for altering his orders, convinced as he was that the Battle of Quatre Bras, of secondary importance though it might now be, was in grave danger of being lost. And Ney so desperately wanted to win. He roared at Napoleon's messenger, Colonel Laurent, that 'the Emperor is sitting on his chair. He can not see what is happening here. The English are in front of me and I am going to beat them.'[10]

There was only one thing to do. A bold counter-stroke must be launched straight into Wellington's army to delay or even contain its advance. Hence Marshal Ney despatched an officer to Lieutenant-General François Kellermann, ordering him to bring forward one of his *cuirassier* brigades from Frasnes.

Some time later, seeing Kellermann arrive on the battlefield, Ney galloped over and vigorously shook his subordinate's hand. Employing the theme of the Fate of France from the orders he had received from Napoleon, Ney worked up to a thundering roar: 'General, the salvation of France is at stake. A supreme effort is required. Take your cavalry, throw yourself into the middle of the English. Crush them! Trample them underfoot!'

Kellermann, courageous to a fault, nevertheless had to question the wisdom of launching a solitary brigade of 800 *cuirassiers* into an army of 25,000 men. Enraged beyond all reason, furious at experiencing the fiasco of one of his army corps marching away without his knowledge, Ney would listen to no objections: 'So what!' he yelled at Kellermann. 'Charge with what you have. Trample them. I will support you with all the cavalry I have here. Off with you! ... Off with you, I say!'

Kellermann had no choice but to obey. He trotted over to Guiton's brigade and formed its two regiments, the 8th and 11th Cuirassiers, in column.[11] As Colonel Baron Adrien Garavaque's 8th Regiment of *cuirassiers* moved off, it cheered Prince Jérôme, commander of an infantry division in Reille's II Corps. Jérôme was the younger brother of the Emperor Napoleon and thus a symbol of what the *cuirassiers* were about to charge for.

It was a poignant moment. Alone of all the eight hundred horsemen, only Kellermann knew that almost certain death lay ahead. Out in front, French guns had redoubled their fire to prepare for the awe-inspiring charge. At the shouted word of command, the horses jerked forward, progressively picking up pace to a trot.

The men wore enormous black jackboots, grey overalls and steel helmets with a brass crest topped by a black horsehair mane. Both regiments wore dark blue coats and the 8th wore breastplates on top; there had been insufficient supplies to issue the 11th with them as well. These glittering, formidable, towering men on strong, energetic, heavy horses were the finest cavalry in the world.

Harnesses creaked. Bits jingled. Hooves thudded. Near the Gemioncourt farm, the order was given: 'Charge at the gallop – Forward march!' They were off. It was to go down as one of the epic cavalry charges of history. Kellermann was out in front. 'I hastened', he related afterwards, 'so as not to give my men the time to reflect on the danger.'

The corn was exceedingly high, some of it as much as seven feet. Ahead, the advancing *cuirassiers* spotted sharp, steel bayonets above the corn. It was a British infantry battalion all but hidden in the vast fields. Down on the massed bayonets homed the avalanche of armoured cavalry. Their hooves drummed. The ground trembled under the mighty impact of the magnificent chargers.

The red-coated British 69th Regiment of Foot hurried to form defensive square formation but it was too late. The square was incomplete. Musketry fire crashed out at thirty paces range, in vain. Thundering through the smoke and musketballs, the 8th Cuirassiers overran the 69th Foot.

'Throw yourself into the middle of the English. Crush them. Trample them underfoot!' Marshal Ney had roared. Now the *cuirassiers* did just that. The British mounted officers fled. The soldiers died where they stood. A cluster of troopers of the 8th Cuirassiers captured the 69th's King's Colour and bore it back in triumph to Prince Jérôme Bonaparte.[12]

Still this fantastic charge ploughed on. The terrified British 33rd and 73rd Regiments broke and ran for the cover of nearby woods before the *cuirassiers* even reached them. The redcoats of the 30th Foot stoutly stood their ground but could not check the impetuous course of the French charge.

Straight up the main road, due north, towards the vital crossroads, stormed the *cuirassiers*. The massed French horsemen galloped past immobile and awestruck Highlanders. They burst through the carnage. Men and horses were shot, hurled back and left behind.

Finally, their horses breathless and covered in sweat, the cuirassiers reigned in on the crossroads. They had captured Quatre Bras. They had achieved the impossible. Against all the odds, they had blown a bloody path straight into the heart of Wellington's army.

But then came the terrible reckoning. Suddenly assailed on three sides by a withering musketry and murderous artillery fire, horse after horse went down. '[The English] infantry, who did not allow themselves to be intimidated, fired with the greatest coolness, as if they were on exercise', reported Kellermann who, along with Colonel Garavaque and Guiton the brigade commander, found himself sprawling on the ground.

Kellermann struggled to his feet. As the *cuirassiers* turned to ride back the way they had come, he grabbed the stirrup leathers of two mounted *cuirassiers* either side of him. Running and bounding over the ground, the quick-witted Kellermann was carried to safety.

The retreat of the decimated *cuirassier* brigade quickly got out of control. Some newly enlisted *cuirassier* officers shouted 'Every man for himself!' Nearby French infantry became caught up and the entire torrent of fugitives swept past Frasnes to the south.

Colonel Levavasseur, an ADC, was at table in an inn at Charleroi, listening to the cannon roaring to the north. Suddenly, the town echoed with a louder noise. Everyone was fleeing. Streets were crammed. The landlord of the inn exclaimed 'we are lost; there is the enemy!' Levavasseur knocked down a fugitive who was trying to steal his horse. Then he rode north out of Charleroi to find merely a few French dragoons talking about a cavalry charge in the distance.[13]

French casualties had been heavy: the *cuirassier* brigade had lost 250 men. The Brussels road leading north up to the crossroads was virtually macadamised with corpses. Kellermann's knee and leg were badly bruised but nevertheless he would lead another remarkable charge two days later at Waterloo.

It had been a magnificent feat. Kellermann had made his name at the Battle of Marengo by falling on the flank of a menacing Austrian infantry column and thus had helped save the day. Now, almost exactly fifteen years later, Kellermann had saved the Battle of Quatre Bras by an equally audacious cavalry charge.

At about 7.00 pm, following the repulse of Kellermann's attack, Marshal Ney received another communication from Napoleon. Its bearer, Colonel Baudus, had nearly been run down by the routed *cuirassiers*. Baudus found Ney on foot and, typically of the man, at the most dangerous spot. Ney had already had two horses shot beneath him.

Baudus handed the marshal a duplicate of the Emperor's direct order to d'Erlon, bidding d'Erlon march to the Battle of Ligny. Baudus had a verbal

CLIMAX OF THE BATTLE OF QUATRE BRAS: 6.30 pm, 16 JUNE

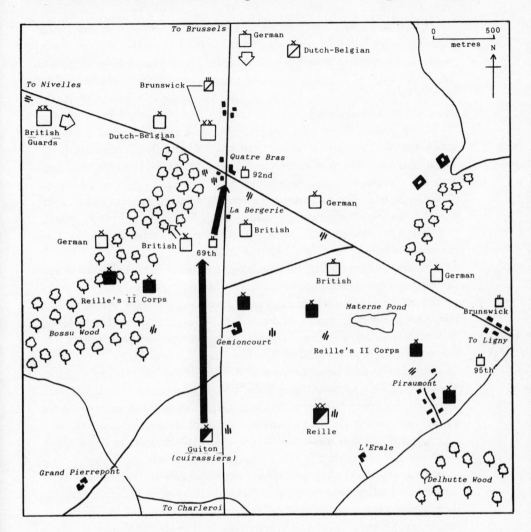

message as well. Napoleon had told him to inform Ney that, whatever the situation might be where Ney was, it was absolutely necessary that the direct order to d'Erlon was executed. Napoleon was not greatly concerned about what happened that day on Ney's wing. The business was all where Napoleon was, because he wanted to get it over with the Prussian army, Baudus said. As for Ney, he was, if he could not do better, to attempt to contain the English army.

But Ney had recalled d'Erlon to Quatre Bras and, in spite of Baudus' pleas, it was hours too late to cancel that recall now. Marshal Ney raged and flung himself back into the front line, crying out in a suicidal rage, 'What, will there not be a musketball or a cannonshot for me?'

Wellington, reinforced to an overwhelming 37,000 against Ney's 21,000, launched an all-out offensive. In spite of Ney's heroic and unceasing efforts, Wellington ground his way south, almost regaining the entire area possessed by his troops when the battle had begun at 2.00 pm.

Towards 8.30 pm, the fighting died down and the bulk of the French troops fell back to Frasnes, leaving advanced posts out in front. In the face of unexpected numbers of Wellington's troops, Marshal Ney had done well to contain the Duke and prevent him from despatching aid to Blücher at Ligny. Nevertheless, Ney is not above reproach, for his generalship at Quatre Bras was unbalanced. He contained Wellington by the bravery of his troops and the sheer force of his personality rather than by superior tactics or strategy. One of Napoleon's ADCs, General Count Flahaut de la Billarderie, wrote: 'I was close to Ney throughout the Quatre Bras engagement. Nobody could have shown greater courage, I might even say greater contempt for death, than he did. But here my praise of him must end, for the affair resolved itself into a series of spasmodic attacks delivered without any semblance of a plan.'[14]

Praise is due to Wellington, whose impeccable conduct on the battlefield denied the vital crossroads to the French. Wellington at Quatre Bras fully demonstrated his renowned tactical skill, sound judgement and cool imperturbability. Quatre Bras was one of his most difficult battles, fought as it was with little of his cavalry or artillery on the scene and on ground not of the Duke's choice. It is undeniable that Wellington had been unable to send direct aid to the Prussians at Ligny. Nevertheless, Wellington's successful defence of the crossroads of Quatre Bras had, allied with the d'Erlon fiasco, prevented Ney from transforming Blücher's defeat into Blücher's destruction.

D'Erlon's I Corps arrived back at Frasnes at 9.00 pm, too late to intervene in Ney's desperate battle. 'And so', wrote Lieutenant Jacques Martin of the 45th Infantry, 'all that remained for us on the evening of this day was to go to sleep like useless logs, without having fired a musket shot. We were ashamed of it.'

But the most curious incident of the fiasco occurred when Ney had sat down to dinner with Prince Jérôme Bonaparte. In came Colonel Forbin-Janson with an order from Napoleon sent at 3.15 pm. It was a copy of the 3.30 pm order received at 5.30 pm, instructing Ney to manoeuvre to fall on Blücher's right wing at Ligny. 'The fate of France is in your hands. Thus do not hesitate even for a moment to carry out the move ordered by the Emperor.'[15]

What had happened? Why had Forbin-Janson taken six hours to bring this order to Ney? More importantly, why had d'Erlon been within marching range of two battles and not participated in either? His intervention in either Ligny or Quatre Bras would have resulted in a tremendous French victory at that battle, and consequently in a resounding French triumph in the entire campaign. If anyone's hands had held the fate of France on 16 June, they were surely d'Erlon's.

Notes

1. Houssaye, *Waterloo 1815*, p.186. Towards the end of the nineteenth century, it was popularly supposed that Wellington had ridden over to consult Blücher at Wavre on the night of 17/18 June. This was later proved to be a myth. Ney's supposed ride to Charleroi on the night of 15/16 June is, likewise, a myth. The only eyewitness to state that Ney returned to Charleroi is the marshal's ADC, Colonel Heymès. But Heymès' account is inaccurate in several places. Ney did have a dinner with Napoleon at Avesnes on 13 June. Heymès seems mistakenly to have placed this dinner at Charleroi on the 15th. General Reille does mention in his account (see Ney, *Documents inédits sur la campagne de 1815*) that 'Ney had returned in the night to Gosselies.' However, Reille meant that Ney had returned from Frasnes, the village he had reached with his leading troops on 15 June, not from Charleroi.

2. Napoleon's failure to send his orders overnight, in order to reach Ney by 7.00 am ready for immediate execution, can be explained as follows:

(1) Napoleon was over-confident that his enemies were in flight (Soult wrote to Ney that Wellington had probably evacuated Nivelles). (2) Napoleon wanted his army to have plenty of rest. Some had been marching since 2.30 am on the 15th June. Moreover, Napoleon intended to march his left wing and reserve to Brussels throughout the night (he wrote to Ney that he wanted to arrive in Brussels at 7.00 am on 17 June).

3. Reille would be cautious once more on 18 June, advising Napoleon on the morning of Waterloo to manoeuvre, not to attack the English head-on. For once, Reille's caution would be justified; for once he would be ignored.

4. Maxwell, *Life of Wellington*, v.2, pp.20–1

5. Chandler, *Waterloo: The Hundred Days*, p.89

6. Lemonnier-Delafosse, *Souvenirs Militaires*, p.361

7. See Appendix Two for a fascinating report of the mourning for the younger Duke of Brunswick in his native land fifty years later.

8. Colonel Heymès, Ney's ADC, states that Laurent mentioned this (Houssaye, *op. cit.*, pp.202–3).

9. Compare Ney's behaviour with Captain François' suicidal rage at seeing the fight at Ligny village so badly conducted.

10. Pétiet, *Souvenirs Militaires*, p.198

11. The other three brigades of Kellermann's III Cavalry Corps were not engaged on 16 June. One was in reserve at Frasnes; the other two were at Liberchies to guard Ney's left rear against any English outflanking move from Nivelles.

12. Report of Kellermann, quoted in de Bas, *La Campagne de 1815 aux Pays-Bas*, v.3, pp.255–6. Becke, *Napoleon and Waterloo*, p.87, records that in 1909 a Captain Jeffcock, late of the 6th (Inniskilling) Dragoons, bought the 69th's flag for 600 francs after seeing it for sale at Azay-le-Rideau in France.

13. Levavasseur, *Souvenirs Militaires*, p.290. Levavasseur asserted that the terror extended into the interior of France like a bolt of lightning.

See also Berton, *Précis historique, militaire et critique des batailles de Fleurus et de Waterloo*, p.37 and de Chaboulon, *Mémoires pour servir à l'histoire*, v.2, pp.166–7. Chaboulon added that the panic caused by the rout of the *cuirassiers* communicated itself as far south as Beaumont. Another eyewitness, General Foy, *Vie Militaire*, p.273, stated that Guiton's brigade fell back in disorder half a league south of Frasnes, sowing terror everywhere and looting baggage: 'the terror and the fugitives were right up to Charleroi and Marchienne-au-Pont.'

The frenzied rout of the *cuirassiers* illustrates the desperate situation Ney had to contend with at Quatre Bras, a situation Napoleon failed to recognise. Furthermore, although Guiton's charge forward was full of elan, skill and daring, when brought to a halt the troopers fled in terror. This was a foretaste of the unstoppable rout on the evening of 18 June, after the Battle of Waterloo.

14. Kerry, *The First Napoleon*, p.119

15. Brett-James, *The Hundred Days*, pp.64–5. Brett-James quotes the account of Quatre Bras by Captain de Vatry, aide-de-camp of Jérôme Bonaparte. Captain de Vatry states Forbin-Janson brought the 3.15 pm order to Ney six hours too late.

7

THE FATAL PEREGRINATIONS OF D'ERLON

Explanations of d'Erlon's almost inexplicable failure abound. They range from Napoleon's poor handwriting and Marshal Ney's pig-headedness in recalling d'Erlon, to d'Erlon's crass stupidity in obeying that recall. A legend has also arisen that one of the Emperor's ADCs, General de La Bédoyère, forged a pencil note supposedly from his imperial master, instructing d'Erlon to march to the battlefield of Ligny. This legend has been repeated by the French historian E. Lenient, and the English historians Archibald Becke and Edith Saunders.

This extraordinary myth can be dismissed out of hand, an action historians have been remarkably reluctant to take, so intriguing has it been. The only eyewitness to assert La Bédoyère was the officer who met d'Erlon's corps south of Frasnes was d'Erlon himself, who in a second narrative left the officer unnamed.

D'Erlon wrote both narratives years after the event and was undoubtedly confused as to the names of officers who brought messages. Moreover, no one, not even an imperial ADC, would have dared to forge Napoleon's signature. The whole legend is ludicrous and patently false.

Much of the confusion surrounding the movements of d'Erlon on 16 June stems from the multiplicity of orders and from contradictory assertions by eyewitnesses as to the identities of the officers bringing these orders. Several participants in the fiasco have made blatantly false declarations as to what happened.

Henry Houssaye's painstaking investigations, relying heavily on the detailed and reliable notes of Colonel Baudus, one of the messengers, are still the best base on which to reconstruct what happened. But Houssaye failed to make certain connections in the evidence, to draw certain conclusions, or to set the evidence out as clearly as possible.

The complex sequence of events surrounding d'Erlon evolved, in fact, as follows:

At 3.15 pm, Chief of Staff Soult wrote an order from Napoleon to Ney: Ney was to bring his force to envelop the Prussians at Ligny. Before a staff officer, Colonel Forbin-Janson, departed with this order, a report arrived from General Lobau, commander of the VI Corps left at Charleroi. Lobau passed on news from his deputy chief of staff, Colonel Janin, who had been with the French left wing, that Marshal Ney was confronted with 20,000 English troops at Quatre Bras.[1]

Consequently, Napoleon realised Ney could in no way leave Quatre Bras and march to Ligny. Napoleon therefore decided to summon merely d'Erlon's I Corps. To save time, this summons, in the form of a pencil note, would go direct to d'Erlon and not through Marshal Ney.[2]

Hence, Colonel Forbin-Janson was entrusted not just with the 3.15 pm order to Ney but also with a pencil note to d'Erlon. After having shown the pencil note to d'Erlon, Forbin-Janson was to proceed to Marshal Ney, give him the 3.15 pm order and explain the situation regarding d'Erlon's corps. Colonel Forbin-Janson departed from Fleurus on his important mission.

At 3.30 pm, Chief of Staff Soult sent another officer, Colonel Laurent, direct to Ney with a duplicate of the 3.15 pm order. Laurent, in addition, was to inform Ney of the direct order to d'Erlon.[3]

At 4.15 pm, Forbin-Janson met the I Corps south of Frasnes, the corps being on the march north to Quatre Bras. Forbin-Janson altered I Corps' direction of march, sending it towards the battlefield of Ligny.

D'Erlon himself had ridden on ahead to Frasnes and was talking to Imperial Guard cavalry officers of Lieutenant-General Charles Lefebvre-Desnouëttes' division. Forbin-Janson therefore continued from I Corps to d'Erlon himself at Frasnes. He showed d'Erlon the pencil note.[4]

This note has not been preserved for posterity, but Henry Houssaye reconstructed it from eyewitness recollections as follows:

> Monsieur the Count d'Erlon, the enemy [Blücher] is falling head first into the trap I have set him. Make immediately with all your troops for the heights of St Amand and fall on Ligny. Monsieur the Count d'Erlon, you are going to save France and cover yourself with glory.
>
> Napoleon.

Forbin-Janson thereupon headed back to Fleurus, completely forgetting to proceed on to the battlefield of Quatre Bras and to hand Marshal Ney the 3.15 pm order and to explain the removal of d'Erlon's corps to the Battle of Ligny.

Houssaye pointed out that Forbin-Janson had no experience whatsoever as a staff officer and that Napoleon was unwise to send him on such an important mission.[5] Forbin-Janson's inexperience may have contributed to Napoleon's 3.30 pm decision to despatch Colonel Laurent with a duplicate of the 3.15 pm order to Ney.

D'Erlon set off to rejoin his I Corps and while heading off with it to the battlefield of Ligny, he sent his Chief of Staff, General Delcambre, to Marshal Ney to inform him that I Corps had been summoned by the Emperor.

Delcambre reached Ney at 5.00 pm. As we have seen, Ney was enraged by the failure of Napoleon to advise him of d'Erlon's move (this being Forbin-Janson's, not the Emperor's, fault). Hence Ney immediately sent Delcambre back to d'Erlon demanding I Corps' return.[6]

Ney foolishly did not reflect that time was too short for the recall message to reach d'Erlon and for his corps to retrace its steps before nightfall.[7] However, the desperate situation of the Battle of Quatre Bras, combined with Ney's understandable fury at not being at least notified, if not consulted, about d'Erlon's move, made him see events in a less than reasoned manner. Moreover, it was not until Colonel Laurent arrived about thirty minutes later that Ney learned from the 3.30 pm order he carried that Napoleon definitely intended Ney to support him, not vice versa.

Thus it was not until Laurent arrived that Napoleon's abduction of d'Erlon's corps made sense to Ney. Laurent would have confirmed that d'Erlon had been summoned by Napoleon, as opposed to marching off on his own initiative, but by then it would have been too late to prevent Delcambre recalling d'Erlon to the left wing.

By 5.30 pm, when Laurent reached Ney, the apparition of d'Erlon's corps heading towards Fleurus was already terrifying the French troops of Vandamme's III Corps. Napoleon himself had summoned d'Erlon but he did not expect him to appear so far south, behind the French lines. For d'Erlon headed in the wrong direction.[8] The pencil note apparently told him to head for the heights of St Amand and to sweep down on Ligny. Napoleon intended d'Erlon to advance due east on to the heights north of St Amand (in other words, the heights on which the village of Brye stood), then on to Ligny village, trapping or destroying the Prussian troops in the vicinity.

But d'Erlon headed not for the heights of St Amand, but for St Amand village. In part the result of an insufficiently precise order from Napoleon,[9] in part the result of d'Erlon's incompetence, the false direction of I Corps was fatal.[10] It undoubtedly crossed Napoleon's mind that the column might be d'Erlon. But until it had been properly reconnoitred and firmly identified as such, Napoleon could not risk ignoring it.

At 5.30 pm Napoleon sent an ADC, probably General La Bédoyère, from Fleurus.[11] This ADC investigated d'Erlon's column, discovering it was not, after all, an enemy formation. At the same time, about 6.00 pm, Delcambre reached d'Erlon with Ney's orders to return. Against the advice of two of his subordinate generals, against the wishes of his troops desperate for action, d'Erlon turned round and headed back west.

Apparently, Napoleon's ADC told, or begged, d'Erlon to continue on to the battlefield of Ligny. Even though the imperial ADCs were important officers with special authority,[12] d'Erlon ignored the ADC's words and conformed with Ney's recall, without reflecting that he would never return in time before nightfall.

D'Erlon did leave two divisions behind but this half measure was useless, reflecting d'Erlon's indecisive, compromising nature. The Emperor's ADC could do nothing but return to Napoleon, whom he reached at 6.30 pm.

Napoleon thereupon sent another officer, or possibly two in succession, to order d'Erlon to attack the Prussians by advancing through Wagnelée. However, by the time these officers reached the detached divisions left by d'Erlon under the command of Lieutenant-General Count Pierre Durutte, d'Erlon himself had vanished, on his way back towards Quatre Bras with the bulk of I Corps.[13]

Durutte, who had been cautioned by d'Erlon to be prudent, nonetheless advanced his infantry through Wagnelée towards 8.00 pm, expelling a Prussian rearguard from that village. But d'Erlon's instructions to be cautious meant Durutte was not in a position to launch a decisive all-out attack on Blücher's troops in support of the other French forces battling their way forward.

'It is incredible that we should be present at the retreat of a beaten army and do nothing, when everything indicates that we have only got to attack in order to destroy it', remonstrated Brigadier-General Brue to his divisional commander.

But Durutte could do nothing. D'Erlon's orders to be prudent were orders, and Brue could count himself lucky he was not responsible for the whole fiasco. 'Would to God that I were!' came the bitter retort. 'We would be fighting right now.'

It is necessary now to return to 5.00 pm, at which point Forbin-Janson re-enters the story. He had just returned to Napoleon, still bearing the 3.15 pm order he was supposed to have delivered to Ney.

Napoleon was angry at Forbin-Janson's failure, for Ney was consequently left uninformed about d'Erlon's move. The Emperor summoned a reliable staff officer, Colonel Baudus, and told him that Forbin-Janson had taken a pencil note to d'Erlon and ought then to have communicated it to Marshal Ney. Owing to Forbin-Janson's failure to do this, Colonel Baudus was to take a copy of the pencil note, together with a verbal message from Napoleon.[14]

Leaving Fleurus just after 5.00 pm, Baudus reached Ney towards 7.00 pm. Baudus handed Ney the duplicate of the pencil note and also conveyed Napoleon's verbal message.

'You will tell him', Napoleon had commanded Baudus, 'that, whatever may be the situation in which he [Ney] finds himself, it is absolutely necessary that this order [the pencil note to d'Erlon] is executed. I am not greatly concerned about what happens today on his wing. The important battle is here, where I am, because I want to finish with the Prussian army. As for the Prince of the Moskowa, he must, if he can not do better, attempt to contain the English army.'[15] When Baudus learned Ney had already summoned d'Erlon to return, he vainly begged the marshal to cancel the recall. But it was too late for such a cancellation.

Forbin-Janson, to conclude the episode, sent back by Napoleon to Ney, left Fleurus sometime between 5.00 and 7.00 pm, and finally brought the 3.15 pm order he had originally been entrusted with to Ney at Frasnes at 9.00 pm: nearly six hours late and after the Battle of Quatre Bras had ended.

At the same time, d'Erlon's corps arrived back at Frasnes, minus the one cavalry and one infantry division left to observe the fight at Ligny.

Clearly, there were several culprits. Forbin-Janson and d'Erlon were the main ones, and Ney and Napoleon the lesser. Napoleon and his Chief of Staff, Marshal Soult, between them failed to keep Ney clearly informed about the Emperor's changing plans. Their orders to Ney were vague and lacked categorical instructions.

Napoleon deserves censure for the insufficiently precise pencil note to d'Erlon, written in his atrocious handwriting. This note may not have made it absolutely clear to d'Erlon that he was to march to the heights north of St Amand rather than to St Amand village.

Secondly, Napoleon failed to envisage the reality of the Battle of Quatre Bras. He clung to the illusion that Ney was confronted by inferior enemy forces. Thus Napoleon made a mistake in appropriating d'Erlon's corps and removing it from Ney's embattled left wing. In place of d'Erlon, Napoleon ought to have remembered, and employed, Lobau's inactive VI Corps left at Charleroi. Napoleon left Lobau's corps too far south – it would have been better positioned further north and ready to lend help to either left or right wing of the French army. When Ney became tied up at Quatre Bras, Napoleon could then have called upon Lobau's corps to perform the outflanking move on Blücher's army that in fact Napoleon ordered d'Erlon to undertake. But Napoleon left Lobau's VI Corps at Charleroi and only remembered it, too late, at 3.15 pm when a report forwarded by Lobau reached the Emperor.

The third criticism that must be levelled at the Emperor in respect of the d'Erlon fiasco is that Napoleon employed the wrong men. Marshal Soult was no replacement for the reliable and recently deceased Marshal Berthier as Chief of Staff. In addition, Napoleon should never have entrusted to Forbin-Janson the transmission of the vitally important pencil note to d'Erlon, and the 3.15 pm order to Ney with the verbal message explaining where d'Erlon had gone. Forbin-Janson was disastrously inexperienced, totally inefficient and monumentally incompetent. Forbin-Janson, consequently, was unable to explain to d'Erlon exactly what Napoleon meant by the somewhat ambiguous words in the pencil note. He also completely overlooked the necessity of continuing on to Ney to deliver the 3.15 pm order and explain the situation regarding d'Erlon.

As a result of Forbin-Janson's mistakes, Ney was left uninformed by Napoleon about d'Erlon's position. Even so, Ney committed a cardinal error in recalling d'Erlon as soon as he discovered that d'Erlon had marched off. Ney, always in the thick of the fight, did not think that d'Erlon would not be able to return before 9.00 pm, by which time the Battle of Quatre Bras would have been irretrievably either won or lost, or brought to a close by a stalemate.

Napoleon commented pointedly on Ney that a general's bravery ought to be different 'from that which a divisional general must have, just as the latter's ought not to be the same as that of a captain of grenadiers.'[16]

The final culprit is d'Erlon. D'Erlon totally misunderstood Napoleon's pencil note, failed to grasp the Emperor's stategy and consequently marched in the wrong direction. Moreover, d'Erlon was wrong to return to Ney when within sight of the battlefield of Ligny, particularly when an imperial ADC was begging him not to return to Quatre Bras.

The eminent historian Sir John Fortescue wrote of d'Erlon: 'we have seen enough of this officer during the campaign in the Pyrenees to know that he was not a man to commit himself upon any side so long as he could find a safe way in the middle.'[17] Indeed, d'Erlon compromised by leaving two divisions behind, while rendering them inactive by instructing them to be prudent, and marching back to Ney with the rest of his corps.

Lieutenant-General Count Maximilien Foy recorded in his diary that on 17 June, 'the Emperor reproached Count d'Erlon for the fact that his corps had not all marched to Marbais [Ligny] on the 16th. His Majesty said that he would have captured half of the Prussian army if the movement of this corps had taken place as he had ordered.'[18]

Another veteran of the campaign, Brigadier-General Jean-Baptiste Berton, noted that Napoleon 'strongly reproached the commander of the I Corps for the great mistake he had committed the previous day in discontinuing his march on the village of Brye as he had been ordered. This mistake, he asserted (to use his own words) had put the salvation of France at risk.'[19]

D'Erlon naturally related this incident differently. He asserted that the Emperor found him at Quatre Bras on 17 June and sadly uttered the following words, which remained forever engraved in his mind: 'France has been ruined. Go, my dear general, put yourself at the head of the cavalry and push the English rearguard vigorously.'

Thus d'Erlon omitted to say that Napoleon accused him in person of having ruined France. Indeed, by criticising Ney's conduct immediately above this passage, d'Erlon gives the impression that Napoleon was blaming Ney.

D'Erlon was not the only corps commander in the 1815 campaign to compromise the Emperor's plans by his excessive caution and tardiness.

Napoleon rightly wrote at St Helena that several of his generals 'had lost something of that dash, that resolution and that self-confidence which had won so much glory for them and had contributed so much to the success of former campaigns.'[20]

None of those responsible for the d'Erlon fiasco afterwards admitted to being guilty. Napoleon at St Helena blamed Ney for not supporting him at Ligny. Napoleon also covered up his vague communications to Ney by falsely asserting he had had from the start the master plan of crushing Blücher in a pitched battle before turning on Wellington. By then Ney was dead and unable to write in his defence. Yet before heroically facing the firing squad on 7 December 1815, Ney had written a letter laying an accusatory finger at Napoleon for having removed d'Erlon's corps from Ney's command.

Forbin-Janson seems to have kept his head down, and hence escaped much criticism.[21] D'Erlon, on the other hand, sought to evade his responsibility for the fiasco by confusing the issue – both by intention and by the forgetfulness brought on by the passage of time. D'Erlon wrote two accounts of the fiasco: a letter to Ney's son in 1829 and a relation of his *Vie Militaire* published in 1844.

These accounts are grossly inconsistent and blatantly self-justificatory. D'Erlon is confused as to who brought the pencil note: he states it was a staff officer in one account, La Bédoyère in another. D'Erlon also tried to make out that the pencil note ordering him to make for Ligny was addressed to Ney and not himself: 'there can be no doubt that had the Emperor addressed his orders to me personally, as many accounts of the battle state, they would have been executed punctually; and that this battle [of Ligny] would have had most important results, and, in all probability, that of Waterloo would not have taken place.'

D'Erlon ended up striving to convince himself, as well as the rest of the world, that he had not 'had the Fate of France in his hands' – and dropped it: 'this is my opinion; and the more I ponder it, the more firmly convinced of it I become.'

Notes

1. This is ironical. When Janin reconnoitred Quatre Bras at about 12.00 pm, there were in fact only 7000 enemy troops around the crossroads. Janin overestimated their numbers. However, by the time his intelligence reached Napoleon, the troops confronting Ney had been reinforced to some 15,000, with an additional 5000 Brunswickers about to arrive.

2. This was in keeping with Napoleon's letter to Ney in the morning: 'according to circumstances, I shall draw troops from one wing to strengthen my reserve.'

3. It was usual for duplicate messages to be sent. The reliable Marshal Berthier, Napoleon's former Chief of Staff, would send twenty copies of the same message, joked Napoleon on one occasion.

4. Houssaye doubted d'Erlon's story that he had ridden on ahead of his corps. Basing his opinion on the eyewitness reports of Durutte and De Salle, Houssaye considered d'Erlon was with his corps when Forbin-Janson joined it, yet there is absolutely nothing in either of these two accounts to justify Houssaye's conclusion. D'Erlon's statement that he rode on ahead of his corps

has a ring of authenticity to it, in that he writes that he talked to some Guard officers at Frasnes. Indeed, Lefebvre-Desnouëttes' Guard light cavalry was stationed at Frasnes.

5. Chesney, *The Waterloo Lectures*, pp.84–5, quotes the Duke of Fezensac (who served on the French staff between 1806 and 1813) as saying: 'as for messages taken on horseback, I have already said that no person took the pains to inquire if we had a horse that could walk, even when it was necessary to go at a gallop; or if we knew the country, or had a map. The order must be executed without waiting for the means ... This habit of attempting everything with the most feeble instruments, this wish to overlook impossibilities, this unbounded assurance of success, which at first helped to win us advantages, in the end became our destruction.'

Baudus, *Etudes sur Napoléon*, v.1, p.210, added that 'if the orders of this prince [Napoleon] had been transmitted in a regular manner, most of the troops which composed [the Prussian army] probably would have fallen into our hands.'

6. General Durutte's account indicates that Ney sent a sequence of officers after Delcambre with the same recall order. This reflects the Marshal's unthinking and implacable rage at d'Erlon's disappearance from his wing.

7. Edith Saunders argues that Ney could not have known that Quatre Bras would end by nightfall (sunset was 8.20 pm). Fighting still raged at the Battle of Wavre at 11.00 pm on 18 June. Yet no decision was reached at Wavre in the night fighting. Generally, nightfall brought battles to a close and hindered attempts at organising and mounting a pursuit – as indeed the Battle of Ligny demonstrates. Waterloo was won, and a pursuit sent off, before nightfall.

Ney should have reflected firstly, that d'Erlon's corps could never return to Quatre Bras in time to save or win that battle. Secondly, Ney should have realised that d'Erlon's presence at Ligny, and hence a French victory there, would have compensated for any defeat at Quatre Bras (on the other hand, it must be admitted that Ney had not yet received Napoleon's 3.30 pm order which made clear to Ney that Ligny not Quatre Bras was the more important battle). Thirdly, Ney, if he needed more troops, should have called on the unemployed cavalry units of the French left wing: the Guard light cavalry and the inactive three brigades of Kellermann's cavalry corps. It is true that Napoleon had told Ney to avoid if possible using the Guard cavalry and to position Kellermann's men at the intersection of the Brussels and Roman roads where Napoleon could draw on them if he had need. But if Ney's situation was truly desperate, Napoleon would have preferred Ney to employ these cavalry formations rather than to recall d'Erlon's corps.

8. Pétiet, *Souvenirs Militaires*, p.197, wrote that 'the Emperor did not expect [I Corps to come] by this direction at all. The direction was undoubtedly more effective for uniting with us, but not for achieving the desired aim of outflanking Blücher's right.'

9. The pencil note, as reconstructed by Houssaye, is certainly imprecise. But did Houssaye reconstruct it accurately? Napoleon's pencil note may have said, like the 3.15 and 3.30 pm orders to Ney, to 'make for the heights of Brye and St Amand', which is more precise. Moreover, General Durutte wrote that 'the Emperor ordered Count d'Erlon to attack the Prussian left [right] flank and to try to seize Brye.' Berton, *Précis historique, militaire et critique des batailles de Fleurus et de Waterloo*, p.27, rightly pointed out that 'the village of Brye became the main key point of the battle.' Whoever held the heights of Brye held the battlefield. If the pencil note did include a reference to Brye, blame should be attached not to the clarity of Napoleon's pencil note but to d'Erlon's failure to understand a simple order.

10. The fact that d'Erlon headed in the wrong direction is partly to be explained by Forbin-Janson's inexperience and inability to explain the precise meaning of Napoleon's pencil note to d'Erlon. A more reliable officer would have known that the heights of St Amand meant the heights north of the village.

11. Napoleon wrongly asserted in his memoirs that this ADC was General Dejean. Grouchy, *Mémoires du maréchal de Grouchy*, v.4, pp.16–7, quotes a letter of 26 July 1839 from Dejean to Marshal Ney's son as saying: 'during this day, I did not see Count d'Erlon's troops at all and I was not commanded to take them any order. I am completely in ignorance of the orders which the Emperor gave Count d'Erlon.' Dejean mentioned in his letter that Napoleon sent him to the French left wing earlier in the day but this was unconnected with d'Erlon's appearance. Napoleon

undoubtedly confused Dejean's earlier mission with the later one by another officer to reconnoitre d'Erlon's column. See also Appendix Three: footnote 7.

12. When they gave orders, the Emperor's ADCs spoke as if with the voice of the Emperor and were to be obeyed as such (Hamilton-Williams, *Waterloo: new perspectives*, p.377).

13. Grouchy, *op. cit.*, v.4, pp.13–14

14. Baudus, *op. cit.*, v.1, pp.210–11

15. *Ibid*, v.1, p.210. After Napoleon had finished speaking, Marshal Soult had added that Baudus was to insist most strongly that Ney was to do nothing to hinder the move that d'Erlon had been ordered to make.

16. Bonaparte, *Napoleon's Memoirs*, p.544

17. Fortescue, *The Campaign of Waterloo*, p.116

18. Foy, *Vie Militaire*, p.275

19. Berton, *op. cit.*, p.33

20. Bonaparte, *Napoleon's Memoirs*, p.544

21. Although he escaped the odium heaped on the other culprits of the d'Erlon fiasco, Forbin-Janson has been criticised for his cowardice on the evening of Waterloo. When the French army dissolved into flight on 18 June, Colonel Levavasseur tried to rally the fugitives. Several, including some generals, tried to push past the colonel, but he stopped them, saying 'you shall not pass!' Levavasseur specifically mentioned Forbin-Janson as one of these individuals who tried to evade him: 'I can cite as an example the Emperor's ADC, Forbin-Janson, who, despite saying he was wounded, was forced by me to stop like the others' (Levavasseur, *Souvenirs Militaires*, p.306).

8

17 AND 18 JUNE 1815

Thus the principal cause of the disaster of Waterloo is the prolonged inaction of the French army following the Battle of Ligny. – A. Grouard[1]

By the early morning of 17 June, Napoleon apparently believed that both Wellington and Blücher were in retreat along their respective, mutually divergent lines of communication. Napoleon's thoughts seem to have been on the lines of a large scale pursuit of the defeated Prussians, similar to the unrelenting pursuit after Jena in 1806, by the French right wing, and a march to Brussels by the left wing. The reserve would support whichever wing needed additional strength.

Napoleon did not order any immediate moves, partly as his renowned energy and decision were sapped by illness,[2] partly as he was waiting for intelligence on his enemies' positions and intentions. Furthermore, he wanted his army to replenish munitions and to rest before the long march to Brussels.

The previous evening, he had ordered the cavalry units of Pajol and Exelmans to follow the Prussians at dawn. These cavalry formations were posted on the French right flank, so it was inevitable that they would find indications of Prussian deserters fleeing eastwards to Liège.

Napoleon omitted to send any of his cavalry units stationed in the centre or left flank of the army at Ligny to reconnoitre to the north. Consequently, the French failed to uncover evidence of the retreat of the Prussian army to Wavre. Hence Napoleon gained an incomplete and misleading picture of the Prussian retrograde movements and believed Blücher's army to be heading east rather than north.

At 7.00 am, while Napoleon was eating breakfast at the Château de la Paix in Fleurus, a report arrived from Pajol saying he was pursuing the Prussians towards Liège and Namur and had taken many prisoners. At about the same time, an ADC arrived from the French left wing with news of the outcome of the action at Quatre Bras on 16 June.

If Napoleon had marched immediately to Quatre Bras, he would have taken Wellington's army, still posted there, in the flank. Wellington would learn of the Prussian defeat at Ligny only at 7.30 am with the return of a British cavalry

IMPACT OF THE LOSSES OF 16 JUNE

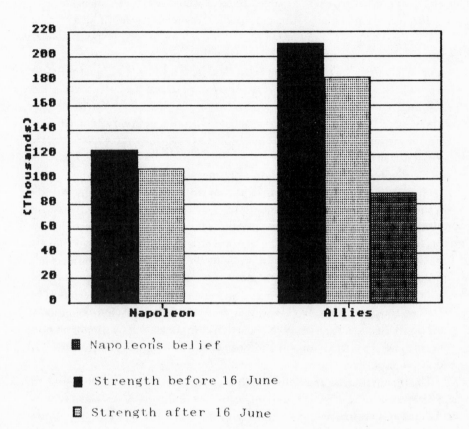

The battles of 16 June failed to have the impact Napoleon hoped for. Before, the allies had enjoyed a numerical superiority of 86,000 men. The fighting at Ligny and Quatre Bras reduced that superiority by 13,000. Yet this was negligible in view of the vast numerical superiority of 73,000 that the allies still enjoyed after 16 June.

Napoleon did not recognise this reality. He wrongly believed that the Prussians had been knocked out of the campaign by their defeat at Ligny. Consequently, Napoleon expected that he had to deal only with Wellington and that it was the French who now possessed the advantage of numbers. This fatal over-confidence would lead Napoleon to his final defeat at Waterloo.

reconnaissance which had communicated with the Prussian rearguard to the north of the battlefield of Ligny.[3] With Wellington's army knocked out of action, if not destroyed, the road to Brussels would have been open.

But Napoleon hesitated still, and the advantages won by his sudden invasion and by his victory at Ligny began to slip through his fingers. Napoleon on the morning of 17 June continued obstinately to believe in the illusion under which he had laboured the previous day: that Wellington was not at Quatre Bras in strength, that he was either in retreat, or about to retreat, to Ostend to embark for England. Napoleon's 8.00 am order to Marshal Ney says it all: 'the intention of His Majesty is that you should take up a position at Quatre Bras; but, in the unlikely event of that not being possible, you must report the fact, giving details.'

Napoleon's fatal lethargy and over-optimism are evident in the same order: 'today is necessary to finish this operation, to replenish munitions, to rally stragglers and to call in detachments.'

At 8.45 am, Napoleon departed from Fleurus, replying as he did so to Marshal Grouchy's request for orders, 'I will give you them when I judge it convenient.'[4] Napoleon rode out to examine the battlefield and to inspect and praise his troops.

When he arrived at the entrance of St Amand, Napoleon was welcomed by General Vandamme who hoped, in vain, for a marshal's baton in recognition of his contribution to the victory. Napoleon had to wait a full quarter of an hour until a passage into St Amand had been opened through a ghastly barrier of slaughtered men.

Thousands of dead and wounded littered the carnage-strewn battleground. The French 82nd Line infantry regiment of Girard's division had been cut down almost to the last man and lay in bloody heaps.[5] Twenty-two of the twenty-seven regimental officers were casualties. A staggering fifty-five per cent of Girard's division had been lost and one in every four of its men was dead.

Sergeant Hippolyte de Mauduit of the Guard wrote that Ligny, unlike most battles, was fought at point-blank range; it consisted of hand-to-hand fighting, of murderous discharges of musketry and of deadly showers of canister. At Ligny village, he wrote, 'more than 4000 dead soldiers were piled on an area less in measurement than the Tuileries garden, some 300 or 400 yards square ... One can picture the rage with which each side dashed against its foes.' The untidy piles of corpses blocking entire streets made it impossible to bring aid to all the wounded.

Members of Napoleon's imperial suite of officers and pages offered aid to the wretched injured troops. Following the Battle of Borodino in 1812, Napoleon had commented soberly that 'after a victory there are no enemies, only men' and he had ordered the wounded from both sides to be carried to a monastery converted into a makeshift hospital. Now, on the battlefield of Ligny, the Emperor noticed a badly wounded Prussian officer and interrogated a Belgian peasant:

'Do you believe in hell?'

The intimidated peasant stammered in the affirmative.

'Good! If you do not want to go to hell, look after this wounded man whom I put in your charge. Otherwise, God will make you burn. He wishes us to be charitable.'[6]

Napoleon's order to the peasant was not merely an exercise in public relations. It rested on a genuine sympathy with the wounded and on the knowledge of the reluctance of the Francophile peasants to aid the Prussians. General Drouot of the Imperial Guard related that 'the peasants carried off the wounded French with the greatest care. They were eager to assist them; but it was necessary to employ menaces to oblige them to carry away the Prussians, towards whom they seemed to entertain great hatred.'[7]

Drouot added that the Emperor left upon the battlefield officers and troops specially charged to take care of the wounded. These men were the survivors of Girard's infantry division, which, all but destroyed by casualties and the loss of its leader, had no further fighting value.

The 'sacred duty', as Napoleon termed it, of providing aid for the wounded had now been seen to. The Emperor pressed on to the heights of the mill of Bussy and here the French units were making soup. At the sight of Napoleon, the troops leapt to their feet, formed up in front of their bivouacs and cheered 'Long live the Emperor!' Napoleon interviewed and congratulated officers and troops, inquiring how many were on parade and how many had been lost the day before and recognising old soldiers with the aid of his phenomenal memory.

Colonel Fantin des Odoards of the 22nd Line infantry heard Napoleon berate the 70th Regiment for fleeing from the Prussian cavalry the day before. The colonel saw the Emperor leave the chastened 70th and proceed slowly along the line to where he stood. After asking him a few routine questions about the state of his unit, the Emperor congratulated Colonel Fantin on his good conduct in repelling the Prussian cavalry during the battle. The Emperor informed him that captured Prussian muskets were to be preserved intact to arm troops back in France and concluded the interview, 'Goodbye, Colonel, I am pleased with you and your regiment.'[8]

The colonel's pride knew no bounds. French soldiers would eagerly exchange an arm or leg for such a brief, factual sentence of praise from that remarkable leader of men, Napoleon.

Napoleon then dismounted to discuss with some of his generals the news from Paris, about the state of public opinion and the politics in the French capital. While Napoleon talked politics and did nothing militarily, Blücher and

Wellington were busy withdrawing their forces to positions at Wavre and Waterloo, and making plans for the Prussians to link up with Wellington at Waterloo, preparing to turn their defeat into victory.

It was a fatal delay. Even at the time, French senior officers were worried. General Vandamme, so used to Napoleon's former campaigns crammed full of activity and speed, was heard to whisper that 'the Napoleon we knew is no more.' General Gérard thought the delay both 'incomprehensible and irremediable.'[9]

It was only from 10.00 am onwards that Napoleon began to receive a clearer picture of the strategic situation. A tardy communication from Marshal Ney reported that at 6.30 am Wellington had still been strongly in possession of Quatre Bras and not in retreat at all. Shortly afterwards, a reconnaissance returned to Napoleon to report that Wellington was still occupying the crossroads.

The veil of illusion was at last lifted from Napoleon's eyes – or at any rate from the eye focused on Wellington, for Napoleon still believed Blücher's Prussians were streaming away to the east. Now at last Napoleon discovered there was a chance of destroying Wellington's army at Quatre Bras, with Ney launching a frontal attack to pin Wellington down until Napoleon and the reserve arrived from the east to roll up the Duke's flank.

Thus, at 11.00 am, Napoleon made his decision. The Reserve – the Guard and two thirds of Lobau's VI Corps – was ordered to march towards Quatre Bras. Meanwhile Marshal Grouchy and the 33,000 men of the French right wing were belatedly ordered to march to Gembloux, to scout in the directions of Namur and Maastricht and to pursue the Prussians. It was important, Napoleon informed Grouchy, to find out the intentions of Blücher and Wellington and whether they intended to unite their armies to fight a battle to cover Brussels and Liège.

But it was too late. The Prussians had had too long a head start. Grouchy thought they were heading east; in fact they had retreated north. Grouchy was an slow, unimaginative bloodhound trying to pick up a long lost scent. Napoleon had given Grouchy too many troops and would have too few to ensure a crushing victory over Wellington.[10]

Napoleon's attempt to destroy Wellington at Quatre Bras by marching west with the reserve was too late as well. By the time Napoleon arrived at the crossroads at 2.00 pm, they were devoid of hostile troops. Marshal Ney had not stirred, in spite of an order from Napoleon at midday to 'attack the enemy at Quatre Bras and chase them from their position.'

Wellington's infantry columns were safely retreating to a position just south of the village of Waterloo. His cavalry rearguard held the French pursuit at bay, aided by a ferocious thunderstorm which turned the Belgian countryside into a muddy morass.

THE 1815 CAMPAIGN: 17–18 JUNE

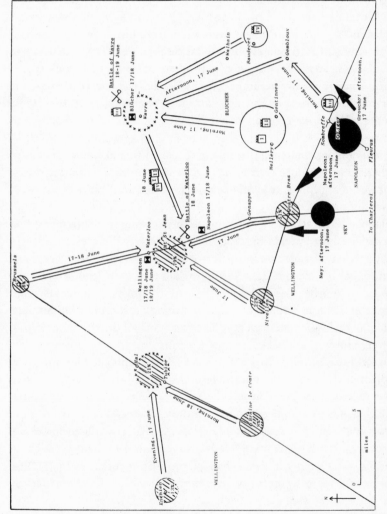

By the close of 17 June Blücher had rallied and massed his resilient army at Wavre, with the fresh IV Corps now arrived from Liège. Wellington had withdrawn to a position just south of Waterloo, joined by units that had been unable to take part in the Battle of Quatre Bras. By confronting the main thrust of Napoleon's offensive at Ligny, Blücher had enabled Wellington to concentrate his army. The fatal French mistake was to delay pursuit after Ligny and to allow Blücher to march west and unite with Wellington.

Napoleon had committed a cardinal error of warfare: to waste time. 'What would I not give today', he lamented in the evening, 'to have Joshua's power and delay [the sun's] progress by two hours!'[11]

By nightfall, the Duke had massed his army and formed it up along the ridge of Mont St Jean, overlooking a shallow valley. Bedraggled French forces bivouacked on the opposite side.

By the close of 17 June, the Prussian army had reassembled around the town of Wavre, in which Blücher had established his headquarters. Much anxiety and effort had accompanied the process of sorting out the muddled units, of preparing the battered army for another terrible battle. The reserve ammunition waggons had gone missing in the confusion of the final hours of 16 June. Only at 5.00 pm did they turn up at Wavre. Lieutenant-Colonel von Röhl, commander of II Corps' artillery, had discovered the waggons on the Nivelles–Namur road and had marched them away to the north and safety. Thanks to Röhl's initiative, I and II Corps could now be restocked with cartridges. Without this resupply of ammunition, these two corps would have been useless as fighting formations.

Unfortunately, the food supply was not as forthcoming as that of munitions. The troops were hungry and tired, battered and footsore. But their morale was intact. They had undergone their baptism of fire and were ready for more. The three corps that had been engaged at Ligny had now been reinforced by the fresh IV Corps. Blücher had ridden alongside his troops, exchanging jokes and encouragements. To an artillery captain bemoaning the loss of one of his guns at Ligny, Blücher replied reassuringly, 'There, now! Don't let that trouble you. We will very soon take it back from them again.'[12]

Blücher's defeat at Ligny had not in the slightest dampened his ardour. If anything, it had made him more determined to fight than ever. 'I shall immediately lead you against the enemy', he declared in a general order to the army. 'We shall beat him, because it is our duty to do so.'

Blücher's inexhaustible energy and determination had crystallised on the one aim of linking up with the Duke of Wellington. It had become an obsession. In the morning of 17 June, Wellington had informed Blücher that he was pulling back to Mont St Jean where he would give battle if he could count on the support of a Prussian corps.[13]

At 5.00 pm the Prussian army had received its vital resupply of ammunition. This enabled Blücher to reply at 6.00 pm to the Duke: 'I shall not come with one corps only, but with my whole army.'[14]

Wellington received this written promise late in the evening, by which time he had repeated his request for Prussian assistance. His letter reached Wavre towards 11.00 pm. Blücher thereupon sent the Duke details of the Prussian plan: IV Corps would march at daybreak, followed by II Corps, towards the

Anglo-Dutch-German army. I and III Corps would be ready to follow. Only the exhaustion of the troops prevented an earlier start.

This welcome message of aid would reach the Duke at 6.00 am on 18 June as he rode forward from his headquarters in Waterloo to tour his battle-line.[15]

At Wavre, Gneisenau was still worried. Only a rash, foolish general could ignore the risks of marching west. Even in peace time a march across the steep and marshy valley of the River Lasne to Waterloo would have been a formidable operation.

Gneisenau's nightmare was the thought of the Prussian army becoming bogged down in this countryside and then abandoned by Wellington to distract the French from an English retreat. Gneisenau's suspicions that Wellington would put his own interests first, and if necessary abandon his Prussian allies, would find a curious echo in a statement the Duke himself made years later: 'I never contemplated a retreat on Brussels. Had I been forced from my position, I should have retreated to my right, towards the coast, the shipping and my resources. I had placed Hill [commander of II Corps] where he could have lent me important assistance in many contingencies, of which this was one. Again I ask – if I had retreated on my right, could Napoleon have ventured to follow me? The Prussians, already on his flank, would have been in his rear.'

But this was exactly the situation Gneisenau feared. If Wellington retreated on Ostend, it would be the Prussians who would have difficulty in extricating themselves. It is noteworthy that on a different occasion, in 1821, Wellington would state, 'I should not have retreated on the wood of Soignes, as Napoleon supposed, thinking I should fall back on Brussels and the sea, but should have taken the direction to my left, that is towards Wavre, which would have given me the substantial advantage of drawing near the Prussian army.'[16]

This self-contradiction by the Duke's statements stems from the salient fact that Napoleon would hold the tactical initiative at Waterloo, and that right up to the end of the battle, Wellington would merely react to French moves. Wellington would never make up his mind in which direction he would retreat because that would depend so much on circumstances. What is certain is that if the French broke through Wellington's left flank, the Duke would be unable to fall back eastwards towards the Prussians. The momentum and direction of the French onslaught would push him back towards Ostend and the Prussians would be trapped between Napoleon and Grouchy. Future historians would interpret Gneisenau's warnings as the wise utterances of a clever strategist; Blücher would be seen as a rash gambler and Wellington as the man who failed his loyal allies.

Therefore it was fortunate for the Prussian army that Wellington was such a consummate master of defensive warfare. He alone would be able to hold out at Waterloo with an inferior army against Napoleon until the Prussians arrived to save him from defeat.

Wellington's achievement at Waterloo would be all the more admirable in that the Prussians were destined to arrive at Waterloo later than expected. In part, their tardiness would be unavoidable and due both to the atrocious weather and a fire in Wavre. Yet it would also be due to the failure of Blücher and Gneisenau to realise the need for speed. The IV Corps would lead the Prussian march to Waterloo. This corps was the strongest and freshest corps of the army and would be the most effective reinforcement for Wellington. On these grounds Blücher had decided from the start that IV Corps would lead the Prussian march to Waterloo.

Yet IV Corps was the easternmost formation of the army. It would have been quicker to send the I Corps first. This corps was not fresh but would not have as far to march to Wellington's aid. Blücher and Gneisenau did not appreciate that speed of reinforcement was more vital than its freshness or strength. This was a serious error and would nearly result in a French victory. The Prussian high command decided to sent first the strong, fresh IV Corps, then the battle-tried II Corps, and then the heavily depleted I Corps. Although relatively fresh and nearer to Waterloo than IV Corps, III Corps would not be sent to Wellington as it was weak in numbers, especially in infantry and artillery, and contained a large proportion of *Landwehr* regiments.

But, whatever the delays that would result in the advance of the Prussian army, at least the vital decision to march to Wellington's aid had been taken. The minutes ticked slowly past; the fourth day of the campaign, 18 June, had begun.

The Prussian IV Corps commenced its march to Waterloo at 4.00 am, but was delayed for two hours by an accidental fire blocking the main street of Wavre. The marching conditions were horrendous. No roads existed. The recent storms had turned the muddy paths and waterlogged tracks into quagmires. Soon these tracks were rendered worse by the passage of thousands of feet, hooves and wheels. The young troops were famished, tired and footsore.

But Blücher was there, urging his troops on. At 9.30 am, he wrote a characteristic note to Müffling who was at Wellington's headquarters. 'I request Your Lordship to tell the Duke of Wellington, in my name, that, ill as I am, I intend to put myself at the head of my troops.' If Wellington found himself under French attack, he could expect Prussian forces to bear down on Napoleon's right flank. 'If, however, today should pass without any enemy action, then I believe that we should make a combined attack on the French army tomorrow.'

To this ebullient despatch, Gneisenau added an anxious note asking Müffling whether Wellington intended to fight a real battle or instead to put up a show of resistance and then to use the arriving Prussians as a diversion to cover his retreat.[17]

'Papa Blücher' had no such doubts as he rode westwards with his troops. 'We must get on', he urged them. 'I have given my word to Wellington, and you will surely not make me break it. Only exert yourselves a few hours longer, children, and certain victory is ours.' The Prussians certainly had the light of battle in their eyes this day. After the campaign, enquiries made of the local Belgian inhabitants would find that no house more than fifty paces either side of the routes taken by the Prussian columns was visited or pillaged.[18]

Ahead, cannon boomed. At 11.30 am, Napoleon had opened the Battle of Waterloo with his first attack on Wellington's army. The ground Wellington had chosen, allied with the atrocious weather, would hinder any French out-flanking attempt. Wellington's flanks were firmly anchored by fortified farms and difficult terrain.

The Prussian approach further guaranteed the Duke's eastern wing. His far right flank was secured by a detachment of 17,000 men around Hal, seven miles to the west.[19] This seven-mile interval was guarded by a chain of bat-talions. If Napoleon had wanted to march undetected round Wellington's flank, he would have had to undertake a huge circular march of more than twenty-five miles. Furthermore, if Napoleon had made such a vast move to the west, he would have lost contact with Marshal Grouchy's detachment.

Moreover, Napoleon had underestimated Wellington's skilful tenacity in defence. 'I tell you', he had boasted, 'that Wellington is a bad general, that the English are bad troops and that this battle will be like eating one's breakfast.'[20] Hence the Emperor had decided on the attritional, frontal attacks employed at Ligny two days before.

First, a diversionary attack would draw Wellington's reserves towards the west. Then the French main assault, preceded by a massed barrage, would hurl back the Duke's left wing. Napoleon would support this onslaught with his entire reserve, including the Guard and heavy cavalry. Wellington's army would be overrun. 'Gentlemen', Napoleon had concluded his pre-battle address to his generals, 'if my orders are carried out well, we will sleep at Brussels.'

Now, desperate fighting was in progress at Hougoumont farm. Waves of French infantry dashed against the rock-like defence. Wellington was already demonstrating that he was the finest defensive general in Europe. He was always at the critical spot, inspiring by example, refusing to be flustered or panicked. At Ligny, Napoleon's attacks had thrown Blücher off balance. They would fail against Wellington at Waterloo. Throughout the day, Wellington would keep as firm a control on his army as habitually he kept on himself.

The cold, proud, chivalrous Duke felt his Honour to be at stake. Two days before, he had been unable to support his Prussian allies as he had indicated he would. So now it was a point of Honour to show Blücher, as well as Napoleon, how he could defend a position and stand by a friend. Like Blücher, Wellington was consumed by a single-minded obsession.

To the east of Waterloo, the Prussian I and II Corps were now following the IV Corps, leaving the III Corps at Wavre as a rearguard. 'Do not forget that you are Prussians', appealed Blücher to his army, 'and that our watchword is *Death or victory!*'

Meanwhile, Marshal Grouchy and the French right wing had picked up the Prussian trail and were moving slowly north to Wavre. Eating strawberries at a farm, Grouchy and a group of officers heard the guns of Waterloo at 11.30 am.

'Where is the action?' demanded an engineer general.

'It is towards Mont St Jean', answered a local guide. 'We can be where they are fighting in three or four hours.'

On this assurance, General Gérard boldly declared, 'we must march on the cannon and join the Emperor.'

But Grouchy stuck blindly to Napoleon's orders to follow the Prussians, and he believed Blücher was at Wavre and not on the march to Waterloo. In any case, Napoleon's lethargy on the morning of 17 June had given the Prussians too great a head start. Even if Grouchy had followed Gérard's advice, he would have been unable to intercept the bulk of Blücher's army. The terrible state of the tracks leading west would have delayed Grouchy's men too long.

Nevertheless, Gérard spoke out again, insisting it was the marshal's duty to march on the cannon. Grouchy closed the dramatic discussion with an absolute refusal. The Emperor had told Grouchy on 17 June that he was going to pursue Wellington and try to bring him to battle. The cannonfire merely indicated that Napoleon had succeeded in engaging Wellington and was, therefore, nothing remarkable. It was certainly no reason for Grouchy to abandon the pursuit of the Prussians and to march west. And so Grouchy's troops renewed their movement northwards to the town of Wavre.

Back on the field of Waterloo, Napoleon was about to launch his second thunderbolt at Wellington when he noticed on the eastern horizon masses of sparkling bayonets. A captured Prussian messenger informed the startled Napoleon that the whole of IV Corps was bearing down on his right flank. French reserve formations marched to protect that flank. In the mean time a British heavy cavalry charge destroyed Napoleon's second attack and captured two eagle standards before being cut to pieces by French lancers.[21]

The Prussians pushed on westward, along sunken lanes, across valleys, through muddy meadows. Conditions were terrible but the fierce fire of vengeance burned in every Prussian heart. Time was running out. Marshal Ney repeatedly led an awesome array of massed French cavalry against Wellington's centre, but failed to break through.

Nevertheless, Napoleon's attritional tactics were beginning to have effect. Wellington's army writhed like an immense, wounded serpent. Still it bellowed defiance but blood spurted forth from innumerable wounds. Some of the less reliable elements of the Duke's army, such as the Dutch–Belgians, were drifting away from the fight. Soon a whole regiment of Hanoverian hussars would turn tail and gallop off, led by its colonel.

In fact, Wellington's army had split into two. One portion still stood proudly immovable on the bloodsoaked ridge. It defied all comers and repelled all attacks. But the other part of the army was already beaten. Demoralised and disintegrated troops roamed around the rear of those who were still fighting. Deserters, prisoners and wounded streamed steadily northwards to Brussels. Never in the history of warfare has such a victorious army presented such an image of defeat.

At 4.30 pm, the leading units of the Prussian IV Corps were on the eastern edge of the battlefield of Waterloo. Blücher's guns opened up at last, and Wellington took heart. Back at Wavre, Grouchy had at last arrived, launching himself into a furious but pointless engagement with Thielmann's Prussian III Corps, which held him at bay.

Successive Prussian formations came up at Waterloo. Blücher focused his attacks on the village of Plancenoit. 'If only we had the damned village!' he roared.[22] Blücher's objective was to cut off Napoleon's line of retreat southwards, surrounding and annihilating the French army. The fighting at Plancenoit was reminiscent in its ferocity and intensity of that at Ligny two days earlier.

Wellington's line began to disintegrate under an attritional all-arms attack brought on by the loss of his stronghold of La Haie Sainte at 6.15 pm. Now Marshal Ney requested French reserve troops with which to achieve the breakthrough. But Napoleon, under increased pressure from the Prussians, turned down Ney's demand. As the appearance of d'Erlon's unidentified column had caused Napoleon to postpone the Guard attack at Ligny, so too did the onslaught of the Prussians cause Napoleon to hold back the Guard at Waterloo. 'Troops!' he exclaimed. 'Where does [Ney] expect me to get them? Does he expect me to make them?'

Napoleon's idleness on the morning of 17 June had cost him his last chance of a decisive victorious campaign. Now, by refusing to release the Guard for an assault on Wellington, Napoleon lost his last opportunity to stave off defeat. The moment passed. Wellington skilfully shored up his line with reinforcements from his reserves.

By 7.30 pm, Napoleon was desperate. He had just vigorously counterattacked and contained the Prussians; so now at last he played his last card against Wellington. Six crack battalions of imperial guardsmen marched against Wellington's line.

To encourage his army to make one last effort, Napoleon ordered his ADCs to spread rumours that Marshal Grouchy's detachment was arriving. It was a lie. Grouchy was still fighting at Wavre, ten miles away, and Napoleon knew it.

THE BATTLE OF WATERLOO: 8.00 pm, 18 JUNE

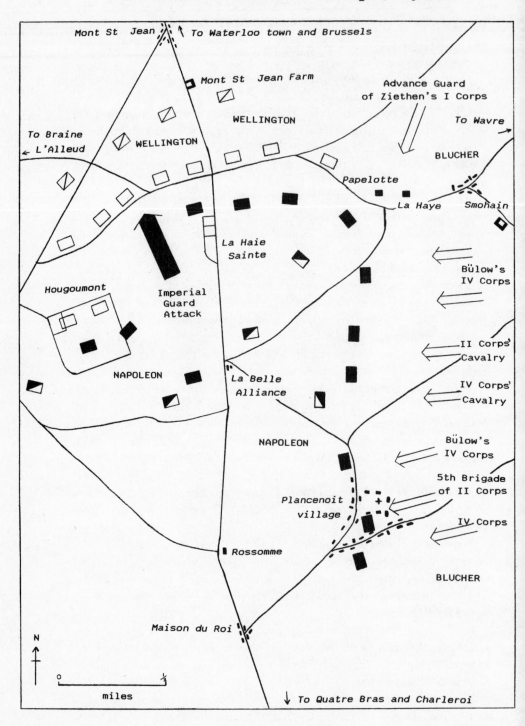

Mont St Jean
To Waterloo town and Brussels
Mont St Jean Farm
WELLINGTON
Advance Guard of Ziethen's I Corps
To Braine L'Alleud
WELLINGTON
To Wavre
BLUCHER
Papelotte
La Haye
Smohain
La Haie Sainte
Hougoumont
Imperial Guard Attack
Bülow's IV Corps
NAPOLEON
II Corps' Cavalry
La Belle Alliance
IV Corps' Cavalry
NAPOLEON
Bülow's IV Corps
5th Brigade of II Corps
Plancenoit village
IV Corps
Rossomme
BLUCHER
N
Maison du Roi
0 ⅓ miles
To Quatre Bras and Charleroi

The end at Waterloo: Wellington's army commences its general advance across the valley. La Haie Sainte farm is on the left; Lord Uxbridge, Wellington's cavalry commander, is in the centre.

But the ruse revived French morale and energy in support of the attack by the Guard.[23]

The Guard's reputation and fighting power were incalculable; it had clinched the victory at Ligny. But at Waterloo, the Guard failed. Shattered by musketry, decimated by gunfire, utterly devastated by a counter-attack by British light infantry and a Dutch–Belgian brigade, the Guard broke. Napoleon's army panicked.

The sun was setting now, and the sky was already darkened with smoke. It was the end.

Wellington ordered a general advance of his whole line, just as the leading units of the Prussian I Corps came up to the battlefield and burst through the French line from the northeast. The French troops, tricked by Napoleon into believing that Grouchy was arriving to save them, suddenly found that overwhelming Prussian reinforcements had come instead. Napoleon's ruse had gained a temporary surge of French fighting spirit, but it was a short-term expedient. With the failure of the Guard attack and the arrival of the Prussian I Corps, the shock of disillusionment caused utter disaster. The French army dissolved into flight.

Napoleon had risked all, had used up his last reserve in a desperate attempt to stave off defeat. Now he had nothing left. The 5th brigade of the Prussian II Corps spearheaded a last, victorious onslaught on Plancenoit, which came just too late to cut off the stream of French fugitives southwards.

'Is it not just like Leuthen?' exclaimed a jubilant Gneisenau. Leuthen had been Frederick the Great's decisive victory of 1757. Indeed, joyous Prussian troops, having reversed their defeat at Ligny two days ago, now burst into the Teutonic battle hymn, *Nun danket alle Gott*, sung at Leuthen by their forefathers.

'We have shown how to conquer; now we will show how to pursue', Gneisenau added.[24] Wellington's army was too exhausted by its hours of strife to move. The Prussians, some of whom had been on the march or in action for seventeen hours, were equally tired. But Blücher's men hated the French with a ferocity that the British lacked. Moreover, Wellington's army fought better in defence than offence.

So an unrelenting Prussian pursuit harried the French through the night. Reminiscent of Napoleon's pursuit of the Prussians after Jena in 1806, it was the exact opposite of the French pursuit after Ligny. It reinforced Gneisenau's reputation as a determined and ruthless man of action, not just an intellectual staff officer. Gneisenau's pursuit was not the least of the contributions by allied generals to the decisively victorious outcome of the campaign.

The French ran. They abandoned muskets and cannon. They surrendered in thousands. They made little attempt to rally. Napoleon's army had not just been physically beaten; it had been psychologically destroyed. Napoleon had

IMPACT OF THE WHOLE CAMPAIGN
ON ARMY STRENGTHS

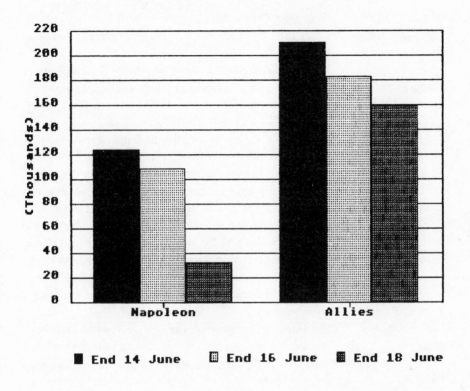

By the close of 18 June the French army, except Marshal Grouchy's detachment at Wavre, had been destroyed. The allies had won, at Waterloo, the knock-out blow which had eluded Napoleon at Ligny.

received at Waterloo the knock-out blow he had sought to inflict on Blücher at Ligny. The Prussians had performed the decisive outflanking move that d'Erlon should have executed on 16 June.

Blücher met Wellington at the inn of La Belle Alliance[25] with an historic greeting: 'Mein lieber Kamerad! Quelle affaire!' That, as Wellington remarked later, was almost the sum total of Blücher's knowledge of French: 'What a fight!'

The following day both Wellington and Blücher's armies began a march by parallel routes on Paris, seeking swiftly to capitalise on their crushing victory of Waterloo. In six days, the allies breached the triple line of French fortresses guarding the northeastern frontier and descended towards Paris.

Napoleon had wanted to fight on, but France was no longer behind him.[26] His political enemies in the Chamber of Deputies and the Senate forced his abdication on 22 June and a Provisional Government replaced him. The new government had little heart for further war. In the east, Austrian and German troops were already across the Rhine and attacking the French frontier formations, which, although outnumbered, resisted well. But the northeast was the decisive sector, and here few units of the beaten and demoralised Grand Army were in any mood to fight. Desertion was rife and the only coherent force of any significant size was Marshal Grouchy's wing which had learnt on 19 June of the outcome of Waterloo and had fallen speedily back into France, skilfully evading Prussian interception.

Grouchy fought a few skirmishes against Blücher on the road to Paris but achieved little. By the evening of 29 June, the Prussians were before the northern outskirts of the capital. Wellington was two days' march behind, owing to the tighter discipline prevailing in his army. Few comparisons do the Duke more honour than that between his conduct and Blücher's during the descent on Paris. Blücher let his Prussians loot, rape and murder their way across France, excusing the barbarous brutalites they inflicted on innocent civilians as revenge for the French treatment of Prussia in 1806.

In strictly military terms, Blücher's swift and merciless sweep to Paris, like the U.S. General William Tecumseh Sherman's destructive march through the Confederacy during the American Civil War, had its justifications. The switch immediately after Waterloo from the defensive in Belgium to the offensive in France prevented any French recovery and a long drawn-out war.

In terms of diplomacy, however, Blücher and the Prussians were doing their best to cause disaster. The conduct of Blücher's army inspired in the French not just fear but hatred. This was no basis on which to build the post-Napoleonic Europe. The very qualities that made Blücher a magnificent war leader fitted him ill for peace.

Wellington as always strove to preserve the utmost discipline within his army. He stated that the enemy was Napoleon and not the French people. To

Wellington greets his loyal Prussian ally at La Belle Alliance

his credit, the Duke wished at all costs to avoid a prolongation of the war. His aim was to win the French people over to Louis XVIII, thus avoiding the horrors of civil war. Since the Bourbons were returning in the baggage carts of the allies, the allies had to be scrupulously fair. Just as a future Irish field marshal, Gerald Templer, won the 'hearts and minds' of the people in his 1952–4 fight against communism in the Malayan Emergency, so Wellington ensured the peaceful transition to Bourbon rule in 1815.

For the Duke was already in touch with the French Provisional Government when Blücher swept round to the unfortified southern side of Paris, prepared to sack the city and requested use of the British rocket battery to set fire to it. The French swiftly agreed to the Convention of St Cloud on 3 July. The French army retired south of the River Loire, evacuating Paris, which the allies entered on 7 July. The following day saw Louis XVIII restored to his throne.

Wellington's task was not yet ended. Placed in command of the 150,000 strong allied army of occupation, he sought to alleviate the burdens placed on France. Blücher's demands for excessive financial reparations were resisted, and the occupation, originally intended for five years, was brought to a close in 1818. The Duke earned the gratitude of France and ensured stability and peace in Europe for decades. Wellington the diplomat was the equal of Wellington the general; his humane treatment of France was at least as important as his actual defeat of Napoleon on the ridge of Waterloo.[27]

By now Napoleon was incarcerated on the remote island of St Helena, having surrendered to HMS *Bellerophon* at Rochefort on 15 July 1815 after attempting to escape to America. Napoleon, having risked all in the Belgian campaign and lost, now paid the penalty of exile for life. Europe breathed a sigh of relief and settled down to half a century of peace.

The 1815 campaign was over; Napoleon's last military victory had led to his final defeat.

Notes

1. Grouard, 'Les derniers historiens de 1815' in *Revue des Etudes Napoléoniennes* (July–Dec. 1917)

2. Howarth, *A Near Run Thing*, pp.52–6; Chandler, *The Campaigns of Napoleon*, pp.1046–7; Holland-Rose, *The Life of Napoleon* I, pp.484–6.

3. A communications breakdown occurred on both sides in the evening of 16 June. In the chaos of defeat, the Prussians failed to notify Wellington that they had been beaten and forced to fall back. This was not wholly their fault. Great confusion was caused by Blücher being temporarily missing. In further mitigation, Gneisenau and Blücher had sent a message before Ligny had been lost to notify Wellington that 'the most we can do is to hold the battlefield until nightfall' (Brett-James, *The Hundred Days*, p.79). The responsibility for notifying Wellington of the defeat of Ligny lay as much with the British liaison officer, Hardinge. But Hardinge had been wounded and had to have his hand amputated. Furthermore, unlike Müffling, Hardinge did not have sufficient messengers at his disposal (Müffling, *Passages from My Life*, p.215). It was the responsibility of the liaison officers to maintain communications between the allies and it was a British responsibility to ensure that Hardinge had a deputy and sufficient resources at his

disposal. To their credit, the Prussians re-established communications early in the morning of 17 June. One of their messengers reached Wellington at Quatre Bras soon after 8.00 am. Similarly, although Wellington failed to inform the Prussians of the outcome of Quatre Bras, he sent a cavalry patrol early in the morning of 17 June to re-establish communications (Chalfont, *Waterloo: Battle of Three Armies*, p.66). On the French side, owing to the incompetence of Marshal Soult, Marshal Ney learnt only at 9.00 am on 17 June that Ligny had been a French victory (Houssaye, *Waterloo 1815*, p.218). Napoleon learnt at 6.00 am of the result of Quatre Bras (Kerry, *The First Napoleon*, p.117).

4. Grouchy has often been blamed for failing to intercept the Prussian march to Waterloo. But in his defence, he had wanted to launch an immediate pursuit of Blücher on the evening of 16 June. The real cause of the Prussian ability to unite with Wellington on 18 June was Napoleon's delay in sending Grouchy off in pursuit until late morning of 17 June (see Grouchy, *Mémoires du maréchal de Grouchy*, v.4, pp.23 and 127).

5. Navez, *Les Quatre Bras, Ligny, Waterloo et Wavre*, p.133, quoting Hippolyte de Mauduit of the 1st Grenadiers. Mauduit asserted that the 82nd lay dead in the cemetery of St Amand, but in fact Girard's division was engaged in La Haye village.

6. Houssaye, *op. cit.*, p.222

7. Jones, *The Battle of Waterloo*, p.225

8. Brett-James, *op. cit.*, pp.72–3

9. Charras, *Histoire de la Campagne de 1815*, p.212

10. From this moment on, Marshal Soult was constantly worried about the strength of the detachment being sent under Grouchy. Soult was not anxious because he believed the Prussians capable of rallying and joining Wellington but because he had fought against the British in Spain. Unlike Napoleon, Soult realised the tenacity of Wellington and his troops in defence. On the morning of 18 June, he advised Napoleon to recall Grouchy but was ignored.

11. Bonaparte, *Napoleon's Memoirs*, p.544

12. *United Service Magazine* (Oct. 1891), p.48

13. Ollech, *Geschichte des Feldzuges von 1815 nach archivalischen Quellen*, pp.180–9

14. Hamilton-Williams, *Waterloo: new perspectives*, p.256

15. Longford, *Wellington: The Years of the Sword*, p.444

16. Weller, *Wellington at Waterloo*, p.248

17. Ollech, *op. cit.*, p.189

18. Navez, *op. cit.*, p.46

19. Innumerable foolish historians have criticised Wellington for not having these 17,000 men with him at the Battle of Waterloo, where they were desperately needed. But Wellington could not have known that Napoleon would attack the Mont St Jean ridge head-on. Only at 10.00 am on 18 June did Napoleon's army form up south of this ridge, and even then it remained unclear whether a detached French force might not be further to the west. The Hal detachment would have delayed any outflanking attempt sufficiently for Wellington's reserves to arrive from Mont St Jean. Moreover, the 17,000 troops at Hal were of poor quality and some would have been a hindrance at Waterloo. Only fifteen per cent of the detachment was British. Nineteen per cent was Hanoverian infantry, mostly *Landwehr*. A further seven per cent consisted of two units of Hanoverian hussars, whose sister regiment was present at the Battle of Waterloo and fled the field *en masse*. A full fifty-nine per cent was Dutch-Belgian, largely militia, and, like many of the Netherlanders, liable to withdraw as soon as the fighting became serious.

20. Houssaye, *op. cit.*, p.311

21. Research by Richard Moore has shown that in the confusion of this stage of the battle other standards were captured and then recaptured. The eagle of the 55th Line appears temporarily to have been in British hands (*The Journal of the Napoleonic Association*, nos. 10 and 11).

22. Chalfont, *op. cit.*, p.135

23. Some historians have criticised Napoleon for this ruse. They are wrong to do so. Napoleon had to win the battle or France would be demoralised and alienated from his cause. Thus there was no question of cutting losses and retreating. Every last man had to be goaded into a last effort to support the Guard. Napoleon's claim that Grouchy was arriving was psychological warfare at

its best. Colonel Baudus of the French staff noted that Napoleon's 'remarkable fib ... not only produced its effect ... on the able bodied but it even revived the wounded – an admirable occurrence. For those who could still drag themselves along, rose and fell on the enemy shouting *Long live the Emperor!*' (Baudus, *Etudes sur Napoléon*, v.1, p.227).

24. Treitschke, *History of Germany in the 19th Century*, v.2, p.192

25. Wellington had ridden along the Brussels–Charleroi road south as far as the cluster of houses called Maison du Roi. Then he returned northwards. As he neared the inn of La Belle Alliance, he noticed a group of horsemen coming from the east. It turned out to be Blücher and his staff (Jackson, *Notes and Reminiscences of a staff officer*, pp.57–8). Wellington would call the fight of 18 June the Battle of Waterloo. But for Blücher and the Prussians it would always be known as the Battle of La Belle Alliance ('the fine alliance'). Indeed, it had been the alliance between the immovable Wellington and the irresistable Blücher that had achieved victory.

26. In the Second World War, by contrast, even after their crushing defeat in Normandy in June to August 1944, the Germans fought on to the end against overwhelming forces because their nation was ideologically brainwashed and ruthlessly controlled by Hitler. Even so, when defeat loomed on the horizon, some Germans were prepared to remove Hitler in order to end the war, as the July Bomb Plot of 1944 demonstrates.

27. By contrast, the Prussians in 1871 and the western allies in 1919 imposed harsh terms on the defeated enemy which would lead to further, even more destructive, wars.

9

AFTER THE 1815 CAMPAIGN

For so many of the combatants, 1815 was their last campaign. Blücher died in 1819, just four years after Ligny. As he passed away, the bugle sounds of Prussian troops skirmishing, on an exercise, drifted gently in through his open window. It was a merciful end, for Blücher was rapidly on his way to senility. Napoleon died in 1821, tortured by pain from a cancerous stomach and by the frustration caused by his restless, caged spirit, in the lonely prison of the island of St Helena. Perhaps he was murdered by arsenic poisoning on Bourbon orders; the evidence for this is inconclusive.

Marshal Ney had died, in December 1815, like the unequalled hero he was – not, alas, at Waterloo fighting to the last but murdered by a firing squad on Bourbon orders. One hundred and twenty nine years later, another energetic and respected soldier, Field Marshal Erwin Rommel, would be murdered in cold blood by the politicians of his country.

Marshal Grouchy stayed in America for a while. He spent most of his later life defending his reputation and his failure to march on the sound of the guns of Waterloo on 18 June 1815. His life ended in 1847, when he was eighty-one years old.

Wellington had, at Waterloo, fought his last military battle, but he had plenty of political ones ahead of him, as did Marshal Soult who reaped high honours from the French state. Both Wellington and Soult attended Queen Victoria's coronation in 1838, Soult as well as the Duke being cheered by the chivalrous British crowds. Soult had rightly been distrusted as an opportunist turncoat by the Bourbons and was allowed back in France only in Louis-Philippe's reign, when he served as Minister of War, Minister of Foreign Affairs and Prime Minister. He died in 1851 aged eighty-two.

Of the Prussian corps commanders who fought at Ligny, the most sucessful was General Ziethen who became a Field Marshal in 1835. He died aged seventy-eight. General Pirch, promoted to lieutenant-general following the 1815 campaign, retired in 1816 and died aged seventy-five in 1838. Thielmann lived until 1824 when he died aged fifty-nine in command of a corps at Koblenz.

As for Gneisenau, he progressed in rank to Governor of Berlin, and Field

Marshal in 1825, and died aged seventy-one of cholera while suppressing a Polish insurrection of 1831. Colonel von Clausewitz died in the same year from the same cause, but he lives on through his epic book *On War*.

Lieutenant-Colonel Count von Nostitz, the loyal ADC who rescued Blücher at the Battle of Ligny, and hence did as much as anyone to win the 1815 campaign, carried Blücher's Field Marshal's baton at Wellington's funeral in 1852. By the time of his own death in 1866, Nostitz was a cavalry general aged eighty-nine.

One young Prussian infantryman, Franz Lieber, would become a university professor in America. Some French veterans, too, ended up on that side of the Atlantic, in order to escape persecution by the restored Bourbon royalist regime.

Many on the French side, having triumphed at Ligny, were doomed to perish in ignominious defeat at Waterloo two days later. Others, who survived, eked out a pitiful existence while living in the dream world of their former days of military glory. The luckiest French soldiers were perhaps those who had fallen on the field of honour at Ligny, when it had still seemed that the path to ultimate victory, not defeat, lay ahead. Colonel Fantin des Odoards, commander of the 22nd Line infantry, was one of the survivors: 'I was not fortunate enough to be killed in the so short and tragic campaign which has brought the enemy into Paris', he wrote bitterly in July 1815. 'I exist to attend the funeral of our wretched country. This is much worse than death.'[1]

Most of the French generals were out of favour with the Second Bourbon Restoration in 1815. For them, it was a matter of living long enough to be pardoned, returning to France in time to reap the rewards to be found following the 1830 Revolution which replaced the Bourbons with the more enlightened monarchy of Louis-Philippe.

Thus, for example, General d'Erlon, condemned to death by the Bourbons, ran a bar at Munich until the 1830 Revolution. Then he returned to France and soon found prominence as Governor-General of Algeria (1834–5) and as a Marshal of France (1843). He died aged seventy-nine in 1844. General Vandamme sought exile in Belgium and America until allowed back in France by the Bourbons in 1819. He died in 1830, just sixty years old. General Lobau, after a wise absence in Belgium, returned to his native land to be General in Chief of the Paris National Guard, and a marshal, in 1831. He died seven years later aged sixty-eight.

A few French generals survived to witness the Second Empire of Napoleon III. General Gérard returned to France from Belgium in 1817 to engage in politics. In 1830 he became Marshal of France, Minister of War and President of the Council under King Louis-Philippe. In 1831–2, Gérard led a French army into Belgium to help the new kingdom, which had broken away from Dutch rule, expel the King of Holland's troops from Antwerp. On the way to

Antwerp, Gérard saved the Prussian Waterloo monument from destruction at French hands. With the advent of the Second Empire in 1851, Gérard became a senator and died in 1852 aged seventy-nine after a brilliant and adventurous life. He had come a long way from being a Revolutionary volunteer in 1791.

General Reille, like Gérard, survived to be a senator in the Second Empire, after appointment to the rank of Marshal in 1847. He died at the age of eighty-five in 1860.

Unlike his colleagues, General Drouot, ever loyal to the Emperor, refused every position offered him by the Bourbons. Aged seventy-three, he died in 1847 as president of the Agricultural Society in Nancy.

And so the French generals of the Battle of Ligny faded away as old soldiers do. Their graves are mostly to be found today in the peaceful, historic cemetery of Père-Lachaise in Paris.

It is fitting to conclude with an ordinary French soldier, brave and loyal but, unlike his superiors, largely unrewarded for his years of devoted service. Captain Charles François, the French officer who fought so bravely at Ligny village, had volunteered at the age of fifteen to serve the endangered Republic in 1792. Thus began a military life of daring adventures and of narrow escapes.

After François had fought at Ligny and under Marshal Grouchy at Wavre in 1815, he eventually settled in Nantes. From 1825 onwards he supervised the building of steamboats for a service on the River Loire between Nantes and St Nazaire. On one dramatic trip, an engineer fell asleep on duty and had his head crushed by an engine beam. The passengers panicked but soon were calmed by François' icy imperturbability. The old soldier brought his ship safely back to Nantes.

Known as the 'Egyptian Dromedary' by the townsfolk, François was elected commandant of the National Guard for fourteen consecutive years. In 1853, he finally faded away aged seventy-seven. A respectful company of the 59th regiment paid the old veteran the last honours.

François was not particularly moral and had numerous love affairs. He was a soldier, and a first class one at that. Brave, determined and experienced, ever loyal to his Emperor, François is a symbol of the magnificent fighting men who served Napoleon: all the imagination, the initiative, the pluck and the elan of France found expression in François and his humble comrades.

It was men like François who won the great Battle of Ligny. It was the generals who took the credit.

Notes

1. Fantin des Odoards, *Journal du général Fantin des Odoards*, pp.427–8

PART TWO

10

ANALYSIS OF NAPOLEON'S LAST MILITARY VICTORY

Napoleon's conduct of the Battle of Ligny has received criticism on several points.

Napoleon is often blamed for beginning the battle as late as 3.00 pm. But he had to wait until that hour before attacking so that the whole of the right wing of his army could mass on the battlefield. Napoleon recognised that the Ligny position would require large forces to capture it.

Second, Colonel von Clausewitz and Marshal Davout criticised Napoleon for not outflanking the Prussian western flank. Davout considered Napoleon's frontal battle of attrition to be at fault and that the Napoleon of Ligny was the same Napoleon of the Battle of Borodino 'who, to make use of a vulgar expression, takes the bull by the horns; this was the reason why the battle was so bloody and so hotly fought.'[1]

Marshal Davout had advised Napoleon to outflank the Russians at Borodino in 1812. Napoleon had rightly rejected this strategy as his army was not numerically strong enough to risk such a move.

Marshal Davout's opinion concerning Ligny is equally faulty. Napoleon's strategy consisted of two parts: first, a frontal battle of attrition, and second, an outflanking move by d'Erlon's I Corps coming from Quatre Bras. That d'Erlon's marching and counter-marching caused Ligny to be solely a battle of attrition with no strategic finesse should not hide, as it hid from Davout, the second part of Napoleon's plan. Brigadier-General Jean-Baptiste Berton, a combatant at Ligny, recognised that Napoleon's frontal attacks were essential in order to absorb Blücher's resources and to distract his attention from the strategic manoeuvre Napoleon wanted to direct against the Prussian right flank.[2]

A more relevant and justifiable criticism is that Napoleon left, and then forgot, Lobau's VI Corps at the town of Charleroi until late in the afternoon of 16 June. Consequently it arrived at the battlefield of Ligny too late to participate in the attack by the Imperial Guard. Yet at the same time as he neglected Lobau's corps, Napoleon was repeatedly ordering Marshal Ney to send some of his troops to Ligny.

A fatal French mistake was the delay in pursuing the defeated Prussians after Ligny. Napoleon could not have done much in the evening of 16 June given that night had fallen, that the Prussians had firmly established a rearguard line on the northern sector of the battlefield and that the French army was too exhausted to move or fight further. The Prussians were equally tired but their defeat acted as a psychological spur to march north. It is more difficult to incite victorious troops to further efforts.

When the Prussians evacuated the battlefield in the early hours of 17 June, Napoleon should have despatched Marshal Grouchy's detachment on their trail immediately, rather than waiting until 11.00 am. By that time, the trail was cold and Grouchy was unsure as to the Prussian direction of retreat and future intentions. In earlier years, the Emperor himself had declared that once a general had decided on the offensive, he should maintain it until the last extremity. In 1815 he failed to follow his own maxim.

Napoleon believed only what he wanted to. After Ligny especially, he acted according to a mental picture of events which was divergent from what was happening in reality. It was as if the Emperor were isolated inside a room whose windows distorted his vision of the situation outside.

For Napoleon could not comprehend, either on 16 June or on the morning of the 17th, that Marshal Ney was facing so powerful an opposition at Quatre Bras.[3] Also, Napoleon came to believe that the Prussians had suffered a devastating defeat at Ligny and would not be able to recover for several days. 'After such a battle as Fleurus', declared Napoleon on the morning of Waterloo, 'the junction between the Allies is impossible for at least two days.' The Prussians would have suffered a devastating defeat if Napoleon's plan for the outflanking of Blücher by d'Erlon's corps from Quatre Bras had become reality. Although this had not happened, Napoleon acted as though it had and as though the Prussians had been decisively knocked out of the campaign.

Napoleon would only be disillusioned on this score on the afternoon of 18 June when powerful Prussian forces closed in on his right flank at Waterloo. In exile on the island of Elba before the 1815 campaign had begun, Napoleon had commented on Blücher: 'that old devil always attacked me with the same vigour. If he was beaten, he would, a moment later, show himself ready to fight again.' Napoleon would have been wise to have recalled those words after beating Blücher at Ligny.

The victory at Ligny boosted the unwarranted over-confidence that permeated the French army. From the start of the campaign, Napoleon had laboured under the fixed idea that Wellington and Blücher would separate and retreat rather than fight and unite. The tough Prussian resistance at Ligny did nothing to shatter this illusion. Indeed, Napoleon exaggerated the effect of his victory and believed that the Prussians were no longer a force to be reckoned with. Thus although Napoleon had not anticipated the Battle of Ligny, it merely strengthened his over-confidence that the allies were separating and retreating.

Over-confidence breeds complacency, which breeds mistakes. Similarly, the allied triumph in Normandy in June–August 1944 bred the belief that Germany was already defeated, could be finished by a daring stroke and was incapable of aggressive action. The setbacks of Arnhem and the Battle of the Bulge were the products of the same over-confidence that led to Waterloo.

Apart from these reservations, Napoleon's generalship at Ligny was superb. Napoleon was a first-rate commander. He kept a firm grip on himself, on his army and on his battle. He improvised to meet the fluctuations of battle. At no point did he lose his nerve. Napoleon's neutralisation of the 5.30 pm crisis at the Battle of Ligny mirrors Marshal Joseph Joffre's imposing imperturbability during the dark days of the Marne in 1914.

Napoleon's style of command is in many ways similar to that of Field Marshal the Viscount Montgomery of Alamein. Both Napoleon and Montgomery were superb leaders of men who boosted their troops' morale and put the light of battle in their eyes. Thus, as Montgomery said, they became 'not only a master but a mascot.'[4]

In terms of strategy, both the generals were experts at defeating an enemy in battles of attrition and of massed firepower. Montgomery at Alamein employed 'wet hen' tactics, attacking the enemy at different points in the line one after another to keep the enemy confused and unbalanced. Then Montgomery broke through the opposing battle front with a massed assault.

Unlike Montgomery, Napoleon at Ligny did not have numerical superiority, but nonetheless wore down and broke into his enemy. In achieving victory, both Montgomery and Napoleon imposed their will on their opponent by seizing and holding the initiative. The only exception during the Battle of Ligny was the panic caused by the appearance of d'Erlon's I Corps at 5.30 pm. This postponed Napoleon's Guard attack and enabled Blücher to put in another two desperate counter-attacks, which served merely to use up more of the Prussian reserves.

Montgomery and Napoleon were two of the finest attacking generals the world has known. Ligny, like Alamein, was a masterpiece of the first order. The enemy were bombarded, tied down, absorbed, confused, exhausted, broken into and, finally, defeated. Napoleon's generalship at Ligny has been underestimated merely because of his defeat at Waterloo two days later.

'The French soldiers surpassed themselves', declared one eyewitness, a French royalist who watched the battle from the Prussian lines.[5] In his memoirs, Napoleon recorded that 'never has the French soldier shown more courage, good will, and enthusiasm.'[6] Yet while the French troops were totally confident in their supremacy and in the abilities of their Emperor, they mistrusted their generals.

The French army's neurotic fear of treason helps explain the dangerous panic which infected Vandamme's III Corps with the appearance of d'Erlon's unidentified column at 5.30 pm. In spite of these psychological flaws in the French soldier, his physical courage was impeccable. 'On no occasion', stated the veteran General Drouot of the Guard, 'on no occasion have I seen French troops fight with a nobler enthusiasm; their spirit, their valour excited the greatest hopes.'[7]

The conduct of the French officers was magnificent as well. Ligny saw fine leadership at all levels. Leadership at the top is not enough. Ligny was won as much by the superb French NCOs and junior officers as by Napoleon and his generals. Napoleon singled out General Gérard for particular praise: 'I intended to give him the baton of a Marshal of the Empire. I regarded him as one of the hopes of France.'[8]

The Prussians have attracted more criticism than have the French for their conduct of the battle. 'Our generals are too much of the opinion that advancing is better than standing and firing. Each has its place', complained Colonel Clausewitz.[9]

Indeed, one of the most telling criticisms of the Prussians' tactics at the Battle of Ligny is that they squandered the strength of their troops. They used up their reserves too quickly. They hurled fresh units into costly offensives rather than conserving their fighting energies by placing them in defensive positions. Counter-attack has a vital role in the defence of a position. But the Prussians were undertaking too many counter-attacks. They were not conserving their energy and biding their time ready to deal a truly decisive counter-blow at an auspicious moment.

Blücher must take much of the brunt of this criticism. 'He was an old hussar who understood nothing of war beyond attacking', wrote one Russian officer who had known him in earlier campaigns. Blücher more than anyone else in the Prussian high command directed the battle operations during Ligny. Blücher galloped from unit to unit, exhorting them to fix bayonets and to charge. Blücher dreamt up grandiose ideas of launching offensives towards Fleurus and Napoleon's observation mill in order to defeat the French at Ligny and to capture Napoleon.

Blücher, in consequence, blindly dissipated the energy of his army, and when the end came the Prussians were exhausted and without reserves. In particular, Blücher sent a mass of five cavalry brigades to Wagnelée to protect and strengthen the west flank of his infantry counter-attacks. Too many squadrons were sent for this task and Lieutenant-Colonel Baron von Lützow's brigade was the only cavalry unit left in the centre to attempt to check the Imperial Guard's advance.

Blücher's disposition of his cavalry indicates that he expected Wellington to advance south from Quatre Bras and then to swing round eastwards to outflank Napoleon. Thus, Blücher positioned five cavalry brigades on his western flank to link up with Wellington and to add weight to Wellington's attack. Ligny was an event full of ironies. One irony was that both generals expected reinforcements from the west that never came. However, Napoleon was able to win the battle despite Ney's failure to arrive. Wellington's failure left Blücher's army dangerously unbalanced.

As Wellington said when asked about Blücher, 'he was a very fine fellow, and whenever there was any question of fighting, always ready and eager – if anything too eager.'[10]

Blücher had in him something of the Spanish fictional hero, Don Quixote. Blücher tilted wildly at the Naveau windmill in Fleurus with ferocious Prussian counter-attacks and ended up in the same predicament as his fictional counterpart: 'tumbling over and over in the plain, in every evil plight.'

Blücher fought the French as implacably as Don Quixote sought to rid the earth of the wicked giants. Both Blücher, and Cervantes' hero, were a little mad. Don Quixote imagined he was killing giants by sabering skins containing red wine. Blücher convinced himself that Napoleon had bribed servants to heat the floor of Blücher's room in order to burn his feet. Consequently, Blücher either sat with his legs in the air or leaped about on tip toe.

By charging at the head of his cavalry in the evening of Ligny and risking death or capture, Blücher put the outcome of the campaign in jeopardy. He might well, with Don Quixote, the 'knight of the lions', have confessed that 'my not acting with proper prudence has ruined me'. Blücher had charged at the head of his cavalry at the end of the Battle of Lützen in 1813 and had nearly been taken in 1814 at Brienne-le-Château.

But Blücher had a Sancho Panza in Gneisenau. While Blücher tilted at windmills, Gneisenau coolly summed up the situation and organised the Prussian army's retreat.

Blücher was a quixotic hero if ever there was one. This had drawbacks as well as advantages. For Blücher's fire-breathing character caused him to fight the Battle of Ligny in a foolish, slap-dash manner that did much to lose the fight.

Unlike the Duke of Wellington, the Prussian commander was not accustomed by character or training to fight a classic defensive battle. Blücher was trained as a hussar. Ligny was simply not a hussar's battle and could not be won using hussar tactics. The attritional Battle of Ligny was a foretaste of the 1914–18 War in which cavalry became obsolete and the big guns ruled the battlefield. 'The struggle was stubborn and bloody', wrote Gneisenau.[11] Ligny was a battle of firepower, particularly artillery firepower, and Napoleon, who had been trained as a gunner, employed his guns to perfection at Ligny. The French artillery pounded the Prussian units mercilessly.

Blücher's qualities as a leader of troops, and as an attacking general in battle, would have to wait until 18 June to be demonstrated to the full. On that historic day, as he urged his troops forward on the tough march to the field of Waterloo and as he directed the repeated onslaughts of the Prussian army on to the French battle line, Blücher would truly come into his own. The battle situation would fit the capabilities and style of the general. Similarly, Wellington was at his best on the defensive at Waterloo, after failing to shine in the early stages of the campaign.

Moreover, it was not simply Blücher's character which caused wasteful Prussian counter-attacks to be undertaken at Ligny. The character of Blücher's troops was a great factor. Two means of defence existed: shock power and firepower. Firepower necessitated bringing all available muskets to bear, and this meant fighting in line. The professional, disciplined and well-trained British troops fought in line two deep but the raw Prussian conscripts lacked the stern, impassive courage necessary to face a French column in line formation.

Hence the Prussian generals were forced to form their battalions in attack columns and to rely on shock power as opposed to defensive volley firing. Criticism of Blücher's extravagance must be tempered by an awareness of the limitations of the resources at his disposal.

The second criticism levelled at the Prussians is their choice of position. Wellington's criticism of the Prussian dispositions, massed columns on a faulty battleground and in full view and range of the French artillery, has been echoed by historians down through the ages. General Baron de Jomini condemned the position as 'detestable'.

Blücher's ADC, Count von Nostitz, throws light and not a little criticism on the choice of the Ligny position:

> Although in the headquarters the subject had been much discussed, and the danger of accepting battle in the position of Sombreffe had often been put forward by many persons, yet Generals von Gneisenau and von Grolmann adhered firmly to the idea. Count Groeben had carefully reconnoitred and surveyed the chosen battlefield, and had described in such lively colours its many advantages as to have given rise to an almost fanatical fondness for it, which the objections put forward by other members of the Headquarters, among them myself, could in no way modify.[12]

Blücher's position at Ligny was to an extent unsatisfactory. Firstly, it exposed the Prussian formations to French artillery fire. But historians have exaggerated this drawback of the battlefield. II Corps was in reserve along the Nivelles–Namur road and consequently was protected by the terrain in front. Some formations of III Corps were exposed but only I Corps occupied seriously exposed positions.

The second disadvantage was that the position was an extensive one, much longer than Wellington's position at Waterloo, for example. A seven-mile stretch of the snaking Ligny brook had to be defended. When the position had been chosen all four corps had been expected to be available for its defence. Bülow's failure to arrive with the IV Corps could not have been foreseen. If Bülow had been present, Blücher would have had ample forces to defend the long Ligny position and even to defeat Napoleon.

As it was, the position was too extensive for the three corps available. This criticism is excerbated by the fact that the whole of Thielmann's III Corps was tied down throughout the day by Grouchy's cavalrymen in the relatively quiet eastern sector of the battlefield. Some III Corps units did shift slightly to the west towards the close of the battle, but it was too little too late for III Corps to influence sufficiently the fight in the western sector of the field.

The choice of the Ligny position has also been criticised on the grounds that it was too close to the frontier to enable the entire Prussian army to be sure of gathering there before the French arrived in force to do battle. This exposed Blücher's army to the threat of being destroyed piecemeal.

In fact, the Prussians had little choice. The Ligny position was the best one available. The Prussians had to concentrate as far south as Sombreffe since they needed if possible to preserve communications with their ally the Duke of Wellington along the lateral Nivelles–Namur road, which traversed the north of the battlefield. The allies had agreed to unite in battle against Napoleon south of Brussels. The simple fact is that the Nivelles–Namur *chaussée* was the only lateral cobbled road, between the two allies, south of Brussels. The marshy Lasne valley made any cross-country march to the north of this road very difficult and time consuming, as the Prussians found on 18 June. Furthermore, to fight further north would have necessitated the abandonment of the easy supply link to Prussia along the Rivers Sambre and Meuse from Charleroi to Namur to Liège.

In short, Blücher had to concentrate at Sombreffe. It was not that Blücher concentrated too far south, rather the Franco-Belgian border was too far north. Recognising this, the allies transferred the territory around Beaumont from France to Belgium in the 1815 Peace Treaties after Waterloo. This lessened the possibilities of another French invasion surprising the defending armies.

Moreover, the Ligny position did have certain strengths: it was defended by a brook, which while not impassible was certainly substantial, and a shallow valley along which lay numerous easily defendable villages. The Italian historian Alberto Pollio correctly asserted that 'in terms of width and of depth of water, this ditch [of the Ligny brook] was negligible or nearly so, but its deep bed, its steep banks and the marshy bottom of the whole of the little valley made for true difficulties in crossing it.'[13]

Lieutenant-General Pierre Berthezène, an eyewitness of the battle, averred that 'this position occupied by the Prussian army was naturally strong', and recalled that he could see very strong Prussian batteries southwest of Ligny and powerful Prussian infantry reserves dominating the villages along the Ligny brook.[14]

The Prussians had not taken the trouble to fortify their chosen position previous to the outbreak of hostilities. Entrenchments and earth works would have made it an even more formidable battlefield. Engineers were, however, in short supply in Blücher's army. Each corps was in theory entitled to two engineer companies but possessed only one.[15] Moreover, fortifications would have revealed to Napoleon where the Prussians intended to fight. A fortified position could always be outflanked.

Even so, the French incurred over 10,000 casualties in clearing the Ligny position, and Napoleon's army was so exhausted it was unable to pursue Blücher until the next morning.

The position, moreover, neutralised the advantages the French possessed in their mounted arm. The French cavalry was better equipped, better mounted, better trained, better led and better organised than that of the Prussians. All of Blücher's cavalry was allocated to individual corps. Consequently, the Prussian cavalry was hampered and tied to supporting the infantry. Unlike the French, the Prussians possessed no large mass of heavy reserve cavalry to achieve a breakthrough nor did they have a celebrated and skilled cavalry general such as Seydlitz of the Seven Years' War. These deficiencies in Blücher's cavalry were demonstrated to the full in the 1815 campaign. The cavalry was the feeblest arm in the Prussian army and the brunt of the fighting in every battle fell overwhelmingly on the infantry as a result.

Fortunately for Blücher, his choice of battle position ensured the magnificent French cavalry would not play as great a role as they usually did. Only infantry could do battle in the numerous villages along the Ligny brook. The obstacles hindering cavalry charges were great and complex. The French cavalry at Ligny was limited to scouting on the west flank and tying down III Corps on the east flank (more by their presence and manoeuvres than by fighting). The only other use of French cavalry at Ligny was in supporting the Guard attack in the evening. Even then, the darkness and confusion, the uneven terrain and the cramped nature of the fighting ensured only relatively small scale charges could be executed. No massed onslaughts on the scale of Joachim Murat at Eylau or of Auguste Caulaincourt at Borodino occurred at Ligny.

Notwithstanding the disadvantageous tactics of the Prussian army and its failure fully to co-ordinate the efforts of the three arms, the troops behaved very well in battle. 'My troops fought like lions', Blücher wrote to his wife after Ligny. Gneisenau wrote of Ligny that 'the battle was lost, but not our honour. Our soldiers had fought with a bravery which equalled every expectation; their fortitude remained unshaken, because every one retained his confidence in his own strength.'[16] Emphasising the resilience of the Prussian troops who, defeated at Ligny, gained complete victory at Waterloo just two days later, Gneisenau added: 'Honour be to troops capable of such firmness and valour!'[17]

Some nine thousand men deserted during the night after Ligny. They fled to Liège and Aix-la-Chapelle, spreading wild rumours that the French were within a mile of Brussels, that their light troops had already entered the suburbs, that all was lost. But these deserters were mostly from areas recently annexed to Prussia. The Prussian army was composed largely of young and inexperienced troops; a defeat was bound to produce some desertion. It is surprising that more Prussian soldiers did not desert after Ligny. In general, Prussian morale remained high, fired as the troops were by a determination to avenge the defeat of Ligny. This fierce determination is reflected in General von Ziethen's orders to I Corps on the morning of the Battle of Waterloo:

'I will count it as one of the luckiest days of my life if the 18th of June shows the same Prussian bravery as the 16th, but greater success.'[18]

One of the most intriguing questions of the campaign is at what stage the Prussians decided to fight at Ligny. From the start, the Prussian headquarters favoured the Ligny position, for reasons already discussed. But in order to fight a full-scale battle there rather than a mere delaying action, Blücher had to have sufficient troops. Originally, Blücher had been confident his army alone could defend the position and had informed Müffling on 15 June that he would give battle there the following day. But after learning of the inability of IV Corps to participate in the battle, Blücher was more dependent on Wellington. 'Hence it was', wrote William Siborne, 'that Blücher was led to place more reliance upon direct support from Wellington.'[19]

Perhaps without the Duke's assurances of support, Blücher would have fought at Ligny anyway but it would probably have been a purely defensive battle, perhaps a mere delaying action to cover an allied retreat to a safer, shared position further north. Wellington's assurances led the Prussians to dream of a joint offensive and this certainly led them to undertake their exhausting onslaughts in the Wagnelée–St Amand sector where Wellington's arrival was expected. It was Wellington's assurances of support, made at the Bussy mill conference, that caused the Prussian headquarters to take the formal decision to give battle at Ligny.[20]

German and British historians have argued bitterly over Wellington's role in this decision. However, it is undeniable that Wellington gave the Prussians over-optimistic information as to when his army would be concentrated and ready to support them at Ligny. In a letter despatched at 11.00 pm on 15 June, Müffling had assured the Prussians that Wellington promised he would 'be in the neighbourhood of Nivelles tomorrow to support your Highness [Prince

Blücher]; or should the enemy have already attacked your Highness, to fall on his flank or on his rear.'[21]

Later, at 10.30 am on 16 June Wellington wrote a letter to Blücher that gave incorrect positions of his units and again grossly underestimated the time they needed to reach Quatre Bras. A couple of hours later the Duke rode to Ligny and conferred with Blücher at Bussy mill. This conference merely strengthened the Prussian belief that support from Wellington would soon be forthcoming.

Gneisenau's biographer, Hans Delbrück, asserted that Wellington deliberately underestimated the time required to concentrate his army at Quatre Bras so as to encourage the Prussians to fight the bulk of Napoleon's army at Ligny. Thus, Delbrück considered, Wellington's aim was to use the Prussians to cover the concentration of his own army.

Delbrück's theory is unjustifiable. Wellington did not mislead the Prussians intentionally; he himself was given false information by his staff.[22] This episode does not do honour to the staff officers, nor to Wellington who relied unhesitatingly on their statements in spite of complaining to Lord Stewart that 'I have ... a very inexperienced Staff.'[23]

But Delbrück was wrong to aver that Wellington deliberately used Blücher to enable himself to concentrate in safety. Delbrück has simply put on paper what Gneisenau came, incorrectly yet understandably, to suspect when Wellington failed to arrive at Ligny.

The German historian Carl von Ollech is more balanced than Delbrück. Ollech concluded that Blücher accepted battle at Ligny with only three-quarters of his army in order to offer his friend Wellington a chance to complete his concentration at Quatre Bras free from the brunt of Napoleon's offensive. This, in turn, would permit the Duke to march to support Blücher at Ligny. Indeed, Baron Müffling noted that:

'Blücher resolved ... to give battle in a position which offered him only a few advantages.... It was only at this moment that Blücher decided to give battle because it was obvious that if he did not do so, the English army would be crushed.'[24]

This was totally in keeping with Blücher's generous and lion-hearted character. Napoleon had totally outwitted and surprised Wellington with his sudden invasion on 15 June. Wellington's paucity of reliable intelligence and his own errors delayed his army's concentration. This nearly had fatal results. But by fighting at Ligny, Blücher saved Wellington's units from being overrun piecemeal.

So Blücher's intention in giving battle at Ligny was to act as a shield. Behind this shield Wellington, in safety, would muster his units into a spear at Quatre Bras. This spear he would then hurl into the flank of the French army at Ligny.

As Blücher had intended, the Battle of Ligny did indeed cover the

The letter which Wellington wrote to Blücher at 10.30 am on 16 June from the heights north of Frasnes. Note how the two allies had to communicate in the language of their foe. Note, too, that the Duke first dated the letter 15 June, then corrected this to 16.

In the letter, Wellington incorrectly describes the dispositions of his army. For instance, he writes that the English Cavalry will be at Nivelles at noon. In fact, at that hour it would be at Enghien, 15 miles northwest of Nivelles. The Prussians accepted battle at Ligny under the false impression that Wellington's army would shortly be massed at Quatre Bras and launching an offensive in their support.

concentration of Wellington's army. But the 'spear' never arrived to save the Prussian army as Wellington had indicated it would. Thus Blücher was left alone to face the brunt of Napoleon's thunderbolts. The 'shield' would be badly dented as a consequence.

The Battle of Ligny is one of the great might-have-beens of history. As Napoleon boasted before the action commenced, 'it is possible that in three hours the issue of the war will be decided. If Ney carries out my orders well, not a single gun of the Prussian army will escape; it is going utterly to be crushed.'[25]

Indeed, if d'Erlon's corps had come up along the Nivelles–Namur road, then a large portion of the Prussian I and II Corps would have been outflanked by d'Erlon, cut off from the Prussian III Corps by the Imperial Guard's storming of the village of Ligny and eventually annihilated or forced into surrender. The rest of the Prussian army would have speedily retired from Belgium, leaving the Duke of Wellington facing the full weight of Napoleon's entire army.

Consequently, with Wellington crushed or having scampered by sea to England, Napoleon would be left with Belgium in his hands. The allies may well have sued for peace, and even if they had fought on, it is possible that Napoleon would have gone on to defeat the Austrians and Russians.

Similar wide-ranging results might have come about simply with the capture of Blücher in the evening of Ligny as he lay unrecognised beneath his dead horse in the midst of a French cavalry charge. So much depended on so little, for Blücher was instrumental in maintaining Prussian morale and his capture would have had a devastating effect.

Truly, the Battle of Ligny could have been a decisive French victory with tremendous implications for the fate of the world.

Historical speculation is fascinating but does not in the slightest alter the cold facts of the past. Victory though Ligny was for the French, Napoleon did not gain there the overwhelming and lasting outcome he had hoped for. Although the Guard broke into the Prussian position at Ligny village, it was halted by the Prussian rearguard line on the battlefield. The Prussians were hurled back but not crushed; they were defeated but their morale remained intact.

Looking back on the campaign, one French colonel wrote that 'the sun of the 16th June shone on a glorious day. But it was like one of those hopeful moments of well-being which fool an invalid on his death bed, the last light of a torch about to go out.'[26] A percipient modern historian, Patrick Maes, has termed Ligny 'the twilight of the eagle.'

The symmetry of the Waterloo campaign is striking. Two sets of 'double-battles' were fought: Ligny–Quatre Bras on 16 June and Waterloo–Wavre on the 18th. In the first, Napoleon defeated Blücher and Wellington; in the second, they beat him. Napoleon seized the strategic initiative with his sudden invasion of 15 June; on the 17th he lost it with Blücher making arrangements to link up with Wellington.

Wellington and Blücher's armies had a combined total of 210,000 men. Napoleon's Army of the North was but 124,000. Thus the allies could absorb casualties and setbacks better than could the French. The vast allied numerical superiority was bound to tell in the long run, unless Napoleon had prolonged, into 17 and 18 June, the brilliance and unremitting activity of the opening of the campaign. Once the allies recovered their balance and Napoleon relaxed his vigilance, the writing was on the wall. After Blücher joined Wellington in force at Waterloo, the French never stood a chance.[27] The mistakes and tardiness committed during the first half of the campaign were primarily those of the allies. Those of the second half were mostly Napoleon's.

Napoleon was a lucky general. Like the German Field Marshal Rommel, he dared to take risks and usually he won. In 1815, from the moment he departed from Elba, Napoleon took appalling risks. He landed in France with just 1000 troops yet regained the country. He invaded Belgium against enemies nearly double the size of his own army yet won the first rounds. Nonetheless, Napoleon could not afford to lose even once and sooner or later he was bound to lose one of his terrifying gambles against the odds. With each throw of the dice, the stakes had become higher and with the final gamble, at Waterloo, Napoleon lost all – his throne, his empire, his ambitions, his freedom and nearly his life.

British historians often assert that Wellington was the victor of Waterloo. He was not. 'The victory', wrote the balanced Italian historian Alberto Pollio, 'was neither English nor Prussian; it was that of the allies.'[28] Waterloo was won by the co-operation of Blücher with Wellington; the victors were both Blücher and Wellington, and not one general alone. 'I should not do justice to my own feelings,' Wellington himself admitted, 'or to Marshal Blücher and the Prussian army, if I did not attribute the successful result of this arduous day to the cordial and timely assistance I received from them.'[29]

Blücher saved Wellington at Waterloo from the defeat from which Wellington had been unable to rescue Blücher at Ligny. Throughout the campaign, Blücher's energy, selflessness and burning determination to defeat Napoleon stand out supreme. Blücher laid the foundations of victory in the 1815 campaign.

Firstly, he tied down Napoleon's main battle strength at Ligny on 16 June and thus afforded the allies time to concentrate their armies and to win the strategic initiative. 'Blücher, although beaten, had attained his goal', wrote the German historian Major Karl von Damitz. 'He had gained a day.'[30] Blücher at Ligny fatally blunted and delayed Napoleon's thrust to Brussels. For this reason, one commentator has asserted that 'the Battle of Ligny was a strategic defeat [for the French].' Indeed, Ligny made Waterloo possible.[31]

Secondly, Blücher rallied his army on 17 June at Wavre and pressured Gneisenau into agreeing that the Prussians join Wellington at Waterloo. Wellington himself called the Prussian retreat to Wavre and the decision to remain in the campaign, as opposed to retiring to Prussia, 'the decisive moment of the century.'[32]

Finally, on 18 June Blücher achieved the uniting of the two allied armies, at Waterloo, which both allies had agreed back in May 1815 was the key to victory. The Battle of Waterloo was primarily Wellington's action in that he provided the stubborn defence against which the main French efforts were expended. But the Waterloo campaign as a whole was primarily Blücher's campaign, in which Blücher's determination and loyalty paved the way to victory.

Notes

1. Ropes, *The Campaign of Waterloo*, p.173
2. Berton, *Précis historique, militaire et critique des batailles de Fleurus et de Waterloo*, p.21
3. Similarly, in 1806 Napoleon had been astounded to learn that Marshal Davout had defeated the bulk of the Prussian army at Auerstädt while he himself had crushed a mere detachment at Jena.
4. Montgomery, *Memoirs*, p.111
5. Houssaye, *Waterloo 1815*, p.174
6. Bonaparte, *Napoleon's Memoirs*, p.545
7. Jones, *The Battle of Waterloo*, p.225
8. Bonaparte, *Napoleon's Memoirs*, p.512
9. Clausewitz, quoted in Chalfont, *Waterloo: Battle of Three Armies*, p.64
10. Stanhope, *Conversations with the Duke of Wellington*, p.120
11. Delbrück, *Das Leben des Feldmarschalls Grafen Neithardt von Gneisenau*, v.2, p.218
12. James, *The Campaign of 1815*, p.149. Count Groeben was a major of the Staff. See also Damitz, *Histoire de la Campagne de 1815*, v.1, pp.87–8.
13. Pollio, *Waterloo (1815) avec de nouveaux documents*, p.201
14. Berthezène, *Souvenirs militaires*, v.2, pp.362–3
15. James, *op. cit.*, p.328
16. Jones, *op. cit.*, p.322
17. *Ibid*, p.326
18. Chalfont, *op. cit.*, p.136
19. Siborne, *History of the Waterloo Campaign*, p.119
20. See Damitz, *op. cit.*, v.1, p.87. See also the testimony of Captain von Reuter, Gneisenau and Müffling quoted in chapter 4 (The Meeting at Bussy Windmill and Final Preparations).
21. Delbrück, *op. cit.*, v.2, pp.170–1
22. Wellington greatly missed his old and trusted Quartermaster-General, Sir George Murray. After the campaign, Wellington wrote to him that 'I regretted much that you went to America at the moment you did ... I regretted it still more since.' It is often forgotten how much famous generals owe to their senior staff officer. Field Marshal Montgomery owed a deep debt to his Chief of Staff, de Guingand. In the 1815 Campaign, Napoleon no longer had the reliable Marshal Berthier as Chief of Staff. Wellington no longer had Murray as Quartermaster-General. As a consequence, both commanders committed errors that might otherwise have been avoided. Only Blücher still had his former right-hand man, General Gneisenau.
23. Longford, *Wellington: The Years of the Sword*, p.402
24. Müffling's notes, quoted in de Bas, *La Campagne de 1815 aux Pays-Bas*, v.1, p.476
25. Bonaparte, *Napoleon's Memoirs*, p.510

26. Fantin des Odoards, *Journal du général Fantin des Odoards*, p.429

27. Jac Weller has rightly pointed out the similarities of the 1815 campaign with the Battle of the Bulge in 1944. The French in 1815 and the Germans in 1944 both achieved initial surprise and advanced speedily. But once the usual frictions of war slowed down their initial advance and once their opponents rushed forces to the area, their eventual repulse was inevitable. An onslaught by a fixed number of troops on an unconcentrated but numerically superior enemy needs to win in a lightning blow. When, on the contrary, the onslaught is made by an initial force due to be reinforced later, the *defenders* have to win in a lightning counter-attack before the attackers achieve numerical superiority. A good example is the Normandy invasion of June 1944.

28. Pollio, *op. cit.*, p.512

29. Booth, *The Battle of Waterloo by a near observer*, p. 165

30. Damitz, *op. cit.*, v.1, p.147

31. Navez, *Les Quatre Bras, Ligny, Waterloo et Wavre*, p.135. Napoleon himself connected Ligny with Waterloo. At Philippeville on 19 June, he exclaimed: 'I thought I was striking a great blow [in Belgium] but I was mistaken. From the sublime [Ligny] to the ridiculous [Waterloo] is but one step.' (Stanhope, *op. cit.*, pp.91 and 150)

32. Longford, *op. cit.*, p.436

11

LOSSES AT LIGNY

Grand totals of troops on battlefield:

Prussians — 83,000 and 224 guns

French   — 63,000 and 230 guns

Losses (killed, wounded and missing):

Prussians — 20,000–25,000, including 8000–10,000 deserters, and 22 guns (24–30% of men, 10% of guns)

French   — 10,000–12,000 (16–19% of men)

NOTE: Percentages to nearest per cent.

It is impossible to gauge precisely the losses suffered by either side. Charles Oman's computations from lists of French officer casualties are the best attempt for the French side (*English Historical Review*, Oct. 1904 and Jan. 1906). Plotho's *Der Krieg des verbundeten Europa gegen Frankreich im Jahre 1815* is invaluable for the Prussian casualties, as is de Bas, *La Campagne de 1815 aux Pays-Bas*, v.3, pp.220–1.

The French General Pierre Berthezène, a divisional commander at the battle, revisited the field of combat some time later accompanied by a comrade. Local inhabitants informed him that they returned to the area after the battle and helped to bury the dead. They asserted that the Prussian dead were more numerous than the French, and assumed the French had taken many of their dead away.[1]

The disparity in numbers was due, in fact, to the French artillery taking heavy toll of the Prussian forces massed in column on the exposed slopes north of the Ligny brook. As a skilled gunner, General Drouot of the Guard, declared, 'I saw with pleasure this cannonade prolonged to our advantage. The troops destined to protect our batteries being at a distance, and masked by the sinuosities of the ground, experienced no injury. Those of the enemy, on the contrary, being placed in masses, in the form of an amphitheatre, behind their batteries, suffered very great losses.'[2]

The two foes' casualties inflicted by hand-to-hand combat inside the villages appear to have been approximately equal.

The losses at Ligny fell unequally on the various units engaged. In the French army, Girard's unfortunate division lost nearly fifty per cent of its complement. III and IV Corps each lost over twenty per cent of their men. But the other French units – the Guard and the three cavalry corps – lost between just five and twelve per cent of their strength.

Of Blücher's army, relatively few casualties were suffered by Thielmann's III Corps. The infantry brigades of II Corps each lost between twenty and twenty-five per cent, except 7th brigade which lost just four per cent of its men. But the brunt of the battle fell on Ziethen's I Corps. The Prussian infantry formations which suffered most severely were 2nd, 3rd and 4th brigades. The last mentioned lost more than fifty per cent of its original strength. The other infantry unit of I Corps, 1st brigade, also lost heavily – about twenty-seven per cent of its complement.

The number of Prussian guns captured is in dispute. General Drouot remarked on 24 June 1815 that 'I do not know what other trophies distinguished this great day; but those which I saw were several colours, and twenty-four pieces of cannon, collected on the same spot.'[3] Colonel Pétiet of the French staff asserted that Napoleon captured 'twenty odd' guns.[4] Gneisenau wrote in the Prussian Official Account that 'in consequence of the sudden irruption of the enemy's cavalry, several of our cannon, in their precipitate retreat, had taken directions which had led them to defiles, in which they necessarily fell into disorder; in this manner fifteen pieces fell into the hands of the enemy.'[5]

From the detailed analyses by the historians August Wagner, William Siborne and Bruno von Treuenfeld, it appears that fifteen guns were captured, and one then recaptured, on 16 June, making a final total of fourteen. Eight others fell into the hands of French cavalry the following morning in direct consequence of the Battle of Ligny.[6] This adds up to twenty-two.[7] The table below sets out these statistics.

Prussian Guns Lost Owing to Blücher's Defeat at Ligny

Battery	Parent corps	Battery commander	No. of lost guns
12-pdr Ft Bty no. 6	I	Captn Reuter	1
6-pdr Ft Bty no. 3	I	1st Lt Neander	1
6-pdr Ft Bty no. 7	I	Captn Schaale	1
12-pdr Ft Bty no. 4	II	Captn Meyer	2
12-pdr Ft Bty no. 8	II	Captn Junghans	3
6-pdr Ft Bty no. 12	II	Captn Bülly	1
Horse Battery no. 14	II	Captn Fritze	8
Horse Battery no. 19	III	1st Lt Dellen	5
		Total lost guns	22

Investigation into these losses reveals much recklessness and even incompetence in the handling of the Prussian artillery. For example, in the evening of 16 June, General Thielmann of III Corps ordered the Horse Battery no. 19 to advance with Count Lottum's cavalry brigade along the Fleurus road on to the French side of the valley. The purpose of this move was to relieve pressure on I and II Corps to the west. However, the artillery had no need to advance with the cavalry brigade, as the French were already in range. This was demonstrated just before the Prussian advance along the Fleurus road when the Horse Battery no. 19 fired a few rounds and incoming fire disabled one of its guns. The remaining seven guns accompanied the cavalry brigade in its foolhardy advance to an exposed position south of the Ligny brook. French dragoons soon captured five pieces. Of the battery, only two guns, posted on the road itself, escaped.

Earlier in the day, a similar rash move had been made by the Horse Battery no. 14 of II Corps. The battery crossed Ligny brook to take post on the hostile side of the valley. Terribly exposed to French fire, it soon lost nineteen gunners and fifty-three horses. Towards the end of the battle, the battery exhausted its ammunition and left the field to search for a resupply. Early on the following morning the battery was driving up and down the main road between Sombreffe and Namur, uncertain of the location of its parent corps. The battery commander disobeyed a strict order from General Thielmann to accompany the III Corps to Gembloux. Pursuing French hussars fell on the battery and seized all eight guns.

These episodes do not do credit to Blücher's artillery. The remaining lost guns were captured when the French broke into the Prussian battleline at Ligny village in the evening. Siborne records, for instance, that the 6-pounder Foot Battery no. 3 lost a gun when overtaken between Bussy mill and Brye.

French cavalry also seized two guns of the 6-pounder Foot Battery no. 12 posted at the outskirts of Sombreffe. Treuenfeld considers that neither of these two guns was recaptured. But Wagner disagrees. So does Siborne, who states that a Prussian infantry counter-attack recaptured one. Several other guns were saved only by the narrowest margins in the midst of French cavalry charges.

In short, the Prussian loss of guns is attributable to two factors: firstly, unavoidable confusion and risk in the aftermath of the French seizure of Ligny village and secondly, senseless risk and incompetent handling. The second factor accounted for thirteen of the twenty-two captured guns. This is a sobering thought.

Eyewitnesses on both sides agree that few prisoners were taken. 'Since no quarter was given on either side we were not troubled with many prisoners', wrote Henri Nieman of the Prussian 6th Uhlans.[8] The French General Berthezène mentioned that few troops were captured from the Prussians.[9]

Although Captain François asserted that his French 30th Infantry regiment seized 500 Prussian captives at Ligny village, he may naturally have been prone to exaggeration.[10] Indeed, Gneisenau asserted that 'the enemy . . . took from us no prisoners, except a part of our wounded.'[11] Colonel Pétiet of the French staff agreed with Gneisenau: 'we collected a great many wounded, but these were the only prisoners that fell into our hands.'[12]

The losses at Quatre Bras were approximately 9000, with Wellington and Ney suffering nearly equal numbers of casualties. A British staff officer, Lieutenant Basil Jackson, wrote that 'the dead lay in every attitude, but generally on their backs, with placid countenances, evincing little trace of suffering in their last moments.'[13] The exceptionally tall standing corn concealed many of the dead and prevented rescuers from finding some of the wounded until too late.[14]

A French infantry lieutenant who passed over the field of Quatre Bras noted the square formation of a Highland regiment etched on to the ground by the bloodied ranks of bodies.[15] The Scots dead were also remarked upon by an imperial guardsman. He related how the flash floods of 17 June swept away the kilted corpses and deposited them at the edge of Bossu wood. There, immersed in water-filled ditches, lay untidy, scarlet heaps of dead.[16]

Count Fleury de Chaboulon, who was attached to Napoleon's headquarters, vividly described the horror of the battlefields after the strife:

> The ferocity with which men fought this day, made even those most accustomed to contemplating calmly the horrors of war tremble. The smoking ruins of Ligny and St Amand were cluttered with the dead and dying, the Ligny brook resembled a river of blood, in which corpses were floating. At Quatre Bras, the same sight! The hollow lane, which bordered the wood, had disappeared under the bloody corpses of the brave Scots and of our cuirassiers.[17]

On 16 June, Lieutenant Jacques Martin of d'Erlon's I Corps missed the fighting but not the sight of the dead:

> But although we had not been engaged, we had seen the battlefields and their approaches at close quarters. It was an unforgettable spectacle. When advancing towards St Amand . . . we found the track covered with carts taking away immense numbers of wounded. More men were groaning on the battlefield. What a horrible sight! I assure you that it takes as much courage to march coolly towards the enemy past dead and dying men as to attack a battery head on. They were certainly not the first casualties that I had seen. But I do not believe it possible without deep feeling to cross such a mass of men, so full of life a moment before, now stained with blood, mutilated in every way, heaped on top of each other and with death and its agonies etched on their faces.[18]

Local Belgian peasants made small fortunes in looting the dead. Soon the stench of decomposition was unbearable. The corpses were hurriedly buried in mass

British Guards burying their slain officers at Quatre Bras

graves; some may have been burned. In a letter dated 16 July 1815, a German officer added that: 'I have visited the field of battle [of Ligny]. The sleep of the dead is sound. On the spot where this day [last] month thousands thronged and fought, where thousands sank and bled, and groaned and died, there is now not a living soul, and over all hovers the stillness of the grave.'[19]

Notes

1. Berthezène, *Souvenirs militaires*, v.2, p.367
2. Jones, *The Battle of Waterloo*, p.224
3. *Ibid*, p.225
4. Pétiet, *Souvenirs Militaires*, p.200
5. Booth, *The Battle of Waterloo by a near observer*, p.177
6. Treuenfeld says six but Siborne and Houssaye say eight. Pajol, the commander of the French cavalry in question, reported to Marshal Grouchy that he had seized eight guns.
7. Bonaparte, *Napoleon's Memoirs*, claims forty Prussian guns were captured. This is either exaggeration or confusion between fourteen and forty. The French words for these numbers are 'quartorze' and 'quarante' respectively. Gneisenau's statement that fifteen guns were lost apparently forgets one was recaptured. Drouot seems to have muddled the total of fourteen at the end of 16 June with the total of twenty-two by the end of the next day, to gain a figure of twenty-four. This confusion is perfectly possible given that Drouot made his statement after a hectic campaign and the trauma of utter defeat.
8. *English Historical Review* (July 1888), p.542
9. Berthezène, *op. cit.*, v.2, p.366

10. François, *Journal du Capitaine François*, v.2, p.881
11. Jones, *op. cit.*, p.322
12. Pétiet, *op. cit.*, p.200
13. Jackson, *Notes and Reminiscences of a staff officer*, pp.27–8
14. Sabine, *Letters of Col. Sir Augustus Frazer*, p.540
15. Martin, *Souvenirs d'un ex-officier*, pp.279–80
16. Barral, *L'Epopée de Waterloo*, p.164
17. De Chaboulon, *Mémoires pour servir à l'histoire*, p.168
18. Martin, *op. cit.*, p.277
19. Jones, *op. cit.*, pp.62–3

12

THE GARRISON OF LIGNY VILLAGE: A CASE STUDY

The village of Ligny was the decisive point of the thunderous battle of 16 June 1815. Napoleon 'considered Ligny to be the key of the enemy position', wrote Brigadier-General Berton, a veteran of the battle.[1]

A review of the Prussian defence of the village yields interesting results. Below is a table of Prussian battalions which fought at the village, specifying the battle phase in which they entered Ligny and the infantry brigade to which they belonged. Included in the table are details of French forces engaged in attacking the village.

This table was compiled by analysing the historian Siborne's detailed description of the battle, which was based on Damitz's history and on information supplied by the Prussian Minister of War and the Prussian General Staff in Berlin. The detailed German work of Treuenfeld, which corrects some errors made by Siborne, was also consulted.

Notable conclusions can be drawn from this table. First, Napoleon's strategy, of attacking the villages along the Ligny brook in order to suck the Prussian reserves into the front line and to wear them down in a battle of attrition, was successful. The initial Prussian garrison of Ligny was 4.5 battalions. The garrison when the French Guard attacked in the evening was 16.5 battalions. A grand total of 21.5 battalions could claim to have fought at the village of Ligny – five battalions having been so exhausted by the fight as to necessitate their being relieved before the French Guard attacked. Nine battalions were sucked into Ligny village from the Prussian reserves of II Corps. In other words, a full twenty-five per cent of II Corps' infantry was absorbed by the fight at Ligny alone.

Evident, too, is that Prussian reinforcements entered Ligny in response to the pressure exerted by the French attackers: when the French sent in fresh units, the Prussians fed in more of their battalions to redress the balance.

One final conclusion to emerge is that in the course of the battle, the Prussian infantry brigades became split up. The only brigade to have all its units in the village was 4th brigade. All the rest possessed other battalions which were

Units Which Entered Ligny Village: A Chronological Table

Battalion INITIAL GARRISON	Brigade	French forces
1/19	4 Bde	
3/19	4 Bde	
2/4 W.L.	4 Bde	
3/4 W.L.	4 Bde	
2nd and 4th companies, Silesian jägers	3 Bde	
PHASE 1		
2/19	4 Bde	One infantry division of Gérard's
1/4 W.L.	4 Bde	IV Corps commences the attack
PHASE 2		
1/7	3 Bde	One infantry brigade of Gérard's
2/7	3 Bde	IV Corps joins the attack
1/3 W.L.	3 Bde	
3/3 W.L.	3 Bde	
3/7	3 Bde	
3/29	3 Bde	
PHASE 3		
2/1 E.L.	6 Bde	Another infantry brigade of Gérard's
1/9	6 Bde	IV Corps joins the attack
2/9	6 Bde	
1/1 E.L.	6 Bde	
3/1 E.L.	6 Bde	
1/21	8 Bde	
2/21	8 Bde	
1/23	8 Bde	
2/3 E.L.	8 Bde	
PHASE 4		
		Five infantry regiments of the Imperial Guard, supported by heavy cavalry and massed artillery, break through the Prussian line at Ligny village. All Prussian battalions evacuate Ligny.

NOTES: (1) Approximate strengths per Prussian battalion: 730 men.
(2) All Prussian battalions entering Ligny in phase 3 are from II Corps; all other Prussian battalions belong to I Corps.
(3) In phase 3, all battalions of the Prussian 4th brigade except 3/4 W.L. are relieved and retire from Ligny village into reserve.

KEY: W.L. = Westphalian Landwehr   E.L. = Elbe Landwehr
1/19 = 1st battalion of the 19th Regiment
1/1 E.L. = 1st battalion of the 1st Elbe Landwehr

fighting elsewhere on the battlefield, mostly in the St Amand–La Haye–Wagnelée sector.

This would have made it difficult for the brigade commander to control all his forces, and this is particularly relevant for the period after the French Imperial Guard broke into the Prussian battle line. With the Prussian brigades already split up, the problem of rallying and sorting out the Prussian battalions was formidable.

The table indicates that even regiments were split up. Two battalions of the 9th Regiment, for example, fought at Ligny while the remaining battalion was at La Haye. In fact, the formations became so intermingled that it was impossible for the corps commanders to control their units. Thus General Ziethen came to command all the troops, both I and II Corps men, in the Wagnelée–St Amand sector, while General Pirch commanded those in the Ligny area.[2]

In this perspective, the confusion and disorder prevalent in the Prussian army at the close of 16 June is not at all surprising. What is surprising is that the army managed to reorganise itself so soon and well, and that only about 9000 troops took the opportunity to desert. The high morale of the greater part of Blücher's army enabled it to survive the traumas of defeat, to remain intact as a fighting force and to reorganise back into an army. The Prussian staff worked hard and competently in sorting out the chaos after Ligny.

Attempts can be made to work out the respective strengths of the Prussian defenders and French attackers at Ligny village throughout the day. These attempts remain but rough estimates owing to the impossibility of gauging accurately the mounting casualties suffered.

When such estimates are plotted on a graph they indicate that the Prussians had a considerable numerical superiority at the village in spite of the fact that they were defending, not attacking, the place. This would suggest that the Prussians sent too many fresh battalions too quickly to Ligny. By regulating a more gradual flow of fresh battalions into the village, the Prussians would have had some intact units at hand to throw against the Imperial Guard attack in the evening.

For the intervention of the Guard was crucial not only in the battle as a whole but also in the local combat at Ligny village. The fresh reinforcements of the veteran guard, backed up by numerous heavy cavalry and a formidable artillery, swung the numerical balance sharply in favour of the French.

In itself, this would be sufficient to explain the French storming of Ligny. But the French appear to have enjoyed not just the advantage of numbers but also that of surprise. Not content with merely battering their way through Ligny village, the French encircled it. In the Prussian Official Account, Gneisenau wrote:

> The evening was already much advanced, and the combat about Ligny continued with the same fury, and the same equality of success. We invoked, but

Troops at Ligny Village

	French	Prussians	Prussian numerical superiority
Phase 1	4700	5100	400
Phase 2	6700	9300	2600
Phase 3	8700	12600	3900
Phase 4	17600	12600	−5000

Note: French strength in phase 4 includes 4100 cavalry

NOTE: Strengths are approximate and are to the nearest hundred. No possibility exists of calculating the mounting casualties suffered by each side throughout the combat. The casualties would have been approximately equal on the two sides. This table therefore takes no account of casualties.

Unfortunately, the data available from an analysis of the historical records do not allow a more sensitive timescale than the four phases to be used. A more detailed timescale might well indicate that on occasions the French gained a short-lived numerical superiority by sending in large reinforcements at the beginning of a phase, thus triggering even larger Prussian reinforcements to enter the village.

Nevertheless, the general trend would still be that the Prussians enjoyed numerical superiority until phase four.

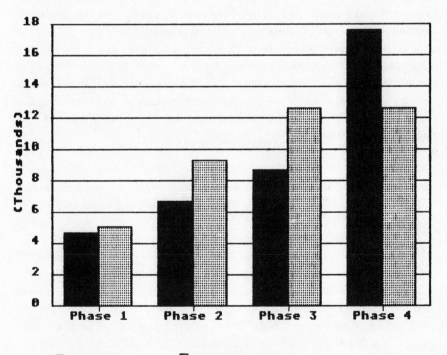

 French   Prussians

in vain, the arrival of those succours [Wellington and the Prussian IV Corps] which were so necessary. The danger became every hour more and more urgent; all the divisions were engaged, or had already been so, and there was not any corps at hand to support them.

Suddenly a division of the enemy's infantry, which, by favour of the night, had made a circuit round the village without being observed, at the same time that some regiments of *Cuirassiers* had forced the passage on the other side, took, in the rear, the main body of our army, which was posted behind the houses. This surprise on the part of the enemy was decisive, especially at the moment when our cavalry, also posted on a height behind the village, was repulsed by the enemy's cavalry in repeated attacks.

Our infantry, posted behind Ligny, though forced to retreat, did not suffer itself to be discouraged, either by being surprised by the enemy in the darkness, a circumstance which exaggerates in the mind of men the dangers to which they find themselves exposed, or, by the idea of seeing themselves surrounded on all sides. Formed in masses, our infantry coolly repulsed all the attacks of the cavalry, and retreated in good order upon the heights.[3]

In short, Napoleon won the Battle of Ligny in spite of fighting against superior numbers. He won by imposing his will on the enemy and by making the enemy react and conform to French moves. Napoleon wore down the Prussian army, exhausted its strength and made it use up its reserves.

Finally, Napoleon broke into the weary Prussian battle line at the decisive point of Ligny village with strong, fresh, crack reserve forces of his own. 'Success in war depends on *coup d'oeil*, and on sensing the pyschological moment in battle', he declared.[4] His timing of the correct psychological moment for the final attack at Ligny was impeccable; the Prussians were hurled back in considerable disorder and evacuated the field.

Whereas the Guard succeeded at Ligny, it failed at Waterloo. Wellington defeated the Imperial Guard's attempt to break through, or even into, his line on 18 June, for at Waterloo many of the factors that had worked in favour of the Guard on 16 June were absent.

Firstly, at Waterloo the Guard did not have numerical superiority. The Guard was supported by other French units, but these were already exhausted and were contained by allied troops. The point of the Guard attack was the decisive sector and here the less than 3000 Guardsmen making the assault were met by about 10,000 of Wellington's infantry. The French Guard was fresh but Wellington's men were not as exhausted as the Prussians had been at Ligny village. The British knew how to ration their strength and the Guard struck one of the least battle-tried sectors of Wellington's line. Moreover, the 3000 guardsmen did not strike Wellington's line simultaneously. The French battalions came up in succession and were defeated in succession. At Ligny, one massed assault broke into the Prussian army.

Secondly, Napoleon had no massed heavy cavalry to support the Waterloo attack. The superb French cavalry had retired a wreck from its mad charges earlier in the day. Cavalry would have forced Wellington's infantry lines into square formations. Squares were highly vulnerable to musketry and artillery salvoes as they massed troops in a small area. They also reduced a unit's firepower by at least seventy-five per cent.

Wellington, unlike Napoleon, did have sufficient cavalry reserves in the evening: two brigades of light cavalry under Vivian and Vandeleur. These cavalrymen formed a cordon behind Wellington's infantry to check any retrograde moves. After the repulse of the French Guard, they moved to the fore and helped precipitate the retreat of Napoleon's army into an irrevocable rout.

Thirdly, at Waterloo the Guard assault lacked the overwhelming long-range artillery preparation so vital to victory. By evening on 18 June, the French artillery was running low on ammunition.[5] Some Guard batteries could not be brought to bear on Wellington's ridge as they were already in action against the Prussians. Napoleon was unable to bring the sheer weight of fire witnessed at Ligny against the target of the Guard assault at Waterloo.

Moreover, Wellington, unlike the Prussians, sheltered his troops on the reverse slopes of a ridge. The British 1st Footguards, who bore the brunt of the Guard attack, sheltered from the pre-assault barrage behind the bank of a ditch. As Guards Captain Powell commented, 'without the protection of this bank every creature must have perished.'[6]

Fourthly, at Ligny, the Guard attack enjoyed superior, integrated, short-range artillery support. At least one Guard battery kept pace with the infantry advance and opened fire with great effect from the west side of Ligny village. At Waterloo, one Guard horse artillery battery under Colonel Duchand did accompany its infantry comrades. Its guns advanced in the intervals between the various battalions and, indeed, had some effect. The British General Maitland wrote that 'the diminished range of the Enemy's Artillery was now felt most severely in our ranks.'[7]

But Wellington's fire caused havoc among the French gunners and reduced the rate of fire of the guns.[8] Although many of Wellington's own guns were out of action, he still had weight and accuracy of fire on his side. One British artillery lieutenant remembered firing canister at the Guard formations which suffered heavily, 'waving, at each discharge, like standing corn blown by the wind.'[9]

Fifthly, Wellington had the edge over the Guard in infantry firepower as well as in that of artillery. The British infantry which met the Guard assault fought in line. Thus they were able to bring all their muskets to bear, unlike the French Guard who advanced in hollow squares.[10] At Ligny, the less disciplined Prussians fought in columns and were more accustomed to charging than to

215

volley firing. Wellington had the added advantage that his front line curved round at the attacked point. Thus his infantry were able to pour a destructive crossfire inwards on to the Guard.

Sixthly, Wellington was able to shatter the Guard's attack because he was prepared for it. Surprise, which had worked in the Guard's favour at Ligny, was on Wellington's side at Waterloo. Forewarned by a French deserter of the impending assault, Wellington ordered his British Guards to lie down and shelter. Only when a French Guard formation appeared on the crest of the ridge did the redcoats stand up.

This sudden apparition, to French troops confident that all before them had fled, was a psychological blow. Together with the physical blow – the actual musketry volley – it paralysed the French advance. 'Those who from a distance and more on the flank could see the affair, tell us that the effect of our fire seemed to force the head of the Column bodily back', wrote one British eye-witness.[11] The momentum of the French unit's attack had been checked; a British bayonet charge caused it to break in terror.

Seventhly, Wellington, the careful general who husbanded his resources, still had reserves in hand in the evening of Waterloo. The 52nd light infantry boldly manoeuvred to outflank and pour a devastating flanking fire into a French Guard unit which tried to renew the attack just defeated by the British Guards. Other French battalions were crushed by a spirited Dutch–Belgian infantry counter-attack aided by the heavy fire of Krahmer's fresh Dutch–Belgian battery.

At Ligny, the Prussians had insufficient reserves to undertake such powerful counter-attacks. In any case, the French cavalry accompanying the Guard infantry would have crushed any Prussian moves.

The final reason why Napoleon's Guard failed at Waterloo was the obstinacy of the British. The Prussians lacked the determination of the British in defence. The British were resolved to resist to the end. The Prussians would yield before an onslaught. They would then counter-attack once the enemy push had exhausted its impetus.[12] Thus at Waterloo the French Guard met a stouter enemy than they had met before.

At Waterloo, Napoleon sent his imperial guardsmen to achieve the victory they had won at Ligny two days before. The same troops were used. But the co-ordination and back-up for the attack were lacking and a different enemy awaited the Guard. Consequently, the troops which had won Napoleon's last military victory failed to prevent his final defeat.

Notes

1. Berton, *Précis historique, militaire et critique des batailles de Fleurus et de Waterloo*, p.27
2. Pollio, *Waterloo (1815) avec de nouveaux documents*, p.215; Damitz, *Histoire de la Campagne de 1815*, v.1, p.151

3. Jones, *The Battle of Waterloo*, pp.321–2

4. Fuller, *The Conduct of War 1789–1961*, p.46

5. Foy, *Vie Militaire*, p.281: 'the great consumption of ammunition at the beginning of the battle caused the lack of it at the end.'

6. Siborne, *The Waterloo Letters*, p.254

7. *Ibid*, p.244

8. Lachouque, *The Anatomy of Glory*, p.487

9. Siborne, *The Waterloo Letters*, p.227

10. Holland Rose, *The Life of Napoleon I*, p.507, quoting Basil Jackson of the British Staff Corps: 'as they [the Guard] lay they formed large squares, of which the centres were hollow.'

11. Siborne, *The Waterloo Letters*, p.255

12. Weller, *Wellington at Waterloo*, p.203

13

GUIDE TO THE BATTLEFIELD OF LIGNY TODAY

Introduction

Visitors familiar with the field of Waterloo will be struck forcibly by the many differences between the battlefields of Ligny and Waterloo. For one thing, Ligny is much more extensive. Fighting at Ligny raged in an area of twenty square miles; the field of Waterloo is but four. The battlefield of Ligny boasts ten important towns and villages, and numerous churches and farms.

Moreover, the visitor to Waterloo has the benefit of the superb viewpoint offered by the Lion Mound monument, an artificial hill topped by a bronze lion which looks out over the entire battlefield. There is no such mound or viewpoint at Ligny.

Ligny benefits from no such protection as that given to Waterloo by Belgian Law on 26 March 1914. At Waterloo, in an area of 1347 acres, the Law forbids any demolition or construction on the battlefield. Luckily, however, Ligny is further from Brussels than is Waterloo and the villages that became the focus of the terrible hours of 16 June 1815 still retain much of their old atmosphere.

The town of Fleurus, on the southern edge of the battlefield, has been less fortunate and has been greatly modernised. Also, much quarrying has occurred through the years near Ligny and the battlefield is slightly disfigured in the vicinity of Ligny and St Amand by the huge piles of waste, now covered with trees, on the north bank of the Ligny brook.

Furthermore, the battlefield is crossed by two railway lines. One of these, leading northeast from Fleurus to Gembloux, is no longer in use. The other line runs north from Fleurus via Ligny to Brussels. The battlefield visitor may obtain some fine views, particularly towards St Amand village, from the trains running along this track.

Since the battlefield is extensive, you will save much time by touring it by car or bicycle. Visitors without a car or bicycle may travel to the battlefield by train and alight either at Fleurus or at Ligny station. To reach the battlefield by train from Brussels, depart from any of the city's three main stations: Midi, Centrale or Nord. Catch any train destined for Namur. Halfway to Namur, leave this

BATTLEFIELD OF LIGNY TODAY

Figures 1–6 identify the main points of interest on the battlefield, as discussed in Part Two, Chapter 13

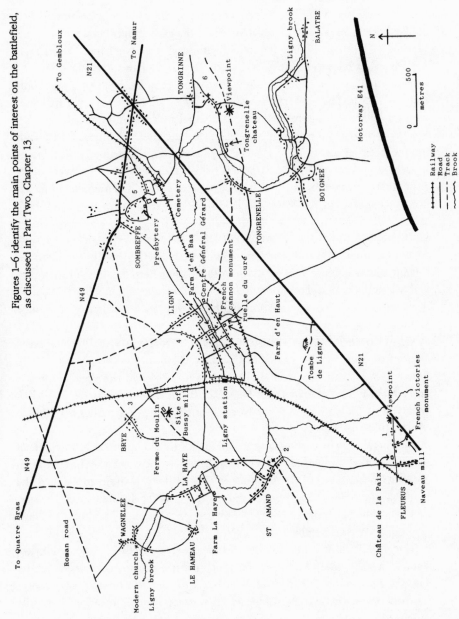

train at Ottignies station. At Ottignies, board any train heading for Charleroi-Sud. This train will stop at both Ligny and Fleurus.

Most of the battlefield consists of private property. Farmers still plough the fields. People still live in the farms. Please respect the local population's privacy.

The success of a visit to the battlefield depends much on good weather. Generals Mist and Rain, the old enemies of the battlefield visitor, are redoubtable adversaries. Moreover, Ligny has none of the souvenir shops and cinemas that cluster about the Waterloo Lion Mound. Even so, you should enjoy your visit. The battlefield has many lessons of military history lying barely beneath its surface. Ligny was, after all, Napoleon's last military victory.

There are six main points of interest on the battlefield. In order of decreasing importance they are: 3,4,5,2,1,6. But if you have sufficient time, visit them all in ascending numerical order. The battlefield tour described below covers all the major relics but those visitors wishing to cover the ground in more detail should obtain a copy of Patrick Maes' excellent booklet, *Ligny: Le Crépuscule de l'Aigle*.

Point one: Fleurus

Fleurus is situated on the southern edge of the battlefield and is a modernised town today. Yet it well merits a visit. Near the northern outskirts of the town, you will find a splendid monument on the western side of the N21. This edifice dates from 1936 and commemorates the three French victories won around Fleurus.

French royalist troops under the hunchbacked genius, Marshal Luxembourg, triumphed over the Germans and Dutch of the Prince of Waldeck in 1690; French republican forces over the Austrians in 1794 and the French imperial army over the Prussians in 1815. Fleurus witnessed yet more battles in 57 BC, when Julius Caesar defeated the Nervii, and in 1622. Skirmishes occurred in 1914, 1940 and 1945.

Although a less important action than the Battle of Ligny, the 1794 Battle of Fleurus is worth some mention, not least beause it witnessed the first use of an observation balloon in a pitched battle. The balloon had already served the French at the actions of Maubeuge and Charleroi earlier the same year. The silk, hydrogen-filled balloon, called *L'Entreprenant*, was tethered at Jumet, a village five miles southwest of Fleurus.

The pilot, Citizen Jean Coutelle, and the observer, General Antoine Morlot, signalled to the ground information which contributed to the French victory. The French commander-in-chief, Jean-Baptiste Jourdan, himself ascended in the balloon on the eve of the battle, in spite of being the target of hostile cannon-shots, some of history's first anti-aircraft fire.

The 1794 Battle of Fleurus was an extensive affair, with the 75,000 French troops occupying a thirty-mile defence line of heights and entrenchments in a semi-circle north of Charleroi. 52,000 Austrians launched attacks on these defences. Some action flared up west of Charleroi, but the most important fighting occurred in the region just south of Fleurus.

Marshal Soult, who fought at Fleurus in 1794 as well as in 1815, wrote of the former battle that 'fifteen hours of the most desperate fighting that I ever saw had considerably weakened the strength of the troops, but their spirit remained the same. They wanted to put an end to it and demanded to be led against the enemy to clinch the victory.' The dense Austrian attack columns were smitten by a fierce French cannon and musket fire and retired in ruins, leaving behind wheatfields set alight by the musketry. The whole scene resembled a volcanic eruption.[1]

Immediately to the west of the French victories monument you will see an old red brick tower in the form of a truncated cone. This is the mill of Naveau, built in 1667 and employed in 1815 as Napoleon's observation post. In 1815, French army sappers constructed a lookout platform on the mill for their Emperor. The owner in 1815 was a French *émigré*, or royalist exile, who had formerly served Louis XVI's Queen, Marie-Antoinette.[2] Today, both the original roof and the sails have disappeared. Unfortunately, the mill of Naveau is private property and visitors are not admitted.

Nevertheless, some idea of the view of the battlefield enjoyed by Napoleon from Fleurus can be gained by advancing 400 metres northwards up the N21 to a viewpoint on the west of the road, just beyond a Shell petrol station. The church spire of St Amand is particularly noticeable from here. However, it is likely that within a few years newly built houses will obscure this view.

The Town Hall is the other relic of 1815 to be found in Fleurus. The Town Hall used to be the Château de la Paix, Napoleon's quarters on the night after the battle. A metal plaque in the entrance courtyard records Napoleon's stay. On the morning of 17 June, eight captured Prussian guns were drawn up in this courtyard under the windows of the *château*.

The Town Hall is open to visitors. You will find Napoleon's room on the first floor, on the north side of the *château*. Today, the room is occupied by the offices of the third secretarial staff. The ladies there are most helpful and will explain how the interior has totally changed since 1815. Nevertheless, a frieze running across the ceiling indicates where Napoleon's bedroom used to be.

After leaving the interior of the Town Hall, proceed past the east wing to the garden on the north side. From here you can see the windows of Napoleon's room on the first floor, just to the left of centre.

Point two: St Amand

St Amand saw the first fighting of the battle. By the end of the day it was a burnt-out wreck of a village. The horror of 16 June 1815 seems far removed from the peaceful, sleepy village of today.

The appearance of St Amand was altered in 1818–19 when the scarred trees in the gardens of the houses were felled. Thus today, the village appears more open and less formidable than it did in 1815. One French imperial guardsman recalled that at the battle, 'the multitude of trees around St Amand caused the area to look like a very dense wood. All our troops could see of St Amand were the church and the few houses that surrounded it.'[3]

You should note the old church of St Amand, which retains its 1815 appearance. According to the Italian historian Alberto Pollio, 'eyewitnesses relate that on the western wing, many soldiers heard distinctly the strokes of 2.30 pm chime at the church tower of St Amand and propagate themselves through an atmosphere rarefied by the heat. For so many heroes, it was the tolling of a funeral bell.'[4]

Prussian and French battalions fought desperately in the cemetery encircling the church. Although this cemetery has been tarmacked over, you will still see a few tombstones affixed to the west wall of the church. After the battle the church was used as a casualty clearing station. Surgeons carried out their grisly task without anaesthetics. Today, the church is fenced off and in need of restoration.

The French General Berthezène, who fought in this sector of the battlefield, described in his memoirs how each individual farm became a small, isolated battlefield, how the ferocious fight raged to and fro and how the streets of St Amand were strewn with dead bodies. Most of the Prussian corpses wore the Iron Cross or medals.[5]

The Prussian defenders of St Amand included two battalions of the 29th Regiment. Formerly part of the forces of the Duchy of Berg, the 29th had only recently been incorporated into the Prussian army and still wore its old white Berg tunics. In order to become less of a conspicuous target, the soldiers donned their grey greatcoats on top. In consequence, they suffered severely from the irksome heat of the warm day, which was aggravated by the exertions of battle.[6]

On your way to point three, pass westwards out of St Amand into the village of La Haye (sometimes called Longpré). La Haye village was the battleground between the Prussian 2nd infantry brigade and General Girard's French division. The old farms, their component buildings whitewashed and grouped around a rectangular farmyard, were in 1815 the bastions and the objectives of the two foes. Each village contained such tactical strongpoints. They were difficult to capture but once they had been seized, the area around them soon fell into the captor's hands.

A bronze plaque on the north-west exterior wall of the farm of La Haye reads:

'Farm of La Haye. Here General Girard was mortally wounded on the 16th June 1815. Association for the Conservation of Napoleonic Monuments 1990.'

Transported back to France, Girard died on 27 June 1815 at Paris and was hence spared the allied occupation of the capital city, after Waterloo, on 7 July.

Napoleon thought highly of General Girard who had, he wrote, 'the sacred spark.' Just before Girard died, Napoleon created him Duke of Ligny, in recognition of his valour at that battle and in his own will, written at St Helena, Napoleon left 100,000 francs to Girard's children.

If time permits, you may also wish to see Wagnelée, the village which marked the westernmost limit of the fighting along the Ligny brook. You will easily spot the old buildings such as the farm south of the modern green-spired village church. The 1815 church has been demolished.

Point three: Brye

This is the heart of the Prussian position. Around Brye stood the Prussian reserves, dotted in columns in full view of the French gunners. Brye church existed in 1815. Although most of the houses are modern, the village has not expanded much since the battle.

Leave the village of Brye and take the road that leads southeast. After 500 metres, turn right on to a narrow road. This will bring you to the site of Blücher's command post, the mill of Bussy.

The mill was destroyed in 1895. It used to stand in the open field immediately southwest of the Ferme du Moulin. Some of the buildings of this farm existed in 1815. In the farm's courtyard a battalion of the Prussian 6th Infantry regiment took up its post before battle opened.

From the site of Bussy mill you will see the battlefield. Around you, battalions of the Prussian I Corps formed up on the gentle slopes down to the Ligny brook. As Wellington had foreseen, they were pounded mercilessly by French guns.

Looking southeast, beyond the railway line you see the village of Ligny (point four), distinguished by its spired grey stone church. Beyond Ligny is the eastern sector of the battlefield.

Turning towards the south, in the foreground on the slope immediately in front of you, there occurred the breathtaking drama of the chaotic Prussian cavalry charges covering the infantry's retreat in the evening, and of the rescue of Prince Blücher from underneath his dead horse. In the distance, screened by trees, is the town of Fleurus, where Napoleon had his observation post: the mill of Naveau. The village of St Amand is partly hidden by trees but its church can be seen.

To the west, beyond the houses of Brye village, you can spot the tall, slender, green spire of the modern church of Wagnelée.

In order to explore the battlefield closer to the scene of the actual fighting, leave the Prussian command post and go down the slopes towards Ligny, following the route taken by Prussian infantry reinforcements marching from reserve into the hell that was Ligny village.

Point four: Ligny

The village that gave its name to the battle lies on both sides of the Ligny brook. Napoleon's *coup de grâce*, the Imperial Guard attack, broke into the Prussian line in this peaceful place. It seems strangely deserted. Few people roam the streets. Little noise assails the ears. Nevertheless, you will find reminders of the battle. One of the streets is named rue Généraux Gérard et Vandamme, after the two French commanders whose troops attacked Ligny and St Amand. The former Mayor of Ligny, Monsieur Léon Ruquoy, inaugurated the plaque bearing the name of the street in 1965.

Ligny is proud of its Napoleonic connection. An enormous bronze siege gun rests under a shelter in the northeastern outskirts of the town. Admirers of the French Emperor placed it there in 1969 to commemorate the bicentenary of his birth. You will soon realise that Ligny is part of the Francophile southern half of Belgium, Wallonia.

The first relic of the actual battle is the Farm d'en Haut, a Prussian bastion taken by General Gérard's troops. To reach this, stand at the eastern end of the street called ruelle du curé and walk towards the village centre. You are following the route taken by Captain François and the French 30th Line infantry regiment when they attacked Ligny at 3.15 pm. At the end of the ruelle du curé stand the solid-looking whitewashed walls of the Farm d'en Haut. A bronze plaque records the struggle of 1815.

Once you reach the Farm d'en Haut, turn left on to the rue d'en Haut and then take the first right. Like the soldiers of the French 30th Regiment in 1815, you find yourself in the small square surrounding Ligny church. This square was once crammed with desperate, fighting troops. Now it is empty. In the square at the end of 16 June 1815 lay, among many other corpses, a dead company of Prussian *Landwehr*, or militia, from the province of Westphalia. They wore soft blue caps and long blue coats with green collars and cuffs.[7]

The church is larger and more elaborate than the edifice that existed in 1815. The cemetery surrounding the 1815 church has also vanished. During the battle this cemetery served as a major strongpoint, into which the French brought two cannon.

Captain von Glasenapp of the Prussian 19th Regiment was one of those who fought in the village and he stated that neither side bothered to take prisoners, that wounded enemy troops were finished off as a matter of course. Glasenapp's regiment formed part of 4th brigade, commanded by General Henkel von Donnersmark. General Henkel was himself in the thick of the fight at Ligny village. Perspiring profusely, he drank out of a soldier's cap filled from a puddle formed of liquid manure. Around him, he saw cannonballs snatching away his men and smashing them into bloody pulp.[8]

A little to the northwest of the church, on the Prussian side of the Ligny brook, stand the remains of the Farm d'en Bas. A plaque on the wall of one of the two surviving wings of the original farm reads:

'Ferme d'en Bas. Last bastion of the Prussian resistance at Ligny, this farm withstood the furious assaults of General Gérard's troops of the French Empire on the 16th June 1815. Captured and lost several times, it was finally taken by Napoleon at the head of his Guard.'

The Château des Comtes de Looz, another Prussian bastion inside the village, used to stand in the southwestern extremity of Ligny, at the end of the rue d'en Haut. Distinguished by towers topped with steeples, the *château* was in a delapidated state even before 1815. The battle itself did not improve the place. It was totally demolished several decades later. The Prussian garrison of the *château* consisted, in the first place, of the 1st battalion of the 19th Regiment. Other troops, including the 2nd and 4th Silesian Schützen companies, reinforced the battalion. In spite of ferocious onslaughts and unremitting bombardment, the *château* held out until the evening.

It is worth while making a small excursion from Ligny village along the rue de Fleurus to the Tombe de Ligny. This shallow rise in the ground – probably a Gallo-Roman tumulus – was the station of the Prussian General Ziethen and his staff during the night of 15/16 June. In the evening of the battle, Napoleon was on this mound as he watched his Guard storming into Ligny.

Point five: Sombreffe

We now pass over to the eastern sector of the battlefield. The main fighting of 16 June 1815 focused on the villages along the Ligny brook to the west of Sombreffe. However, the eastern sector does merit a visit.

At Mont, a locality within Sombreffe,[9] find the church and stand facing it across the open square. During the battle, this square was occupied by the 3rd battalion of the Prussian 8th Infantry. The church dates from only 1860 but occupies the site of the church existing in 1815. To the right of the two-storey house adjoining the church is the cemetery. Immediately on entering the cemetery, turn to the left and note a cannonball, which has smashed into the cemetery wall. Thanks to its sheltered position it has escaped the effects of weathering.

From its position, it is clear that this cannonball came from the French side of the valley. We know that the Prussian Foot Artillery battery no. 18 was posted on the south side of the cemetery. We can infer that this battery would have attracted French counter fire endeavouring to silence it. The cannonball embedded in the cemetery wall is clearly a French round which overshot its target.

Now proceed from the cemetery 100 metres along the road leading west. To the north of this road you will see the Sombreffe presbytery, built in about 1760 and half hidden behind two magnificent plane trees planted about the same time. The presbytery is the finest house at Sombreffe and for this reason Blücher made it his headquarters on the eve of the battle. He arrived in the evening of 15 June and left on the morning of the 16th to ride over to the Bussy mill. The building is practically unchanged except that the high wall that stood between the plane trees and the road has been demolished.

The parish priest residing at the presbytery today is very knowledgable about its history. He is especially well informed about the two mysteries of the interior of the house. First, the top of one of the wooden doors is full of indentations. Legend has it that Blücher cut these in anger or frustration with his sword. Blücher was certainly anxious on the night before the battle, for at that time he had only Ziethen's I Corps in position to block the French invasion. But why should a fiery Blücher hack at the top of the outside face of the door? The dents seem to be deliberately inflicted in cold blood. Perhaps after the battle a local Belgian damaged the door so that he could add realism to his story of Blücher's stay at the presbytery.

The second mystery of the house is the cannonball embedded in a wall just above the fine, original, oak staircase. The mystery is how this cannonball entered the house. You will note that it could not have entered through a window. The parish priest will inform you that the exterior of the house bears no indication of the ball having passed through the northern wall. It might just have entered through the main door on the south façade, skimmed past a corner of the corridor and embedded itself into the wall, but the angle is very tight. Moreover, if this were the flight path of the cannonball, it would have been fired from the Prussian side of the valley. Prussian gunners are unlikely to have fired on a house previously used as Blücher's headquarters. Perhaps the cannonball was found soon after the fight on the battlefield and cemented into the wall of the presbytery to attract tourists.

Point six: Tongrinne

The village of Tongrinne is posted on top of a hill at the heart of the position occupied by Thielmann's Prussian III Corps. Tongrinne church is the original edifice which witnessed the battle; it has a choir dating from the thirteenth century and a tower from the sixteenth.

The best viewpoint over the eastern sector of the battlefield is in the fields 250 metres south of Tongrinne church. Note the strength of this dominating position. The relatively steep valley sides contrast strikingly with the more gentle slopes on the western sector of the battlefield. Indeed, the Prussian artillery posted on the heights of Tongrinne inflicted considerable casualties on the French right wing.[10]

Looking to the south and west, you spot the houses of Boignée and Tongrenelle lying in the valley of the Ligny brook. On the western horizon is the tree-lined Fleurus–Sombreffe highroad. Ligny village is out of sight beyond this road. To the northwest you see Sombreffe church reposing on a height above the trees.

Antagonism in the eastern sector of the battlefield was limited to the ritual of two sides trying to tie the other down: mutual observance and skirmishing. Thus no serious combats occurred here and there was much less slaughter than to the west. Nevertheless, the small, picturesque villages of Boignée, Balâtre and Tongrenelle merit a visit. The French eventually cleared all three villages of Prussian troops.

You should also visit Tongrenelle *château*. This château, a formidable fort on the Prussian bank of the brook, was garrisoned by elements of the Prussian 27th Regiment. Still extant today, it is surrounded by water – a good defensive barrier.

To the north of Tongrenelle, the bridge bearing the N21 over the Ligny brook is a modern one. During the battle of 16 June, Prussian forces barricaded the old bridge and it was not until nightfall that French infantry under General Hulot managed to capture it. The brook itself is less of an obstacle today. In particular, its banks are not as marshy as they were in 1815.

To conclude your battlefield tour, advance from the bridge along the N21 towards Fleurus. After 1075 metres, take the track on your right leading to Ligny village. Halfway along this track, you will find yourself on the summit of a shallow hill. This is the point to which the Prussian 30th Regiment advanced in the evening in an attempt to relieve the pressure on its I and II Corps comrades further west by intimidating the French attackers. For in the darkness of late evening, the French could not have seen that a mere two Prussian battalions had gained the hill top.

Note, too, how close Ligny village is to where you are standing. This proximity can scarcely have reassured the French troops attacking northwest out of Ligny. With the situation in their right rear under threat from the Prussian 30th Regiment, they would have been discouraged from pushing too far forward.

Continue from the hill top into Ligny village. As you leave the track, turn right and enter the General Gérard Centre. The Centre is owned by Ligny's tourist information office and it forms a fitting conclusion to your tour of the battlefield. The Centre includes a first-rate museum on Napoleon and on the Battle of Ligny. Exhibits include a diorama of the Guard attack on the Farm d'en Bas and cannonballs found on the battlefield. The General Gérard Centre is open every day except Monday from 2.00 pm to 5.00 pm. On weekends, opening hours are longer but in winter visits are by appointment.

You are encouraged, if possible, to visit Ligny in early June. On the first weekend of that month, Napoleon's Imperial Guard marches again through the streets of Ligny. The recreated 1st Chasseurs, resplendent in towering bearskins and blue wool jackets, keep alive the memory of Napoleon and his crack 'grumblers'.

This brings our tour of the battlefield of Ligny to a close.

Keen and dedicated military historians may wish to extend their tour beyond the battlefield of Ligny to encompass other relics of the events of the 16th June 1815; in particular, to follow Marshal Ney's movements and actions on the ground. A brief description of important places to visit, relating to the operations of the French left wing, is therefore appended.

Charleroi

Start in the town of Charleroi. It was founded by the Spanish in the seventeenth century and expanded rapidly in the nineteenth and twentieth centuries, being an important industrial and mining centre situated on the River Sambre. The River Sambre's course has been diverted by a canal immediately to the north of Charleroi-Sud railway station. The original channel of the river through the town has been filled in – it used to run along the line of the Boulevard Tirou. Consequently, Charleroi has altered much since 1815. Even so, the military historian will benefit from a visit.

The French captured Charleroi in their invasion of Belgium on 15 June. Towards midday, French Imperial Guard sappers and marines seized the bridge over the River Sambre. You will find a road named rue Pont de Sambre (Bridge of the Sambre Street) leading north from the Boulevard Tirou. This is the site of the bridge of 1815. From here, French hussars pushed after the retreating Prussians up the steep rue de la Montagne. This street will lead you to the Place Charles II, on the opposite side of which is a pub with a large painting of Napoleon on its facade.

On the afternoon of the 15th, Napoleon dozed in a chair outside the Belle Vue tavern as his troops passed by. This long since vanished tavern used to stand at the junction of the modern streets, rue Zénobe Gramme and rue Fagnart. Marshal Ney here received Napoleon's orders to push northwards along the Brussels road. From the site of the Belle Vue tavern, follow Ney's route north.

Gosselies

The first relic connected with the 'bravest of the brave' is the site of the house of Monsieur Dumont at Gosselies, where Ney spent the night of 15/16 June 1815. Unfortunately, the ancient house collapsed around 1937, but a park occupies the former location of the house and its grounds. You will find this park west of the main Brussels road. From the Place Albert 1er, at the centre of Gosselies, head west along the rue Vandervelde. After 300 metres, turn south into the rue St Roch, which is also known as the rue Stranard. Proceed 50 metres down this street and to the west you will see the entrance to the park.

CHARLEROI TODAY

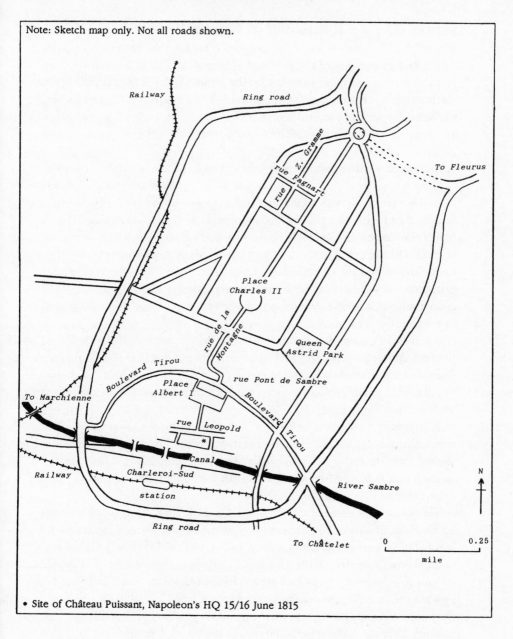

Note: Sketch map only. Not all roads shown.

Railway

Ring road

rue Fagnart

rue

To Fleurus

Place
Charles II

rue de la
Montagne

Queen
Astrid Park

Boulevard Tirou

rue Pont de Sambre

Place
Albert I

Boulevard Tirou

To Marchienne

rue Leopold

*

Canal

Railway

Charleroi-Sud
station

River Sambre

Ring road

To Châtelet

N

0   0.25
mile

• Site of Château Puissant, Napoleon's HQ 15/16 June 1815

Battlefield of Quatre Bras

Ney left M. Dumont's house at 7.00 am on 16 June to ride north to Frasnes. By 2.00 pm, he was fighting the Battle of Quatre Bras. The battle was confused and its events are difficult to follow on the ground today. The main change at the battlefield is the disappearance, in 1816–17, of the Wood of Bossu, which bordered the west of the field. Nevertheless, six farms, three monuments and two plaques bear witness to the fight which resulted in a bloody stalemate with about 9000 casualties.

Quatre Bras farm occupies the northeast corner of the important crossroads of Quatre Bras (where you will find ample parking). Although modernised and altered in places, the farm retains much of its former appearance. Towards 6.30 pm, the 92nd Highlanders, deployed in front of this farm, poured a devastating hail of musketry into General Kellermann's French *cuirassiers* which, after their splendid charge, reined in on these very crossroads. A small cluster of *cuirassiers* even charged into the courtyard of Quatre Bras farm. Unable to find another exit, they charged back through the entrance gateway and were shot down.[11] After the battle, the British employed the breastplates of dead *cuirassiers* as pans in which to cook provisions.

The farm of Quatre Bras was employed during the battle as a makeshift field hospital. At one point, nearly 1000 wounded troops are said to have lain in the courtyard. One horrified Scotsman commented that 'while I live, I shall ever retain a vivid recollection of the farmyard at Quatre Bras on the evening of the 16th and morning of the 17th.'[12]

A German officer wrote, 'at the inn [farm] by the cross-roads at Quatre Bras the contest was the hottest. Here are the most graves. The wounded reeled into the inn-yard, leaned against the walls, and then sank down. There are still traces of the blood on the walls, as it spouted forth from the wounds with departing life.'[13]

The house of La Bergerie was the scene of a spirited yet costly counter-attack by the 92nd (Gordon) Highlanders at about 7.00 pm. French infantry were occupying La Bergerie and its garden. Wellington needed to take the strongpoint in order to be free to launch a general offensive southwards – you can see for yourself the proximity of La Bergerie to the crossroads. The 92nd were led by their commander, Lieutenant-Colonel John Cameron, and by Wellington's fiery Adjutant-General, Sir Edward Barnes. 'Come on, my old 92nd!' roared Sir Edward, yielding to the temptation to join the attack himself.

La Bergerie fell to the Highlanders and Wellington's infantry rolled forward to drive Ney's forces towards Frasnes. But this success was won at a heavy price, including the life of Lieutenant-Colonel Cameron. The colonel, struck by French fire, was carried away on his frenzied horse up to Quatre Bras. There, the horse suddenly halted and Cameron was thrown head-first on to the cobbles.

Proceed from La Bergerie 200 metres further south down the Brussels road.

BATTLEFIELD OF QUATRE BRAS TODAY

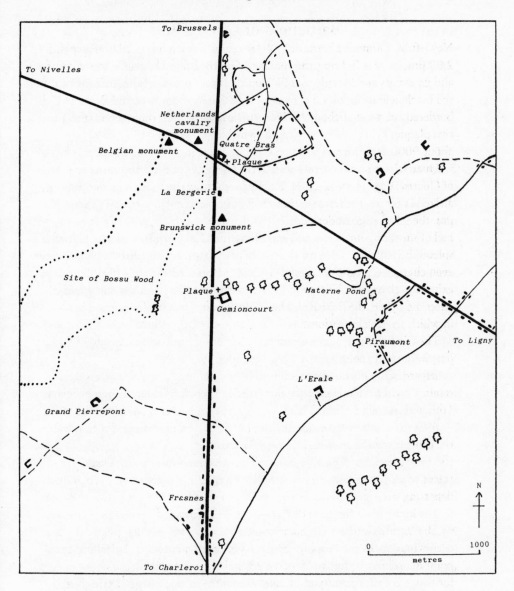

To Brussels

To Nivelles

Netherlands cavalry monument

Belgian monument

Quatre Bras
+ Plaque

La Bergerie

Brunswick monument

Site of Bossu Wood

Plaque +
Gemioncourt

Materne Pond

Piraumont

To Ligny

L'Erale

Grand Pierrepont

Fresnes

N

To Charleroi

0   1000
metres

To the east of the road stands a monument to the slain 44-year-old Duke of Brunswick. It was inaugurated on the seventy-fifth anniversary of Quatre Bras. On the summit of the granite pedestal stands a lion holding a shield which depicts the Brunswick symbol of a leaping horse. Below a bronze image of the Duke's head is inscribed: 'Frederick William, Duke of Brunswick and Lunebourg, fell not far from this spot at the head of his troops on the 16th June 1815.'

The fifteenth-century farm of Gemioncourt is 750 metres south of the Brunswick monument. On the wall of the entrance gate is a plaque inaugurated on 4 June 1988. It is dedicated 'To the memory of the soldiers of the [French] Grand Army who fell before these walls on the 16th June 1815.' This is the only French memorial on the battlefield.

Gemioncourt was garrisoned initially by the Dutch 5th Battalion of National Militia. But it soon fell at the start of the battle to Marshal Ney's general advance of 2.00 pm. The Dutch Prince of Orange ordered the militia battalion out of the farm to attack some French batteries. The battalion was promptly routed by French light cavalry. The Prince himself, waving his plumed hat over his head, nearly shared the fate of one of his ADCs, who was wounded and captured. The Dutch survivors rallied at the farm but were soon expelled by French footsoldiers.

The French held Gemioncourt until the evening, when it was retaken by Major Thomas Chambers and the British 30th Regiment. Gemioncourt is typical of the Belgian farms that featured so prominently in all the battles of the campaign. Note the solid, loopholed buildings arranged around a courtyard. Attackers invariably suffered enormous casualties.

On the southern edge of the battlefield are the farms of l'Erâle and Grand Pierrepont, neither of which witnessed much fighting. Marshal Ney seized them from Dutch–Belgian forces at the commencement of the battle. Bossu Wood stood to the north of Grand Pierrepont and extended up to the Nivelles–Namur highroad. This wood, contested all day, was finally cleared by the British Guards in the evening. Many guardsmen were killed by falling branches, which French cannonshot severed from the tree-tops.

The village of Piraumont and the large farm in the village centre were the battleground between a French infantry division under General Bachelu and the 1st battalion of the green-coated British 95th Rifles. The crack riflemen successfully prevented the French from driving north from Piraumont to cut the Nivelles–Namur road. This road was the vital direct route between Wellington at Quatre Bras and Blücher at Ligny.

The riflemen were supported by a Brunswick battalion, and reinforced after 6.00 pm by a Hanoverian brigade. The arrival of the Hanoverians in this sector of the field caused Piraumont to fall into Wellington's hands.

Two monuments northwest of Quatre Bras, three hundred metres or so along the N49 towards Nivelles, pay tribute to the Dutch–Belgians of Wellington's army. On the south side of the road, you will find a plain, stone memorial. The inscription reads: 'To the memory of the Belgians killed at the Battle of Quatre Bras for the defence of the flag and the honour of arms.'

The site for this monument was chosen before the Great War. In June 1914, General Baron de Heusch led a pilgrimage to the site and eulogized the Dutch–Belgian soldiers who died at Quatre Bras. The erection and inauguration of the memorial were delayed by the 1914–18 war, until 1926.

On the opposite side of the road, and nearer the crossroads, is a striking commemorative structure. It is in the shape of a cross, formed by the blade, hilt and crosspiece of a great stone sword. Dedicated on 21 September 1990, it bears a bronze plaque remembering the Dutch–Belgian cavalrymen of 1815.

The 5th (Belgian) Light Dragoons had a particularly trying time at Quatre Bras. Many of the dragoons had in previous years fought under Napoleon. So when charged by the French 5th Lancers, they had to endure former comrades, now enemies, addressing them by name and urging them to desert. The Belgians steadfastly remained loyal to their new allegiance to the Netherlands but were routed by the French 6th Chasseurs à cheval. Further tragedy ensued as a British battalion fired by error on the Belgians, who wore almost exactly the same green and yellow coats as the French *chasseurs à cheval*.

A plaque on the wall of Quatre Bras farm at the crossroads likewise pays tribute to the Dutch–Belgians. It reads: 'To the memory of the Netherlanders and their allies, the defenders of Quatre Bras.'

The battlefield as a whole is small and complex, with rolling terrain. It is difficult to ascertain exactly where the rival troops were positioned, for example the spot on which the 8th Cuirassiers overran the British 69th Foot. The 69th was probably cut up in the low lying ground to the west of the Brussels road 150 metres south of the Brunswick monument.

The crops today are much shorter than they were two centuries ago. In 1815, after the battle, observers could follow the march of various battalions in all directions by the swathes of trodden down corn. Sergeant James Anton of the 42nd Highlanders commented that the crops were as high as his bonnet.[14] Inevitably, the line of his battalion was much disordered after struggling through a field of rye. Before charging British infantry squares, the French cavalry often had to send forward an intrepid horseman to plant a lance before a square to indicate its position amidst the rye. The French would then charge towards the lance pennon.[15]

Since 1815, the battlefield has lost numerous hedges and ditches and the terrain is now much easier for troops to traverse. Nevertheless, it is an evocative and well preserved small patch of historical ground. Hopefully, the relics of the battlefield of Ligny will soon be signposted, as those of Quatre Bras already are.

In the footsteps of d'Erlon

You will reap great benefits by following, on foot, the route taken by d'Erlon's I Corps on 16 June, synchronising the timing of your march to that related by eyewitnesses of 1815. The distance of the march is sixteen miles. At first you will have to walk along the edge of the busy Brussels road but a pavement exists for much of the way.

Begin at Jumet, on the Brussels road. Here General d'Erlon arrived with two divisions of his I Corps on the evening of 15 June. During the morning of 16 June, the rest of the corps, strung out during the marching of the previous day, closed up and massed around Jumet.

At 12.15 pm, d'Erlon received an order from Ney to put his corps on the march, but had to wait until 1.00 pm for Reille's II Corps immediately to the north to move off to Quatre Bras. Owing to the heavy burdens carried by the troops and the difficulties of manoeuvring large units in those days, the first of d'Erlon's men arrived at Gosselies only between 1.30 and 2.00 pm. At Gosselies, d'Erlon halted for about an hour to allow a force to reconnoitre a village seven-and-a-half miles to the west, where peasants mistakenly asserted enemy troops were massed.[16]

At 3.00 pm, d'Erlon got his men back on the march, moving along the Brussels road north out of Gosselies. About two miles north of Gosselies, you will find that the Brussels road forks. Take the eastern route. This is the route of the Brussels road in 1815; the other route is the modern bypass. One-and-a-fifth miles beyond the fork, you arrive at the intersection of the Brussels *chaussée* and the Roman road. Between 4.00 and 4.15 pm, d'Erlon's corps was passing this intersection of the Brussels and Roman roads when Colonel Forbin-Janson brought Napoleon's order for d'Erlon to head for the Battle of Ligny. Accordingly, d'Erlon moved east.

D'Erlon passed either through or nearby the village of Villers-Perwin.[17] You will do best to walk northeast along the Roman road. The last section of the road is in its original condition of 1815: a mere earth track. You arrive at a crossroads and should follow d'Erlon's route southeast along a track signposted 'Redebel'. Pass the old red brick mill, which possibly existed in 1815, and the farms of Chassart, which definitely existed then, and head for Fleurus.

Already, Vandamme's troops would have seen d'Erlon's column and would have panicked. Unfortunately, the embankment of a disused railway line blocks your view towards the positions occupied by Vandamme. But note, to the northeast, the slender, modern church spire of Wagnelée, marking Blücher's extreme right flank, which d'Erlon was supposed to fall upon. Instead d'Erlon continued along the track towards Fleurus.

At 6.00 pm, d'Erlon, somewhere beyond the Chapelle St Bernard, received his recall from Ney and marched back. He passed through the centre of Villers-Perwin to reach Frasnes. Before following d'Erlon's return route, you should

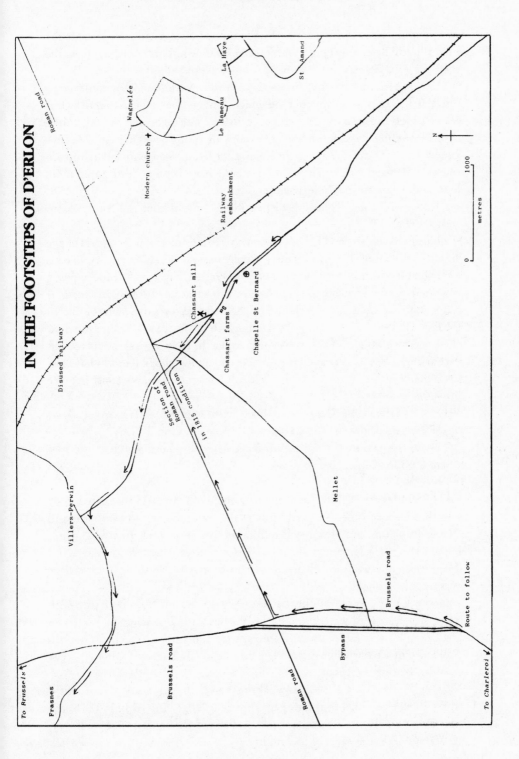

IN THE FOOTSTEPS OF D'ERLON

To Brussels

Frasnes

Villers–Perwin

Disused railway

Roman road

Modern church

Wagnelée

Le Hameau

La Haye

St Amand

Railway embankment

Chassart mill

Chassart farms

Chapelle St Bernard

Section of Roman road in 1815 condition

Mellet

Brussels road

Brussels road

Roman road

Bypass

Route to follow

To Charleroi

N

0   1000

metres

position yourself at Fleurus and in Vandamme's position and look towards the path where d'Erlon first appeared. You can see Chassart mill distinctly from the road between Fleurus and St Amand.

D'Erlon arrived back at Frasnes at 9.00 pm. Note how long you take to return to Frasnes – it will not be much longer than ninety minutes. But d'Erlon took three hours. This reflects d'Erlon's indecision and the difficulties of manoeuvring large formations of troops in the pre-wireless era. Messengers would have to ride along the column ordering the commanders to turn round and march back. The column would have been at least three miles long and a horseman would have required half an hour at the very least to reach its rear, while explaining to bewildered officers that the corps was to turn about.[18]

One of the soldiers in d'Erlon's corps was Louis Canler, eighteen years of age and in the ranks of the 28th Infantry. Canler described in his memoirs how his regiment arrived at its bivouac position near Frasnes. The troops trudged past a wretched young Frenchman sprawled on the verge of the Brussels road. A cannonball had obliterated both his legs. Someone had tried in vain to staunch the flow of blood by bandaging the stumps with a shirt. Blood trickled too from chest and face wounds. He was bleeding to death. Nevertheless, he roared out encouragement to Canler and his comrades: 'Long live the Emperor! I have lost both my legs but I couldn't give a damn! Victory is ours! Long live the Emperor!'

Decades later, Louis Canler still shook with emotion when he recalled the noble stoicism of that unknown hero of Napoleon's Grand Army.[19]

Today, the cars from Charleroi to Brussels rush unheedingly past the spot where the Frenchman bled to death.

This concludes the exploration of the battlefield of Ligny and the surrounding area. If you have time, you could follow the route of the Prussian retreat to Wavre on 17 June, via Mellery where Blücher spent the night after the Battle of Ligny. Alternatively, you could drive to Gembloux, then on to Wavre. By doing this you will be following in the footsteps of Marshal Grouchy's pursuit.

You will find relics of another battle at Wavre, where Grouchy clashed with a Prussian rearguard while the bulk of Blücher's army marched to Waterloo. For example, the Eglise Saint Jean-Baptiste contains a French cannonball embedded in a pillar while the modern Bridge of Christ bears a bronze plaque commemorating the battle.

From Wavre a short drive west will bring you to the better known battlefield where Blücher and his Prussians gained their revenge. On 16 June 1815, the sun set on Napoleon's last military victory. Forty-eight hours later it would set, at Waterloo, on the ruins of his empire.

Notes

1. Dupuis, *Les opérations militaires sur la Sambre en 1794*, pp.368–9
2. Garros, *Le Champ de Bataille de Waterloo*, p.88
3. Navez, *Les Quatre Bras, Ligny, Waterloo et Wavre*, p.116
4. Pollio, *Waterloo (1815) avec de nouveaux documents*, p.210
5. Berthezène, *Souvenirs militaires*, v.2, p.364
6. Reiche, *Memoiren*, p.180
7. Booth, *The Battle of Waterloo by a near observer*, p.72
8. Königer, *Der Krieg von 1815*, p.250
9. The terminology of this part of the battlefield is confused, partly owing to Napoleon's administrative reforms which amalgamated the village of Mont with other houses to form the commune of Sombreffe. I am grateful to the parish priest of Sombreffe and to Guy Delvaux for explaining these complexities to me.
10. Pajol, *Pajol, Général en chef*, v.3, pp.206–7
11. Jackson, *Notes and Reminiscences of a staff officer*, p.27. For a slightly different version, see Maxwell, *Life of Wellington*, v.2, pp.28–9.
12. Gardyne, *The Life of a Regiment*, p.437
13. Jones, *The Battle of Waterloo*, p.63
14. Brett-James, *The Hundred Days*, p.58
15. Siborne, *The Waterloo Letters*, p.348
16. Houssaye, *Waterloo 1815*, p.200
17. Houssaye, *op. cit.*, p.204, believed that when the I Corps headed east, it merely left the main road and moved across country before marching along the Roman road and turning on to the track running past Chassart mill (see maps nos. 13 and 20 in this book, and the map in Müffling's *Geschichte des Feldzuges*). General Durutte wrote that the corps passed near Villers-Perwin. However, Captain Chapuis of the 85th Infantry of I Corps asserted that the corps passed through Villers-Perwin (James, *The Campaign of 1815*, p.126). Perhaps Chapuis assumed that the farms beside the Roman road, many of which you can see today, formed part of Villers-Perwin village to the north.
18. Hamilton-Williams, *Waterloo: new perspectives*, p.380, writes that d'Erlon's column would have been five miles long. He bases his estimate on a German military manual of 1912, which allowed for columns of troops four men abreast. However, the tracks d'Erlon used can accomodate more than four and so his column may have been shorter.
19. Canler, *Mémoires de Canler*, p.15

APPENDICES

Appendix 1

The Miller at Ligny

From J. Booth, The Battle of Waterloo by a near observer *(1816), p.91*

24th November 1815:
Prince Blücher on his way to the Prussian dominions, gave occasion to several fêtes. In passing through Belgium, he desired to see again, at Ligny, the place where, thrown from his horse, he lay upon the ground during the pursuit and hasty return of a part of the French army. After remaining there some time conversing with his aide-de-camp, he generously recompensed a miller who had assisted him in his critical situation.

The miller at Ligny, recompensed by Prince Blücher on his return from France, addressed the following letter to the editor of the Brussels Oracle:

'Prince Blücher, on his return, called at my house with his aides-de-camp; his modesty concealed his illustrious name, and I did not recollect him. He asked me many questions concerning my losses, and my melancholy situation. Alas! it was easy for me to answer that I had saved nothing, either in my house, or on the lands which I farm, and that the war had reduced my family to misery, so that I could not pay my contributions. He asked me the amount of them. I told him 80 francs, which he immediately gave me. He departed, and when he got to Namur, he sent me four pieces of 40 francs each, and one of 20 francs. It was from this messenger, that I learnt the name of this great Prince; his generosity honours him; his modesty enobles him; and my heart thanks him.'

It has, alas, been impossible to confirm the miller's tale. The miller, a Belgian civilian, is unlikely to have been present at the battle to help rescue Blücher. But generous Blücher quite possibly recompensed Belgians in the area for losses caused by the war, when he passed by on his return to Prussia. If the miller had aided Blücher at the battle, he would have recognised him when Blücher passed by in November.

APPENDIX 2

Extracts from *The Times*

Monday, 25 October 1937

NEY'S QUARTERS BEFORE WATERLOO

OLD HOTEL FALLING TO RUIN

FROM OUR CORRESPONDENT

Brusssels, Oct. 24

Many houses in the town of Gosselies, near Charleroi, are undermined by the workings of a local colliery, and several have collapsed in recent years. Among those now threatened with ruin is a deserted eighteenth century inn with cracked walls, called the Maison Dumont. This building is known to old citizens as the 'Maison de Waterloo,' as it was here that Marshal Ney took up his quarters on June 15, 1815, after having been given by the Emperor Napoleon the command of the I and II Infantry Corps.

According to local tradition Ney's first care was to have a bed prepared 'with two or three mattresses'. Then he proceeded to do honour to his host's cuisine and excellent Burgundy. During this time Napoleon had sent several messages to the Marshal enjoining him to advance at once. But Ney liked M. Dumont's wine, and as the bottles were emptied lined them up before him on the table. He resumed his march next morning, but it was then too late, and on June 18 he met defeat.

Napoleon, in company with a few followers, passed through Gosselies on his way back after Waterloo, and took a cold meal in the Maison Dumont. But the Prussians were close behind him, and Napoleon and his generals reached the Courcelles road by a hidden gate at the end of the park. Blücher and his staff entered Gosselies on June 19, and installed themselves in the Maison Dumont for the night.

Thus in the space of a few days the hotel sheltered three of the principal actors in the drama of Waterloo. Nothing can now save the old building, and the news of its collapse is only a matter of time.

The local tradition that Ney ignored Napoleon's instructions to advance is false: Napoleon's first message reached Ney at 11.00 am. Ney left the house at 7.00 am, which was not too late. Nevertheless, Ney's failure to mass his troops at this early hour was a fatal delay which allowed Wellington to maintain his hold on Quatre Bras.

Tuesday, 27 June 1865

WATERLOO FESTIVAL AT BRUNSWICK

(FROM A CORRESPONDENT.)

Brunswick, June 19.

Our Waterloo Festival came off yesterday, and, as I think some account of it may interest you, I send you a slight sketch of the proceedings.

Friday being the 50th anniversary of Quatre Bras, where Friedrich Wilhelm fought his last battle, and died the death of a hero, after living the life of one, was celebrated by a solemn Cathedral service, at 6.30 in the evening, and by all the bells in Brunswick tolling the parting knell for half an hour. The Cathedral-place was crowded, and there was no possibility of getting within the doors, even officers being obliged to stand outside. From every house hung a flag or banner of some kind. But in every case, whether the colours were those of the town or country, of Brunswick or Hanover, the long black weepers of crêpe never failed, marking thus the mourning of the Bruns-wickers for their gallant and unforgotten Duke. In many cases there was simply a black flag in solitary gloom, hanging from the staff, which, however, like the crêpe weeper, was to be removed the next day in order to give way to the ducal, municipal, or national colour.

Saturday passed over very quietly. It was bitterly cold, a biting north-east wind blowing up clouds of dust, and searching one's very bones; yet many persons went to

The Duke of Brunswick falls mortally wounded at Quatre Bras

see the veterans arrive at the railway station at 6.30. Nine hundred odd had announced themselves – an almost incredible number, when one thinks of the age of all and of the 50 years come and gone since the great battle which sealed Napoleon's fate. The old warriors – chiefly, of course, men in a very humble class of life – were met at the station by the youths attending the Gymnasium. These are here called the Gymnasts, and belong to a society for the promotion of athletic exercises. They wear a simple uniform, and their captains marching at the head of the corps give their orders in military fashion. One of the young athletes had a drum suspended at his waistband; beating a muster-roll, all the veterans came to call; they were then conducted by the Gymnasts to a Bureau, where they received their tickets of billet, the number of the house and the name of the street where they were to be freely lodged; they were then conducted to their quarters by the young athletes.

At 6 on Sunday morning a general réveille was sounded, and all met on the Monumentz-platz, a very beautiful open space, surrounded by a double row of chestnut trees, and in the centre of which, in the middle of a closely shaven lawn, stands an obelisk to the memory of those two gallant Dukes of Brunswick, Earl Wilhelm Ferdinand, Napoleon's 'General Brunswick' (who met with his death, as you remember, at the unfortunate battle of Jena), and that of Friedrich Wilhelm, the father of the reigning Duke, who fell 50 years ago at Quatre Bras. A solemn morning hymn was played, and other appropriate music followed. At 9.30 there was a Cathedral service. We knew there was no possibility of getting in, but we drove to the Cathedral-square to see the Waterloo heroes come out of the church.

Everybody almost who had a carriage to send had placed it at the disposal of those gallant old fellows, prefering to walk or take some public vehicle themselves; and indeed, the poor old men could never have tottered out to the parade ground before the town gates, for many of them were already exhausted with the unusual excitement and all that they had already gone through that morning.

I never saw anything more touching than when the cathedral doors opened, and the solemn notes of the great organ came grandly pealing out into the morning air, – all these old men, halt and maimed, feeble, infirm, and furrowed, each with a sprig of the traditional German oakleaf in his hat, many with a second sprig in their buttonholes, and not a few with a scarf of oakleaves interwoven and worn order-wise across the breast and over the shoulder – people of a gone-by generation, men who had lived in times of excitement, and who had seen bloodshed and tyranny, pestilence and famine, had stood side by side in the midst of battle and sudden death, had gone through hardships untold, had (not a few of them) crossed the Alps, and escaped as by a miracle the snowy death of Russia, now standing helpless and weak as little children in summer sunshine, supported by one, tenderly guided by another, looked at with reverence almost savouring of awe by all, themselves, perhaps, the least affected of any by the touching scene.

The Platz was densely crowded, and, of course, there were not nearly carriages enough for all 'the nine hundred'. We took two in our drosky. One of them helped to carry the Duke from the field of battle at Quatre Bras, after the fatal bullet had gone home doing its cruel work. They were both only Waterloo [campaign] men. But the day before I spoke to one who had been all through the Russian campaign, a hale hearty old fellow, whom it did one's heart good to see. And, indeed, though many were sadly feeble, it was very cheering to see how many had work in them yet; their old faces rosy, and their eyes still bright, while they marched away as well as the best of their pioneers, the Gymnasts.

It was some time before the line of carriages got into motion, and then we went at a foot-pace, with frequent stoppages. This was rather trying, as the sun was pouring its fiercest rays down upon us, a bitter cold wind blowing, and clouds of dust flying; for in these primitive parts we are as yet unblest with water-carts. But we had ample amusement in looking about us.

Across the street was suspended wreaths and chains of oak leaves, forming sort of triumphal arches; from every house hung flags and banners, with appropriate legends and inscriptions. In many cases the windows were completely garlanded with flowers, and up to the housetops human faces crowded one above the other. All the beauty of Brunswick was to be seen. The variety of pink, white, blue, and mauve bonnets was perfectly bewildering. If 'none but the brave deserve the fair', I am sure the valour of those poor old veterans must be incontestable, for the brightest eyes, the rosiest cheeks and lips were there to do them honour, and the whitest hands flung bouquets by the hundred into the carriages and among the crowd for 'Waterloo heroes'.

The procession passed up the principal streets, leaving the blackened ruins of the burnt down Schloss to the right, and so across the market-place, and out of the town gates to the 'Exercier-platz', or parade-ground, a large open green space, bordered on all four sides by fine old elm and lime trees. Here all the soldiery were drawn up; the Generals and the staffs in a cluster looked very gay, with their dress uniforms and all their manifold decorations and orders; but every eye was directed to the gallant nine hundred in every variety of costume, but with the unfailing Waterloo medal and the emblematical though simple decoration of oak leaves.

The troops were then paraded. The bands played 'God save the Queen'. The General Commandant of the town (Erichsen) at the head of his staff crossed the parade-ground to where the veterans stood, and gave them a short address, which we were too distant to hear. The bands then played some German national airs, and the troops, defiling before the General, left the parade-ground.

The Waterloo heroes were then conducted to a banquet provided for them, and at which, I believe, 1,100 sat down to dinner. In the evening there was a grand display of fireworks, and military music in the grounds adjoining the infantry barracks. These were on a very grand scale, and all Brunswick was there; not only the populace, but also the élite.

The festivities were over between 11 and 12, but I trust the poor old Waterloo heroes were in bed long before that hour. Of course, they were all brought hither free of expense, and had free quarters and food, but they must have been three trying days for the dear old men. It was really good of them to arise out of their distant villages to go through all the excitement and fatigue, but it shows the true old spirit was alive in them yet.

It was not a day for observing convenances, so I asked our warrior how old he was. 'Seventy-five', he said; whereupon I told him he was nothing but a youth, at which he chuckled, not dissatisfied. I think all the old men would have liked a look at the son of the man for whom they had fought and bled; it would have been good for them to have seen their Duke if but this once more; but the Duke was in Venice, and their poor old eyes, which have seen many strange sights, were denied the loyal desire of their true old hearts.

In the hall where the banquet was given, and which was very prettily decorated with evergreens, oak wreaths, inscriptions, and banners, were also a number of tattered old flags, all of which had been borne by the gallant corps of Black Brunswickers at Waterloo. There were also swords and guns which had been in that mighty battle, arranged in stars, and intermixed with other trophies.

The whole sight was one worth seeing, and one we are not likely to look upon again. When I heard 'God save the Queen', and the word 'Waterloo' in everybody's mouth, I felt that the truest ties of blood are perhaps those won side by side on the battlefield. The memory of Waterloo alone made one feel one with every old warrior there.

APPENDIX 3

Extracts from Eyewitness Accounts Relating to the Movements of d'Erlon's I Corps on 16 June 1815.

1. Marshal Ney (letter to Joseph Fouché, Duke of Otranto, 26 June 1815).[1]

Reports of the most false and defamatory nature have for some days been publicly circulated respecting my conduct in this short and unfortunate campaign. The journals repeat these odious calumnies and appear to lend them credit. After having during twenty-five years fought and bled for the glory and independence of my country, it is I against whom the charge of treason is thus daringly made; it is I who am pointed out to the people, and even to the army, as the author of the disaster which has occurred!

Compelled to break silence – for, as it is always painful to speak of one's self, it is particularly so when the object is to repel calumny – I address myself to you, as President of the Provisional Government, in order to lay before you a faithful relation of the circumstances which came under my observation.

On the 11th of June I received an order from the Minister at War [Marshal Davout] to repair to the Imperial headquarters. I had no command, and possessed no information on the force and composition of the army. Neither the Emperor nor the Minister had previously said anything to me which could give me the slightest idea that I was to be employed in this campaign. I was consequently called upon in a state quite unprepared, without horses, equipage, or money, and I was obliged to borrow in order to enable me to reach my destination.

I arrived on the 12th at Laon, on the 13th at Avesnes, and on the 14th at Beaumont; in which last place I purchased from the Duke of Treviso [Marshal Mortier] two horses, with which I proceeded on the 15th to Charleroi, accompanied by my first aide-de-camp [Colonel Heymès], the only officer I had with me. I arrived at the moment when the enemy, having been attacked by our light troops, were falling back upon Fleurus and Gosselies.

The Emperor immediately ordered me to put myself at the head of the I and II Corps of infantry, commanded by Lieutenant-Generals d'Erlon and Reille, of the light cavalry of the Guard, under the orders of Lieutenant-Generals Lefebvre-Desnouëttes and Colbert, and of two divisions of [Kellermann,] the Count of Valmy's cavalry, forming altogether eight divisions of infantry and ... [five] divisions of cavalry. With these troops, of which, however, I had only a part disposable, I pushed the enemy, and obliged him to evacuate Gosselies, Frasnes, Mellet and Heppignies; there the troops took position, with the exception of the I Corps, which was still at Marchiennes, and which did not join me until next day.

On the 16th I was ordered to attack the English in their position at Quatre Bras. We advanced towards the enemy with an enthusiasm difficult to be described. Nothing resisted our impetuosity. The battle became general, and victory was no longer doubtful when, at the moment in which I wished to bring forward the I Corps of infantry which I had left in reserve at Frasnes, I learnt that the Emperor had disposed of it without informing me, as well as of Girard's division of the II Corps.[2] His purpose was to direct these units upon St. Amand and to strengthen his left wing, which was vigorously engaged with the Prussians. The mortification I received from this news was terrible. Having now under my command only three divisions instead of the eight on which I had calculated, I was obliged to renounce hope of victory; and in spite of all my efforts, in spite of the intrepidity and devotion of my troops, my utmost efforts after that could do no more than maintain myself in my position until the close of the day.

About nine o'clock the I Corps was returned to me by the Emperor, to whom it had been of no service.[3] Thus between 25,000 and 30,000 men were, as it were, paralysed, having been obliged during the whole of the battle to parade from the left to the right and from the right to the left, without firing a single shot.

Here I cannot help arresting your attention for a moment upon these details, to bring before your view all the consequences of this false movement and in general, to the bad dispositions adopted that day.

By what fatality, for example, did the Emperor, instead of directing all his forces against Lord Wellington, who would have been taken unawares and unprepared, regard this attack as secondary? How could the Emperor, after the passage of the Sambre, conceive it possible to fight two battles in one day? This was, however, what took place against forces the double of ours, and which the officers who saw it can still with difficulty comprehend.

Had he, instead of doing that, left a corps of observation to hold the Prussians in check, and marched with his most powerful masses to support me, the English army would undoubtedly have been destroyed between Quatre Bras and Genappe. And once this position, which separated the two allied armies, was in our power, it would have opened for the Emperor the opportunity of outflanking the right of the Prussians and crushing them in their turn. The general opinion in France, and particularly in the army was that the Emperor would in the first place turn his attention solely to the destruction of the English army, and for that circumstances were very favourable, but fate has ordered it otherwise.

2.(a) *Count d'Erlon (Letter of 9 February 1829 to the Prince of the Moskowa, Marshal Ney's son).*[4]

You ask me, Prince, for information on the activities of my army corps during the 16th June 1815.

I hasten to send you this information.

Towards 11.00 a.m. or midday, Marshal Ney sent me the order to place my army corps under arms and to direct it towards Frasnes and Quatre Bras, where I would receive further orders. Therefore my army corps began to move immediately.[5] After ordering the general in command of the head of the column to make haste, I went on ahead to see what was happening at Quatre Bras, where it seemed to me that General Reille's corps was engaged.

Beyond Frasnes, I stopped with some generals of the Guard,[6] where I was joined by General La Bédoyère,[7] who showed me a pencilled note that he was bearing to Marshal Ney and which enjoined the marshal to direct my army corps on Ligny. General La Bédoyère informed me that he had already given the order for this movement by changing the direction of my column, and he indicated to me where I could rejoin it. I immediately took this road and sent my Chief of Staff, General Delcambre, to the Marshal [Ney] to inform him of my new destination.

Marshal Ney sent him back to me ordering me imperatively to return to Quatre Bras, where he was heavily engaged and counted on the cooperation of my army corps. Hence I had to imagine the situation was desperate, since the marshal had taken it on himself to recall me, although he had received the note about which I have spoken above.[8] In consequence, I ordered the column to make a return march. But, in spite of all the haste that could be put into this march, my column could not appear to the rear of Quatre Bras until nightfall.

Did General La Bédoyère have the authority to change the direction of my column before having seen the marshal? I do not think so. But in any case, this circumstance alone caused all the marches and counter-marches that paralysed my corps on the 16th June.

2.(b) Count d'Erlon (Extract from his autobiography, Vie Militaire, 1844)[9]

I beg the reader to read the following paragraph carefully, because it is important that the truth be known at last.

The Emperor, heavily engaged at Ligny, sent a staff officer to Marshal Ney to tell him to direct the I Corps on Ligny, so as to turn the Prussian right wing. This officer met the head of the I Corps, which was coming up to Frasnes, and before he had transmitted these imperial orders to Marshal Ney, sent this column off in the direction of Ligny. I had gone on ahead and had no knowledge of the new direction which my army corps had just taken. Towards 4.00 p.m., having learnt about it indirectly, I immediately hurried to rejoin my corps. I sent my Chief of Staff to notify Marshal Ney of my movement.

Marshal Ney, about to be forced back at Quatre Bras, disregarded the Emperor's orders and recalled my army corps to him.

This was a wretched idea and a very great mistake. It prevented the Battle of Ligny having the results the Emperor expected of it.[10] It totally paralysed the I Corps by the marching and counter-marching it was ordered to undertake during the entire day. The corps was unable to participate in either of the two actions.

I hope that this explanation will dispel all the lies that have been said and written about my inaction on this day.

There can be no doubt that had the Emperor addressed his orders to me directly – as many accounts of the battle state – they would have been executed punctually. Nor can there be any doubt that this battle [of Ligny] would have had most important results, and, in all probability, that of Waterloo would not have taken place. This is my opinion and the more I ponder it, the more firmly convinced of it I become.

3. Lieutenant-General Baron Pierre Durutte (From La Sentinelle de l'Armée, *8 March 1838). Durutte writes in the third person singular.*[11]

Towards 10.00 a.m. on the morning of the 16th [June], the I Corps was ordered to march to Frasnes, on the Brussels road. The 4th division, under the orders of General Durutte, was at the head of the column.

While this movement was being executed, an order was received to march towards Quatre Bras [Ligny?]: the right wing was fighting heavily in the direction of Fleurus. The Emperor ordered Count d'Erlon to attack the left [right?] flank of the Prussians and to try to capture Brye. The I Corps passed near Villers-Perwin to execute this movement. While it was on the march, several commands from Marshal Ney arrived in a hurry to stop the I Corps and to make it march to Quatre Bras. The officers bringing these orders said that Marshal Ney had found superior forces at Quatre Bras and that he had been pushed back. This second order greatly troubled Count d'Erlon, for at the same time he received new entreaties from the right wing to march on Brye. Nevertheless, he made up his mind to return towards Marshal Ney. But, as he and General Durutte observed that an enemy column could emerge in the plain which lies between Brye and Delhutte Wood, which would have completely cut the Emperor's wing of the army off from that commanded by Marshal Ney, he decided to leave General Durutte in this plain. Under his orders, he left him, besides his own division, three regiments of cavalry commanded by General Jacquinot.

General Durutte, when leaving General d'Erlon, asked him clearly if he should march on Brye. D'Erlon replied to him that, in the circumstances, he could give him no orders and that he relied on his experience and caution. General Durutte directed his cavalry towards the road running from Sombreffe to Quatre Bras, leaving Wagnée [Wagnelée] and Brye on his right, but still pressing on those two villages. His infantry followed this movement.

General d'Erlon had told him to be cautious because things were going badly at Quatre Bras. This caused General Durutte to observe Delhutte Woods well, for at the slightest retrograde movement by Marshal Ney, the enemy would be behind Durutte.

When General Jacquinot arrived at a cannon shot from the Sombreffe to Quatre Bras road, he met an enemy formation with which he began a cannonade whch lasted three quarters of an hour. General Durutte advanced his infantry towards him in support . . .

The enemy troops who were exchanging cannonfire with General Jacquinot had been retired and General Durutte, receiving no more unfortunate news from the left wing, decided to march on Brye.

4. Count Fleury de Chaboulon (Napoleon in his Memoirs avoided detailed discussion of the d'Erlon fiasco. For Napoleon's viewpoint, it is necessary therefore to turn to Count Fleury de Chaboulon, imperial secretary:)[12]

The Emperor hoped that at any moment Marshal Ney would come to take part in the action [of Ligny]. Since the start of the battle, he had reiterated the order to Ney to move so as to outflank the Prussian right wing. The Emperor counted on this diversion so much that he wrote to the marshal and told him several times that the Fate of France was in his hands. Ney replied 'that he had on his hands the entire English army, that he promised to hold out the whole day but he could promise nothing more.' The Emperor, who was better informed, assured Ney 'that he was at odds with only Wellington's advance guard', and again ordered him 'to seize Quatre Bras whatever it cost.' The marshal persisted in his fatal mistake. Napoleon, convinced of the move which Marshal Ney refused to understand and to execute, sent a direct order to the I Corps to make haste and to fall on the Prussian right wing.[13] But after losing precious time waiting for it, he reckoned that the battle could not safely go on any more. He ordered General Girard, who had with him only 5000 men, to carry out the move that the 20,000 men of Count d'Erlon should have made, that is to say, to turn St Amand and to fall on the enemy rear.[14]

This move, ably executed and seconded by a head-on attack by the Guard, and by a brilliant charge, of the *cuirassiers* of General Delort and of the Guard Grenadiers à cheval, decided the victory. The Prussians, weakened everywhere, retired in disorder and abandoned to us, besides the battlefield, 40 cannon and several flags.

De Chaboulon adds the following about Ney's role in the fiasco:

He immediately sent off a command on the tracks of Count d'Erlon, that whatever orders he might have received from the Emperor himself, d'Erlon was to march back. Count d'Erlon was feeble and wretched enough to obey.

Notes

1. Jones, *The Battle of Waterloo*, pp.385–9
2. In fact, Girard's division had already been attached to the French right wing, during the operations of 15 June.
3. Ney, keen to justify himself, omits any mention of his own recall of d'Erlon.
4. Ney, *Documents inédits*, pp.64–5
5. In fact, it had to wait about an hour for Reille's II Corps in front to move off.
6. These generals were of Lefebvre-Desnouëttes' Guard light cavalry division at Frasnes.
7. Houssaye, *Waterloo 1815*, p.204, asserted that d'Erlon was clearly mistaken in asserting that La Bédoyère bore the pencil note as Pétiet's *Souvenirs Militaires* state that La Bédoyère was close to the Emperor at 5.00 pm. Yet, just two pages later, Houssaye added that Forbin-Janson, the real bearer of the pencil note, returned to Fleurus towards 5.00 pm. Hence La Bédoyère could in theory have delivered the pencil note to d'Erlon and have been back at Fleurus at 5.00 pm, as

Pétiet testifies. But in fact the bearer of the pencil note was Forbin-Janson, not La Bédoyère. Only d'Erlon asserts that La Bédoyère brought the pencil note, and he states it only in one of his two accounts. La Bédoyère may have been the imperial ADC Napoleon sent to reconnoitre and meet d'Erlon's column, as it approached Fleurus at 5.30 pm. Thus d'Erlon probably confused La Bédoyère in this meeting with meeting Forbin-Janson at Frasnes. Colonel Baudus, the most reliable eyewitness for the d'Erlon fiasco, states the officer carrying the pencil note was Forbin-Janson. 'No one', Baudus wrote, 'knows better than I do the circumstances which caused I Corps to be useless on 16 June to both Marshal Ney and the Emperor.'

8. D'Erlon could not have known that Forbin-Janson had forgotten to proceed to Quatre Bras to give Ney the pencil note.

9. D'Erlon, *Vie Militaire*, pp.95–6

10. Here d'Erlon expressly blames Ney for the fiasco. But note that in the 1829 letter addressed to Ney's son, d'Erlon criticises not the marshal but La Bédoyère. D'Erlon clearly wished to spare the feelings of Ney's son.

11. Ney, *Documents inédits*, pp.71–3

12. De Chaboulon, *Mémoires pour servir à l'histoire*, v.2, pp.164–7

13. This was the famous pencil note carried by Forbin-Janson. De Chaboulon's testimony makes nonsense of Becke and other historians' theory that La Bédoyère forged the pencil note and that it was not sent by Napoleon. Certain historians object that this pencil note is not entered on Marshal Soult's register of orders and correspondence. But this does not mean the pencil note was not sent. It seems that only important orders were included in Soult's register. Notes were not included. For example, Napoleon's 1.00 pm note to Ney, auctioned at Sotheby's in 1970 and telling the marshal to attack at Quatre Bras 'with the greatest impetuosity', does not appear on Soult's register.

14. Girard by this time (6.00 pm) had been mortally wounded and his division severely depleted. De Chaboulon is probably confused and is refering to the order Napoleon sent to d'Erlon, on discovering his column's identity, to attack the Prussians. By the time this order had arrived, only Durutte's infantry division of 4000 men plus a light cavalry division remained, for d'Erlon had taken the rest of his corps back to Quatre Bras. Durutte eventually attacked Wagnelée and advanced towards Brye.

BIBLIOGRAPHY

M ore sentences must have been written on the Battle of Ligny than cannonshots were fired in it. Moreover, just as those cannonshots were fired at an enemy, so too nearly all the multitude of books dealing with the campaign look at the Battle of Ligny from only one side of the valley. Compare a Prussian account and a French narrative and you will scarcely believe they describe the same action. The following list of books contains many titles – some good and others not so good. The most noteworthy deserve a few words of explanation.

The best primary account of the Battle of Ligny is by Charles François, a French infantry captain. No other eyewitness achieved such a vivid, detailed and accurate narration.

Baron Carl von Müffling's *Passages from my Life* is valuable in affording the reader an insight into high level Anglo-Prussian relations throughout the campaign. But treat Müffling with caution as he exaggerated his own role (compare Müffling's highly self-centred account of the Bussy mill conference with Dörnberg's more objective, though less detailed, description: Holland Rose, *Napoleonic Studies*, pp.281–3). The great French historian, Henry Houssaye, writes that Müffling 'always attributes good advice to himself.' Müffling boasts of his prestige and influence at Wellington's headquarters. He certainly possessed diplomatic charm for Wellington stated, 'I was acting on the very best terms with Müffling' (Ellesmere, *Personal Recollections of the Duke of Wellington*, p.188). However, the Duke also asserted that he had little regard for Müffling's abilities (*Conversations of the First Duke of Wellington with George William Chad*, p.15: "The D. [Duke] had not a high opinion either of Gneisenau or of Müfflin [sic]". By his own account, Müffling believed that Hougoumont farm at Waterloo was indefensible, in spite of the obvious strength of the post).

Müffling detested Gneisenau and portrays him in a bad light. Nevertheless, Müffling provides some good vignettes of Prince Blücher.

Napoleon's Memoirs are worth consultation but do rewrite history at the cost of the reputations of Marshals Ney and Grouchy.

Anthony Brett-James' collection of primary accounts, *The Hundred Days*, is vital reading.

Secondary accounts usually treat Ligny as a minor prelude to the great drama of Waterloo. William Siborne's reputation as a towering giant in the world of historiography of 1815 is still largely intact after more than 150 years. Yet Siborne was subjective and wrote mainly to glorify Wellington and the feats of the British Army.

The majority of his source material was taken from letters by surviving British officers who participated in the battle. To an extent, Siborne also denigrates Napoleon and the French troops as well as the non-British elements of Wellington's army.

Siborne's account of Ligny was based largely on information supplied by the Prussian General Staff in Berlin or culled from Major Karl von Damitz, an early German author. But Siborne is not wholly accurate, either in the initial set-out of the Prussian formations or in the progress of the battle. Siborne was overwhelmed by the mass of information which he, as the first of the noteworthy secondary historians of 1815, encountered. He neglected to impose a framework of the four constituent battle phases on the detailed material at his disposal. This contributed to some confusion in his account. To take just one example, on page 121, Siborne asserts that the 2nd battalion of the 19th Regiment repelled a French column advancing on Ligny village. Just one page later, Siborne mentions the same battalion entering the village from reserve for the first time.

In his recent revisionalist book, David Hamilton-Williams mercilessly denounces Siborne's subjectivity and flawed research. Nevertheless, he exaggerates when he accuses Siborne of a 'bad deed' against history. Siborne's faults are more than compensated for by his energy in amassing a wealth of invaluable eyewitness accounts which has helped make Waterloo the best documented battle of the age. Indeed, that Hamilton-Williams decided to immerse himself for three years in the Siborne archives is recognition enough of Siborne's service to future historians. If Hamilton-Williams is the first to consult the original Siborne archives rather than relying unhesitatingly on all that Siborne wrote, it is no fault of Siborne's.

In spite of overstating his main argument, Hamilton-Williams has placed a refreshing, new interpretation on the campaign and his work is only slightly marred by his over-partial defence of Ney. For instance, he gives a false picture of a cool and level-headed Ney calmly weighing up his decisions during the d'Erlon fiasco (pp.216–7). Even so, Hamilton-Williams' work is liberated as far as possible from any xenophobic pride and in years to come will rank as one of the most important to appear this century.

The best German histories of the 1815 campaign are by Bruno von Treuenfeld and Carl von Ollech. These are both well written with Teutonic thoroughness and detail and impose an ordered framework on the historical material. Treuenfeld's work includes eleven fine colour maps of the campaign, including one setting out the disposition of Prussian units at the start of the Battle of Ligny, correcting the mistakes made by Siborne.

On the French side, Henry Houssaye is the outstanding historian. Houssaye has been the nearest to the truth behind the d'Erlon fiasco and has based his account on painstaking research of material in English, French and German. Houssaye can be criticised for a certain overconfidence and rashness in jumping to conclusions and believing what he wanted to believe. Some of his arguments, based on a cavalier treatment of evidence, have been demolished by Lady Elizabeth Longford and Edith Saunders. In the *Revue des Etudes Napoléoniennes*, Messieurs Emile Gallo and Emile Mayer have criticised Houssaye for inaccurate quotations from primary sources. In places, Houssaye dramatises his account at the cost of accuracy.

Jean-Baptiste Charras is the other eminent French authority. His work includes a particularly fine, large map of the battlefield of Ligny. The key to understanding Charras is the fact that he went into exile, in opposition to the French Emperor Napoleon III. Charras' sympathy for the Belgian contingent of Wellington's army springs from his exile in Belgium. His exile also lies behind his criticism of Napoleon III's uncle as general, as head of state and as human being.

Edgar Quinet, like Charras, goes over the top in criticising Napoleon and even writes that 'one might really suppose that the man who led the French army during that fatal campaign had never waged war at all, or had lost his head.'

Readers wishing to enlighten themselves further on Wellington's role in the Waterloo campaign should consult Jac Weller's book and Lady Elizabeth Longford's masterly two-volume biography of which the first volume, *Wellington: The Years of the Sword*, deals with the Duke's military career. Superbly and sympathetically written, evocative and readable, Lady Longford's work eclipses all other lives of Wellington and will never be surpassed. Jac Weller has provided a detailed and expert examination of Wellington and his army in the 1815 campaign, but ignored the Battle of Ligny and consulted only English language books.

Several other works must be mentioned. The Italian writer Alberto Pollio enjoyed the great advantage that his nation did not participate in the 1815 campaign and hence was better placed to resist the temptations of subjectivity. Written in 1908, Pollio's book is somewhat out of date. Nonetheless, his sound and measured criticism of the conduct of the Prussian high command at Ligny is eminently sensible. On other matters he reached surprising conclusions. For example, he asserted on page 223 that Napoleon's 3.15 pm order to Ney on 16 June 'was a magnificent order. In giving it, Napoleon had such a clear vision of the present situation ... [Ney], who received it, must have been electrified by it. It was truly the Napoleon of history and of legend who wrote to Ney. The greatest of captains who appeals to the bravest of his lieutenants!' Furthermore, Sir John Fortescue is heavily critical in his *The Campaign of Waterloo*, p.82, of Pollio's ignorance of Wellington's character and relations with his allies and political superiors.

Archibald Becke's *Napoleon and Waterloo* (1936) is an improved, revised version of his 1914 two-volume work. He competently discussed the campaign strategy and mistakes of the three armies but was totally confused by the d'Erlon fiasco and the reasons for it.

The Belgian historians F. de Bas and Count J. t'Serclaes de Wommerson collaborated on a weighty three-tome work published in 1908. Jacques Logie states that their book, which strongly defends the conduct of the Dutch–Belgian contingent of Wellington's army, received secret funding from the Belgian government (Logie, *Waterloo: L'évitable défaite*, p.213). In spite of their subjectivity, the authors have researched the topic in great depth, particularly in the Dutch archives. Furthermore, the reader gains a clear picture of the actions of the Dutch generals Constant-Rebecque and Perponcher on 15 June, and of the sequence of intelligence and orders on which those two generals based their decisions. This section of the book is one of the best guides History can offer as to when and how subordinates should exercise initiative and informed disobedience. All Belgian officer cadets ought to read de Bas and de Wommerson as part of their course at the Brussels Military School.

Ernest Henderson and Hans Delbrück strive to defend Gneisenau. But they are hopelessly biased against Wellington. Some English diatribes, on the other hand, give all credit for victory to Wellington and ignore the roles of Blücher, Gneisenau and their Prussians.

Roger Parkinson's two books are both extremely readable accounts from the Prussian side of the Ligny brook.

Henry Lachouque also provides vivid, energetic and readable narratives, but with a strong French flavour and a rehabilitation of Grouchy and Ney. His works are note-worthy but he fails to provide references to support his assertions, many of which are debatable.

David Chandler is the foremost contemporary scholar of Napoleon the soldier. His monumental *The Campaigns of Napoleon* has no equal and sets Ligny into the back-ground of Napoleon's strategy in 1815, and of his method of making war. *Waterloo: The Hundred Days* is the best introduction to more detailed works on the campaign.

The various Osprey Men-at-Arms series of books are excellent on the uniforms, equipment and tactics of the troops at Ligny. Also of value in this respect is Philip Haythornthwaite's compact and well-illustrated *The Uniforms of Waterloo*.

Patrick Maes' booklet, *Ligny: Le Crépuscule de l'aigle*, is the product of deep research and original thought by an expert.

The most comprehensive guide to the relics, in Belgium, of the 1815 campaign is a French-language work by Georges Speekaert and Isabelle Baeker. The book is on sale in the museums and souvenir shops of the battlefield of Waterloo.

Finally, by far the finest historical novel involving Ligny is by Emile Erckmann and Louis Chatrian. Sometimes assumed by historians to be eyewitness recollections, the book is in fact an imaginative recreation of the fierce fighting along Ligny brook. The book refights the epic battle through the eyes of an infantryman in the 6th Light infantry regiment of General Gérard's IV Corps.

Sources

PRIMARY

Ali, M., *Souvenirs du mameluck Ali sur l'empereur Napoléon* (1926)

Anon, *The Journal of the three days of the Battle of Waterloo* (1816) [the author was in the French II Corps]

Anon, 'Operations of the Fifth or Picton's Division in the Campaign of Waterloo', in *United Service Magazine* (June 1841)

Baudus, A., *Etudes sur Napoléon* (1841) v.1

Beaufroy, M., 'The Battle of Waterloo by an eyewitness', in *History* (July–Sept. 1915)

Berthezène, J., *Souvenirs militaires* (1855) v.2

Berton, J., *Précis historique, militaire et critique des batailles de Fleurus et de Waterloo* (1818)

Bonaparte, M., *Porte-feuille de Buonaparte, pris à Charleroi le 18 juin 1815* (1815)

Bonaparte, N., *Correspondance de Napoléon 1er* (1869) v.28

Bonaparte, N., *Napoleon's Memoirs* ed. S. de Chair (1985)

Brett-James, A., *The Hundred Days* (1964)

Bro, H., *Mémoires du Général Bro* (1914)

Canler, L., *Mémoires de Canler, Ancien Chef de la Police de Sûreté* (1882) v.1

Coignet, J., *The Notebooks of Captain Coignet* (1897, 1986)

Combier, A., *Mémoires du général Radet* (1892)

Curely, J., *Itinéraire d'un cavalier léger de la grande armée* (1887)

de Chaboulon, F., *Mémoires pour servir à l'histoire de la vie privée du retour, et du règne de Napoléon en 1815* (1819) v.2

de Civrieux, L., *Souvenirs d'un cadet* (1912)

d'Erlon, D., *Vie Militaire* (1844)

DeLancey, Lady, *A Week at Waterloo* ed. B Ward (1906)

de Pontécoulant, L., *Souvenirs Historiques et Parlementaires* (1863)

des Odoards, F., *Journal du général Fantin des Odouards* (1895)

du Casse, A., *Mémoires et correspondance du Roi Jérôme et de la Reine Cathérine* (1866) v.7

Eaton, C., *Waterloo Days* (1888)

Ellesmere, F., *Personal Recollections of the Duke of Wellington* (1903)

Foy, M., *Vie Militaire* (1900)

François, C., *Journal du Capitaine François* (1904) v.2

Gérard, E., *Quelques documents sur la bataille de Waterloo* (1829)

Gourgaud, G., *The Campaign of 1815* (1818, 1982)

Grouchy, E., *Fragments historiques relatifs à la campagne de 1815, et à la bataille de Waterloo* (1829)

Grouchy, G., *Mémoires du maréchal de Grouchy* (1873) v.4

Gurwood, J., *The Dispatches of the Duke of Wellington* (1838) v.12

Henegan, R., *Seven Years Campaigning* (1846)

Jackson, B., *Notes and Reminiscences of a staff officer* (1903)

Kerry, Earl of, *The First Napoleon* (1925)

Larrey, J., *Memoir of Baron Larrey* (1861)

Lecestre, L., ed., *Lettres Inédites de Napoleon 1er* (1897)

Lemonnier-Delafosse, M., *Souvenirs Militaires* (1850)

Levavasseur, O., *Souvenirs Militaires* (1914)

Marbot, M., *The Memoirs of Baron Marbot* (1893, 1988)

Martin, J., *Souvenirs d'un ex-officier* (1867)

Maxwell, H., ed., *The Creevy Papers* (1904)

McGrigor, J., *Autobiography and Services* (1861)

Müffling, C., *Geschichte des Feldzuges der ... Armee unter Wellington und der Armee unter Blücher, im Jahre 1815* (1817)

Müffling, C., *A Sketch of the Battle of Waterloo* (1842, 1983)

Müffling, C., *Passages from my Life* (1853)

Ney, J., *Documents inédits sur la campagne de 1815* (1840)

Ney, M., *Military Studies* trans. by G. Caunter (1833)

Ney, M., *Mémoires du maréchal Ney, publiées par sa famille* (1833)

Nieman, H., 'The Journal of Henri Nieman of the 6th Prussian Black Hussars' ed. F. Thorpe, in *English Historical Review* (July, 1888)

Pétiet, A., *Souvenirs Militaires* (1844)

Petit, J., 'General Petit's account of the Waterloo Campaign' ed. G. Smith, in *English Historical Review* (1903)

Reiche, L., *Memoiren des Koniglich preussichen Generals der Infanterie Ludwig von Reiche. Herausgegeben von seinem neffen Louis von Weltzien, grossherzoglich oldenburgischem Hauptmann und Brigademajor* (1857)

Reuter, C., 'A Prussian gunner's adventures in 1815' ed. E. May, in *United Service Magazine* (Oct. 1891)

Sabine, E., ed., *Letters of Col. Sir Augustus Frazer* (1859)

Schlumberger, G., *Journal de route du capitaine Robinaux* (1908)

Siborne, H., ed., *The Waterloo Letters* (1891, 1993)

Stanhope, Earl of, *Conversations with the Duke of Wellington* (1938)

Thornton, J., *Your most obedient servant* (ed. E. Longford) (1985)

Wellington, Duke of, *The Dispatches of the Duke of Wellington* ed. J. Gurwood (1838) v.12

Wellington, Duke of, ed., *Supplementary Despatches* (1863) v.10

Wellington, 7th Duke of, ed, *Conversations of the First Duke of Wellington with George William Chad* (1956)

SECONDARY

Acton, Lord, 'German Schools of History' in *English Historical Review* (Jan. 1886)

Anon, *An Account of the Battle of Waterloo* (1815) [by a British Officer on the Staff]

Anon, *Beaumont 1815* (1992)

Aron, R., *Clausewitz* (1983)

Atkinson, C., *A History of Germany 1715–1815* (1908)

Barral, G., *L'Epopée de Waterloo* (1895)

Barthorp, M., 'The Imperial Guard at Waterloo', in *History Today* (Nov. 1966)

Beamish, N., *History of the King's German Legion* (1837, 1993)

Beauchamp, A., *Histoire des Campagnes de 1814 et de 1815* (1817) v.2

Becke, A., *Napoleon and Waterloo* (1936)

Bell, D., *Wellington's Officers* (1938)

Belloc, H., *Waterloo* (1912)

Bonnal, H., *La Vie Militaire du Maréchal Ney* (1911)

Booth, L., *The Battle of Waterloo by a near observer* (1816)

Boulger, D., *The Belgians at Waterloo* (1901)

Brett-James, A., *Europe Against Napoleon* (1970)

Brett-James, A., 'Picton at Waterloo', in *History Today* (April 1958)

Bryant, A., *The Great Duke* (1971)

Bukhari, E., *Napoleon's Guard Cavalry* (1985)

Bukhari, E., *Napoleon's Marshals* (1986)

Bukhari, E., *Napoleon's Hussars* (1987)

Bukhari, E., *Napoleon's Dragoons and Lancers* (1988)

Bukhari, E., *Napoleon's Cuirassiers and Carabiniers* (1988)

Bukhari, E., *Napoleon's Line Chasseurs* (1988)

Camon, C., *La Guerre Napoléonienne. Les Systèmes d'opérations* (1907)

Camon, C., *La Guerre Napoléonienne. Atlas* (1910)

Camon, C., *La Guerre Napoléonienne. Les batailles* (1910)

Camon, C., *La Guerre Napoléonienne. Précis des campagnes* (1911)

Casse, A., *Le Général Vandamme et sa correspondance* (1870) v.2

Cassin-Scott, J., *Uniforms of the Napoleonic Wars* (1977)

Caldwell, G., *Rifle Green at Waterloo* (1990)

Chalfont, Lord, ed., *Waterloo: Battle of Three Armies* (1979)

Champney, E., *Romance of Old Belgium* (1915)

Chandler, D., *Dictionary of the Napoleonic Wars* (1979, 1993)

Chandler, D., *The Campaigns of Napoleon* (1966)

Chandler, D., *Waterloo: The Hundred Days* (1980)

Chandler, D., *The Illustrated Napoleon* (1991)

Chandler, D., *On the Napoleonic Wars* (1994)

Chandler, D., ed., *Napoleon's Marshals* (1987)

Chandler, D., ed., *The Military Maxims of Napoleon* (1987)

Chappet, A., *Guide Napoléonien* (1981)

Chapuisart, E., 'Les Régiments Suisses de l'Empire' in *Revue des Etudes Napoléoniennes* (1914)

Chapuisart, E., 'Les Etudes Napoléoniennes en Suisse: 1913' in *Revue des Etudes Napoléoniennes* (1915)

Charras, J., *Histoire de la Campagne de 1815* (1857)

Cherry, R., 'Some Aspects of Great Campaigns. Waterloo' in *The Journal of the Royal Artillery* (Sept. 1915)

Chesney, C., *The Waterloo Lectures* (1907)

Chevalier, E., *Histoire de la marine française sous le Consulat et l'Empire* (1866)

Clausewitz, C., *On War* (1984)

Colin, J., *Napoleon* (1914)

Connelly, O., *Blundering to Glory* (1988)

Conreur, M., *De Thuin à Waterloo* (1990)

Couvreur, H., *Le Drame Belge de Waterloo* (1957)

Cotton, E., *A Voice from Waterloo* (1900, 1974)

Creasy, E., *The Fifteen Decisive Battles of the Western World* (1909)

Cronin, V., *Napoleon* (1971)

Dalton, C., *The Waterloo Roll Call* (1978)

Damitz, K., *Histoire de la Campagne de 1815* trans. by L. Griffon (1840)

Davson, H., 'Napoleon's Marshals. Ney', in *The Journal of the Royal Artillery* (Feb. 1908)

de Bas, F., and J. de Wommerson, *La Campagne de 1815 aux Pays-Bas* (1908)

de Gaulle, C., *La France et son armée* (1948)

de Goutelle, H., 'Les Derniers Jours de l'Empire' in *Revue des Etudes Napoléoniennes* (1918)

Delbrück, H., *Das Leben des Feldmarschalls Grafen Neithardt von Gneisenau* (1882) v.2

Dilks, T., 'The Campaign of 1815 and His Majesty's Opposition', in *History* (July–Sept. 1915)

Dupuis, V., *Les Opérations Militaires sur la Sambre en 1794* (1907)

Ellis, G., *The Napoleonic Empire* (1991)

Erckmann-Chatrian, E., *Waterloo, Suite du Conscrit de 1813* (1865) [English translation by H. Dulcken published in 1972]

Esposito V., & J. Elting, *A Military History and Atlas of the Napoleonic Wars* (1964, 1980)

Fitchett, W., *How England Saved Europe* (1900) v.4

Fletcher I., and R. Poulter, *Gentlemen's sons. The Guards in the Peninsula and at Waterloo, 1808–15* (1992)

Fortescue, J., *The Campaign of Waterloo* (1987) (Reprint from v.10 of the *History of the British Army*)

Fraser, E., *War Drama of the Eagles* (1912)

Fraser, W., *The Waterloo Ball* (1897)

Fraser, W., *Words on Wellington* (1900)

Fuller, J.F.C., *The Conduct of War 1789–1961* (1962)

Fuller, J.F.C., *The Decisive Battles of the Western World* (1985)

Gallo, E., 'Le "Waterloo" de Henry Houssaye' in *Revue des Etudes Napoléoniennes* (1915)

Gamot, M., *Réfutation en ce qui concerne le maréchal Ney* (1818)

Gardner, D., *Quatre Bras, Ligny and Waterloo* (1882)

Gardyne, C., *The Life of a Regiment. The History of the Gordon Highlanders* (1901)

Garros, L., *Itinéraire de Napoleon Bonaparte* (1947)

Garros, L., *Le Champ de Bataille de Waterloo* (1952)

George, H., Review of W. O'Connor Morris, *The Campaign of 1815*, in *English Historical Review* (Oct. 1900, p.811–6)

Germain, P., *Drouet d'Erlon. Maréchal de France* (1985)

Geyl, P., *Napoleon. For and Against* (1986)

Girod de l'Ain, M., *Le Général Drouot* (1890)

Glover, M., *Wellington as Military Commander* (1968)

Glover, M., *1815 The Armies at Waterloo* (1973)

Glover, M., *The Napoleonic Wars* (1979)

Glover, M., *Warfare in the Age of Bonaparte* (1980)

Glover, M., *The Velvet Glove* (1982)

Godwin, J., *Beaudesert, the Pagets and Waterloo* (1992)

Grant, C., *Waterloo. Wargaming in History* (1990)

Griffith, P., *Wellington, Commander* (1983)

Griffith, P., *Forward into Battle* (1990)

Griffiths, A., *Wellington and Waterloo* (1898) part 10

Grouard, A., *Critique de la Campagne de 1815* (1904)

Grouard, A., 'Les Derniers Historiens de 1815' in *Revue des Etudes Napoléoniennes* (1913)

Grouard, A., 'Les Derniers Historiens de 1815' in *Revue des Etudes Napoléoniennes* (1917)

Guedalla, P., *The Duke* (1931)

Guedalla, P., *The Hundred Days* (1939)

Hamilton-Williams, D., *Waterloo: New Perspectives. The Great Battle Reappraised* (1993)

Hamley, E., *Wellington's Career* (1860)

Haswell, J., *The First Respectable Spy* (1969)

Hayman, P., *Soult. Napoleon's Maligned Marshal* (1990)

Haythornthwaite, P., *Uniforms of Waterloo* (1979)

Haythornthwaite, P., *Weapons and Equipment of the Napoleonic Wars* (1979)

Haythornthwaite, P., *Napoleon's Line Infantry* (1984)

Haythornthwaite, P., *Napoleon's Light Infantry* (1987)

Haythornthwaite, P., *The Napoleonic Source Book* (1990)

Henderson, E., *Blücher and the Uprising of Prussia against Napoleon* (1911)

Herold, J., *The Age of Napoleon* (1963)

Herold, J., *The Battle of Waterloo* (1967)

Hofschröer, P., *Prussian Light Infantry 1792–1815* (1984)

Holland Rose, J., 'Sir Hudson Lowe and the Campaign of 1815' in *English Historical Review* (July 1901)

Holland Rose, J., *Napoleonic Studies* (1904) chapter 9

Holland Rose, J., *Pitt and Napoleon* (1912) (pp.157–83)

Holland Rose, J., 'Wellington dans la Campagne de Waterloo' in *Revue des Etudes Napoléoniennes* (1915)

Holland Rose, J., *The Life of Napoleon I* (1924)

Holland Rose, J., *The Personality of Napoleon* (1929)

Horricks, R., *Marshal Ney. The Romance and the Real* (1982)

Horricks, R., *In Flight with the Eagle* (1988)

Horward, D., ed., *Napoleonic Military History* (1986)

Houssaye, H., *Waterloo 1815* (1987)

Howard, M., ed., *Wellingtonian Studies* (1959)

Howard, M., *Clausewitz* (1983)

Howarth, D., *A Near Run Thing* (1968)

Hurren, B., *The Battle of Waterloo* (1975)

Hutchinson, H., *The Story of Waterloo* (1890)

James, W., *The Campaign of 1815* (1908)

Janin, E., *Campagne de 1815* (1820)

Johnson, D., *The French Cavalry 1792–1815* (1989)

Johnson, R., *Napoleonic Armies* (1984)

Jomini, A., *Précis politique et militaire de la campagne de 1815* (1839)

Jomini, A., *Souvenirs de 1815. Atlas portatif pour servir à l'explorateur des champs de bataille de Waterloo et de Ligny* (1851)

Jomini, A., *Life of Napoleon* trans. by H. Halleck (1864)

Jomini, A., *The Art of War* (1862, 1992)

Jones, G., *The Battle of Waterloo* (1852)

Kausler, F., *Die Kriege von 1792 bis 1815 in Europa und Aegypten, mit besonderer Rucksicht auf die Schlachten Napoleons und seiner Zeit. {With} Karten* (1842)

Keegan, J., *The Face of Battle* (1976)

Kelly, C., *The Battle of Waterloo* (1831)

Kircheisen, F., *Napoleon* (1931)

Königer, J., *Der Krieg von 1815* (1865)

Lachouque, H., *The Anatomy of Glory* (1961, 1978)

Lachouque, H., *Napoleon's Battles* (1966)

Lachouque, H., *Waterloo: Wallonie, Art et Histoire* (1972)

Lachouque, H., *Waterloo* (1975)

Lachouque, H., *Napoleon à Waterloo* (1965)

Lachouque, H., *Le Secret de Waterloo* (1952)

Lamb, R., 'Napoleon's Last Victory' in *War Monthly* (March 1981)

Lasserre, J., 'Musiques et Batteries des Grenadiers à pied et des Chasseurs à pied de la vieille garde impériale' in *Revue des Etudes Napoléoniennes* (1922)

Lawford, J., *Napoleon. The Last Campaigns 1813–15* (1977)

Lefebvre, G., *Napoleon 1807–1815* (1969)

Lenient, E., *La solution des énigmes de Waterloo* (1915)

Lenient, E., 'La solution des énigmes de Waterloo' in *Revue des Etudes Napoléoniennes* (1917)

Logie, J., *Waterloo. L'évitable défaite* (1989)

Logie, J., *L'Europe face à Napoleon* (1990)

Longford, E., *Wellington: The Years of the Sword* (1972)

Longford, E., *Wellington: Pillar of State* (1972)

Macbride, M., *With Napoleon at Waterloo* (1911)

MacKenzie, N., *The Escape from Elba* (1982)

Macready, E., 'On a part of captain Siborne's History of the Waterloo Campaign', in *United Service Magazine* (March and June 1845)

Maes, P., *Ligny. Le Crépuscule de l'Aigle* (1991)

Maes, P., *Le Premier Corps d'Armee en 1815* (1993)

Markham, F., *Napoleon* (1963)

Marshall-Cornwall, J., *Napoleon as Military Commander* (1967)

Martinien, A., *Liste des officiers généraux tués ou blessés sous le premier empire de 1805 à 1815* (1896)

Maurice, F., 'Waterloo': articles in *United Service Magazine* (April, May, June, July, September and October 1890 and January 1891)

Mayer, E., 'Henry Houssaye. Notes sur sa documentation' in *Revue des Etudes Napoléoniennes* (1913)

Maxwell, H., *Life of Wellington* (1900) v.2

Maxwell, H., 'Our allies at Waterloo', in *The Nineteenth Century* (Sept. 1900)

McGuffie, T., 'The British Soldier at Waterloo', in *History Today* (June 1965)

Montgomery, B., *The Path to Leadership* (1961)

Montgomery, B., *A History of Warfare* (1968)

Morris, W., *The Campaign of 1815* (1900)

Morton, J., *Marshal Ney* (1958)

Myatt, F., *Peninsular general. Sir Thomas Picton* (1980)

Navez, L., *Les Quatre Bras, Ligny, Waterloo et Wavre* (1903)

Naylor, J., *Waterloo* (1960)

Nicholson, H., *The Congress of Vienna* (1948)

Nofi, A., *The Waterloo Campaign. June 1815* (1993)

Ollech, C., *Geschichte des Feldzuges von 1815 nach archivalischen Quellen* (1876)

Oman, C., 'The Dutch–Belgians at Waterloo', in *The Nineteenth Century* (Oct. 1900)

Oman, C., 'The French Losses in the Waterloo Campaign' in *English Historical Review* (Oct. 1904 and Jan. 1906)

Page, F., *Following the Drum* (1986)

Pajol, C., *Pajol, Général en chef* (1874) v.3

Palmer, A., *An Encyclopaedia of Napoleon's Europe* (1984)

Parker, H., *Three Napoleonic Battles* (1983)

Parkinson, R., *Clausewitz* (1970)

Parkinson,R., *The Hussar General* (1975)

Petrie, C., *Wellington. A Reassessment* (1956)

Pflugk-Harttung, J., *Vorgeschichte der Schlacht bei Belle-Alliance – Wellington* (1903)

Plotho, C., *Der Krieg des verbundeten Europa gegen Frankreich im Jahre 1815* (1818)

Pollio, A., *Waterloo (1815) avec de nouveaux documents* trans. from Italian by Goiran (1908)

Quennevat, J., *Atlas de la Grande Armée* (1966)

Quinet, E., *Histoire de la Campagne de 1815* (1861)

Regnault, J., *Les Aigles Impériales* (1967)

Robertson, W., 'The French Official Account of Waterloo' in *United Service Magazine* (March 1890)

Rogers, H., *Napoleon's Army* (1982)

Ropes, J., *The Campaign of Waterloo* (1893)

Rothenberg, G., *The Art of Warfare in the Age of Napoleon* (1977)

Ruquoy, L., ed., *A Ligny j'avais gagné!* (1990)

Saunders, E., *The Hundred Days* (1964)

Savant, J., *Les Mamelouks de Napoleon* (1949)

Schom, A., *The Hundred Days. Napoleon's Road to Waterloo* (1993)

Selwyn, W., *Waterloo. A lay of jubilee* (1865)

Seymour, W., *Decisive Factors in Twenty Great Battles of the World* (1988)

Sheppard, E., *The Study of Military History* (1952)

Siborne, W., 'The Waterloo Campaign', in *United Service Magazine* (April and July 1845)

Siborne, W., *History of the Waterloo Campaign* (1848, 1990)

Six, G., *Dictionnaire biographique des généraux et amiraux français 1792–1814* (1934)

Speekaert M., & I. Baeker, *Les 135 vestiges et monuments commemoratifs des combats de 1815 en Belgique* (1990)

Sutherland, J., *Men of Waterloo* (1966)

Sweetman, J., *Raglan. From the Peninsula to the Crimea*

Terraine, J., 'Big Battalions: the Napoleonic Legacy' in *History Today* (June 1962)

Thiry, J., *La seconde abdication de Napoléon 1er* (1945)

Thorburn, W., 'Napoleon's soldiers and their uniforms' in *History Today* (Sept. 1959)

Thornhill, P., *The Waterloo Campaign* (1965)

Treitschke, H., *History of Germany in the 19th Century* trans. by E. & C. Paul (1916) v.2

Treuenfeld, B., *Die Tage von Ligny und Belle-Alliance* (1880)

Tulard, J., *Napoleon. The Myth of the Saviour* (1985)

Tulard, J., *Nouvelle bibliographie critique des mémoires sur l'époque napoléonienne* (1991)

Vivian, C., *Richard Hussey Vivian* (1897)

Watson, S., *Carnot* (1954)

Wauters, A., *Histoire des Environs de Bruxelles* (1855)

Weller, J., *Wellington at Waterloo* (1967, 1992)

Whitehead, J., 'Wellington at Waterloo' and 'Waterloo – Wellington's Right Flank', in *The Army Quarterly* (1965 and 1972)

Wise, T., *Artillery Equipments of the Napoleonic Wars* (1989)

Wootten, G., *Waterloo 1815. The Birth of Modern Europe* (1992)

Young, P., *Blücher's Army 1813–15* (1973)

MAPS

J. de Ferraris, *Nouvelle carte chorographique des Pays-Bas autrichiens* (1777) 1:86,000

J. Cloché, *Plan des batailles de Waterloo ... des 15, 16, 17 et 18 juin, 1815* (1815) 1:135,000

Capt. Salucci, *Bataille de Waterloo. Dressé par Salucci* (1815) 1:40,000

W. Craan, *Plan du champ de bataille de Waterloo dit de la Belle Alliance* (1816) 1:12,500

L'Institut Cartographique Militaire, *Carte topographique de Belgique* (1881) 1:20,000

German General Staff, *Belgien* (1941) 1:40,000

Institut Géographique National, *Fleurus–Spy* (no. 47/1-2) (1980) 1:25,000

Institut Géographique National, *Gouy-lez-Piéton–Gosselies* (no. 46/3-4) (1982) 1:25,000

Institut Géographique National, *Nivelles–Genappe* (no. 39/7-8) (1983) 1:25,000

Institut Géographique National, *Thuin* (no. 52) (1984) 1:50,000

Michelin, *Oostende–Bruxelles–Liège* (no. 2) (1983) 1:200,000

Michelin, *Mons–Luxembourg* (no. 4) (1982) 1:200,000

INDEX

French divisions are indexed by name of commander rather than by number as part of the French Army. Divisional commanders are given in the French order of battle, which starts on p. 87.